A Sense
of the
Enemy

———

A SENSE
OF THE
ENEMY

THE HIGH-STAKES HISTORY OF
READING YOUR RIVAL'S MIND

by

Zachary Shore

OXFORD
UNIVERSITY PRESS

OXFORD
UNIVERSITY PRESS

Oxford University Press is a department of the University of Oxford.
It furthers the University's objective of excellence in research, scholarship,
and education by publishing worldwide.

Oxford   New York
Auckland   Cape Town   Dar es Salaam   Hong Kong   Karachi
Kuala Lumpur   Madrid   Melbourne   Mexico City   Nairobi
New Delhi   Shanghai   Taipei   Toronto

With offices in
Argentina   Austria   Brazil   Chile   Czech Republic   France   Greece
Guatemala   Hungary   Italy   Japan   Poland   Portugal   Singapore
South Korea   Switzerland   Thailand   Turkey   Ukraine   Vietnam

Oxford is a registered trade mark of Oxford University Press
in the UK and certain other countries.

Published in the United States of America by
Oxford University Press
198 Madison Avenue, New York, NY 10016

Library of Congress Cataloging-in-Publication Data
Shore, Zachary.
A sense of the enemy : the high stakes history of reading your rival's mind / Zachary Shore.
p.   cm.
Summary: "A bold explanation of how and why national leaders are able—or unable—to correctly
analyze and predict the intentions of foreign rivals"—Provided by publisher.
Includes bibliographical references and index.
ISBN 978–0–19–998737–5 (hardback)
1. Political leadership—Psychological aspects. 2. Heads of state—Psychology.
3. Enemies—Psychology. 4. Psychology, Military. I. Title.
JC330.3.S56 2014
320.01'9—dc23
2013035543

9780199987375

1   3   5   7   9   8   6   4   2

Printed in the United States of America on acid-free paper

For my parents

CONTENTS

———

vii

Introduction

Seeking Strategic Empathy

DESPITE A DECADE OF military operations across Afghanistan, by the winter of 2010 it had become clear that the United States was not succeeding. Hoping to induce the Afghan insurgents into peace talks, U.S. and NATO officials tried to bribe the Taliban to the conference table. They paid an undisclosed and hefty sum to Mullah Akhtar Muhammad Mansour for his participation, at one point flying the Taliban's second-in-command to meet with President Hamid Karzai in Kabul. The talks seemed to be proceeding well. Mansour's demands were remarkably reasonable. Yet one thing did trouble some officials. Mansour was several inches shorter than he should have been.

Unfortunately, the Taliban commander was a fake, a shopkeeper from Quetta, Pakistan.[1] Following the third round of negotiations, the clever merchant made off with a fortune, no doubt laughing as he spirited his wealth away. The episode exposed how poorly the United States knew its enemy in this ongoing war. On a superficial level, American and NATO officials could not even identify the number-two man in their opponent's organization. On the more strategic level, they did not notice that throughout three separate meetings, the impostor never once requested that foreign troops withdraw from Afghan soil—a staple of Taliban demands. Without concrete descriptions of Mansour's appearance, the U.S. and NATO had to focus on his behavior. Did he think the way a Taliban commander would? In a sense, they needed to read Mansour's mind.

What NATO and U.S. officials lacked was strategic empathy: the ability to think like their opponent. Strategic empathy is the skill of stepping out of our own heads and into the minds of others. It is what allows us to pinpoint what truly drives and constrains the other side. Unlike stereotypes, which lump people into simplistic categories, strategic empathy distinguishes what is unique about individuals and their situation. To achieve strategic empathy, you must first identify the information that matters most.

Knowing how another thinks depends initially on gathering and analyzing information. Most leaders use the "great mass" approach. Drawing on intelligence networks, they gather up as much data as they can. The problem is that it is too easy to drown in an ocean of information. Determining which data matter and connecting the dots then grows even harder. In contrast to the great mass approach, others believe that a "thin slice" of information is more effective at revealing someone's true nature. The danger is that we often choose the wrong slice, leading us painfully astray.[2] The conclusion here is inescapable. The quantity of information is irrelevant; it's the relevance of any quantity that matters. The key is not to collect a great mass or a thin slice but the right chunk.

The challenge that has long bedeviled leaders is to find heuristics—decision-making shortcuts—to help them locate those right chunks. Such shortcuts would not generate omniscience, but they would equip us with a sense for what makes our enemies tick. And that sense would greatly improve our odds of anticipating the enemy's actions. This is what strategic empathy enables, and you can imagine how valuable this skill would be.

This is a book about prediction, though not of the ordinary kind. It is not about predicting sports matches, stock markets, elections, or any of the typical things people bet on. Instead, it's about predicting other people's behavior when the stakes are the highest they can be—over matters of war and peace. It's a book about how we get out of our own minds and into someone else's head, and it focuses on how national leaders in modern times have struggled to do it well.

This is specifically a history of how leaders within governments have tried to think like their enemies. It explores the zig-zag stories when each side in a conflict sought to outmaneuver the other. It is a walk through one of the twentieth-century's most challenging yet crucial quests: reading the enemy mind.

The Question

A Sense of the Enemy addresses two questions. First, what produces strategic empathy? Second, how has strategic empathy, or the lack of it, shaped pivotal periods in twentieth-century international conflict?

More than 2,000 years ago the Chinese military philosopher Sun Tzu advised generals to know thy enemy. The question has always been how to do it. Though millennia have passed, we are still searching for the answer. Writing in 1996, the philosopher Isaiah Berlin argued that political genius, the ability to synthesize "the fleeting, broken, infinitely various wisps and fragments that make up life at any level," is simply a sense—you either have it or you don't.[3] But what if Berlin was wrong? What if that sense could actually be learned and improved?

Using the masterful nineteenth-century statesman Otto von Bismarck as a prime example of one who was exceedingly gifted at divining an opponent's reactions, Berlin observed that the German Chancellor managed to integrate vast amounts of disparate data over a breathtakingly expansive range. Then, rather disappointingly, Berlin asserted that any careful study of this sense could never lead to any meaningful guides. As he saw it, the gift of political judgment came from seeing the unique in any situation, and any generalizations would be useless in future contexts. Berlin is so uncommonly sensible, so thoroughly compelling, that I am almost tempted to agree.

As a historian of international relations, I find myself deeply planted in Berlin's camp. I am dubious about the value of international relations theories, and I seek no predictive models of behavior. Yet I question his conviction that a rigorous investigation of the ability to know one's enemy would yield nothing of value. Leaders who possess this skill are adept at identifying, as well as synthesizing, the data relevant to a given problem. A careful look at such leaders would bring us closer to comprehending how they thought and in that way further illuminate why events unfolded as they did. It might also help us understand how they knew which information to scrutinize and which to ignore. As the psychologists Christopher Chabris and Daniel Simons observe: "For the human brain, attention is necessarily a zero-sum game. If we pay more attention to one place, object, or event, we necessarily pay less attention to others."[4]

We often assume that the experts in any field have absorbed and retained vast amounts of data on their given subject. Though it has been more than a century and a half since he first assumed the German Chancellorship, Bismarck is still viewed in this light. Christoph Tiedemann served as the Chancellor's personal assistant from 1875 to 1880. Though steadfast in his work ethic, even he struggled to keep pace with the indefatigable statesman. Sessions with the Chancellor typically lasted all day. Once Bismarck dictated a single letter to the Emperor for five hours straight, without interruption. At one point in the dictation, Tiedemann's arms began to cramp, so he swiftly removed his jacket. Bismarck gazed at him with amazement, astonished that Tiedemann should require a break in the action. Bismarck's ability to dictate for such long stretches stemmed from his total mastery of the relevant information. His aim, as the Chancellor's most recent biographer put it, was to know everything about everything in "a constant, furious absorption of material."[5] Yet today we know more about how the mind works. Chabris and Simons, among other psychologists, have shown that a central aspect of decision-making is not the absorption of massive amounts of material but instead the capacity to ignore the bulk of it while focusing on the few key data points that truly matter. "Intuitively, most people think that experts consider more alternatives and more possible diagnoses rather than fewer. Yet the mark of true expertise is not the ability to consider more options," Chabris says, "but the ability to filter out irrelevant ones."[6] As leaders filter out the noise, they must also sense where to find the signal.

The Argument

One key to strategic empathy comes not from the pattern of past behavior but from the behavior at pattern breaks.

We can better understand the past century of international conflict by scrutinizing how leaders struggled to think like their enemies. When they did it poorly, they tended either to assume that their opponents' future behavior would resemble their past behavior or they assumed that their enemies would think and act as they themselves would do. But when leaders succeeded in thinking like their enemies, they focused on the enemy's behavior during meaningful pattern breaks.

In a twenty-first century marked by mind-boggling amounts of accessible data, we naturally assume that pattern recognition is supreme. When sophisticated algorithms met super-fast computing, and when network analysis joined with social science, we dramatically expanded our predictive power over individuals as well as masses. Today whole industries have arisen on the backs of pattern spotters. Nearly every major corporation hopes to transform mass consumer behavior into profit streams. Amazon can suggest the books we might enjoy. Netflix does the same for films. And Pandora predicts what songs we'll like to hear. These types of predictions of our preferences rely on pattern recognition. What many people may not realize is that, although these preference predictions seem targeted specifically at you and me, they are largely based on analysis of how vast numbers of people similar to us have previously behaved. As impressive as these algorithms are, there remains a limit to their magic.

Quantitative analysis fails us when statesmen are the subject. Knowing what past dictators have done in similar situations, for example, cannot shed much light on what the current autocrat may do. Each case of international conflict and every ruler is sufficiently unique to make analogical reasoning a dangerous endeavor.[7] Left to consider only the past behavior of a particular ruler, foreign leaders are caught in a quandary. Most of the time, the record of actions is mixed—full of seemingly conflicting behavior, out of which opposing interpretations can easily be drawn. In other words, if one seeks evidence of malignant or benign intentions, both can usually be found. This is why fixating on the patterns in enemy behavior can easily lead us in circles. We need to be aware of prior patterns, but we also need a better heuristic for making sense of what drives the other side.

Consider two historical examples that make this point. Throughout the 1930s, some British and French officials concluded it was best not to confront Hitler because they believed in his repeated assurances of peace. They observed his pattern of conciliatory behavior after each new demand, and they assumed he could therefore be appeased. In contrast, during the Cuban Missile Crisis, some American officials, such as Air

Force General Curtis LeMay, insisted that war with the Soviet Union was inevitable based on evidence of prior Soviet aggression. For that reason, LeMay strenuously argued for a full-scale attack on Cuba. Both sets of officials advocated policies based on patterns they perceived—patterns drawn from a selected sampling of data—and both sets of officials were wrong. If these policymakers had focused on a different sampling of data, they could have located the opposite patterns in their enemies' behavior. Winston Churchill, for example, saw in Hitler's behavior a pattern of insatiable aggression, whereas President John F. Kennedy saw evidence of Nikita Khrushchev's reluctance for war. Had statesmen in the 1930s correctly read Hitler, many lives might have been saved. Had statesmen in 1962 forced a direct confrontation with the Soviets, in the age of nuclear weapons, many more lives might have been lost. Reading the enemy right is clearly a priceless skill, and leaders cannot afford to ground their assessments in a select sampling of past behavior. Instead, they must understand what makes the current enemy tick. But how can we know in the moment which patterns reveal the enemy's true motives?

Leaders are better served not by straining to perceive patterns of behavior but by focusing their attention on behaviors at pattern breaks. It is at these moments when statesmen typically reveal their underlying drivers—those goals that are most important to them. These episodes can also expose much about a leader's character, showing the kind of measures he is willing to employ.

What Are Pattern Breaks?

Pattern breaks are merely deviations from the routine. These deviations can involve sudden spikes in violence, sharp reversals of policy, unexpected alterations in relations, or any substantial disruption from the norm. There are two main types of pattern breaks: pattern-break events and pattern-break behaviors. The behaviors provide valuable information about an enemy but only under certain conditions.

Naturally, pattern breaks frequently occur. Most are meaningless, but some are meaningful. To distinguish one from the other we must focus on costs. Henry Kissinger, the American National Security Adviser who negotiated with the North Vietnamese over an end to the war, offered an excellent example of a meaningless pattern break.

In his reflections on those negotiations, Kissinger explained how Hanoi invariably lectured America in its pronouncements, always insisting that the United States "must" do this or that. At one point Hanoi suddenly used a different word, declaring that the United States "should" meet a particular demand. Kissinger and his team thought they were on the brink of a major breakthrough. It proved a fleeting fancy. The next communication returned to the usual insistent language.[8] This momentary word change cost Hanoi nothing. In theory it could have marked a shift in Hanoi's attitude, but it revealed nothing about Hanoi's underlying intentions.

In contrast to Kissinger's experience, consider the Chernobyl nuclear accident of 1986 for a brief example of a meaningful pattern break. Although it took him more than two weeks to issue a public announcement, Gorbachev did disclose the true horror of what had occurred. Prior to that moment, Soviet leaders had typically denied any weaknesses in their economy or their society, invariably extolling the superiority of communism. By admitting that the nuclear disaster had occurred, and by inviting American medical experts into the Soviet Union to assist in caring for the sick, Gorbachev openly acknowledged certain failings of the Soviet system. He thereby risked incurring the enmity of the old-school hardliners within his regime. This was a pattern-break behavior, and it revealed much about the Soviet Premier. When he first came to power, Gorbachev initiated the reforms dubbed *Glasnost* and *Perestroika* (an openness to free speech and a rebuilding of the economy). For those outside observers who doubted the sincerity of these reforms, Gorbachev's behavior during Chernobyl indicated that he was a truly different leader from those who had preceded him. Chernobyl itself was a pattern-break event, and Gorbachev's behavior surrounding it revealed much about his underlying intentions.[9]

We must first be able to recognize patterns before we can spot a pattern break. When no breaks are apparent, we may have no better option than to assume that the enemy's future behavior will resemble his past. I call that the "continuity heuristic," and I will say more about it in chapter 8. It is a method with many flaws, though at times it is all we have to go on. Sometimes, however, there is a better way, a way that leaders have employed to good effect and one that can be just as valuable today.

To summarize, meaningful pattern breaks are those episodes that expose an enemy's underlying drivers or constraints. Those less obvious factors become apparent when an opponent behaves in a way that imposes genuine costs upon himself—costs with long-term implications. The enemy need not change his behavior at those times. He might continue on exactly as he had done before. The pattern break simply provides an opportunity for revealing what he values most. It acts as a spotlight, illuminating qualities that might otherwise be hidden. In the chapters that follow, we will witness cases of pattern-break events as well as pattern-break behaviors, and we will dig deeply into examples of meaningful pattern breaks that involved behaviors costly to the enemy in question. Above all, we will see how talented strategic empaths used those pattern breaks as teachable moments to help them gain a sharper sense of their enemy. As you encounter their stories, remember that strategic empathy is not a trait—a superior quality with which one is simply born. This might be true of empathy itself, though it is possible that empathy can be cultivated, but this would be the subject for a different book. *Strategic* empathy, on the other hand, should be thought of as a skill that you can develop and enhance. Like all skills, no matter how much you might practice, you can never achieve perfect results every time. Focusing on behaviors at pattern-break moments cannot guarantee an accurate reading of your rival's mind, but it can certainly up the odds.

The Overview

Each chapter investigates cases of how particular statesmen struggled with strategic empathy. Chapter 1 considers how Mahatma Gandhi read British leaders shortly after World War I, when the Indian independence movement was just about to blossom. Chapters 2 and 3 center on German Foreign Minister Gustav Stresemann's attempts to read the Russians in the 1920s. Amid the tumult of ever-changing Weimar coalitions, Stresemann remained the one steady leader of German foreign policy. His diplomatic acumen helped restore his defeated nation to a position of strength. These chapters ask how he did it.

Chapters 4 and 5 explore both Stalin's and Roosevelt's attempts to read Hitler in the years prior to Hitler's invasion of Russia. The central question is this: How did Stalin and FDR think about Hitler? To borrow a term from cognitive science, I am asking how they "mentalized" about their enemies. I explain what it means to mentalize by discussing the findings of cognitive scientists and relating their discoveries to historical subjects. Chapters 6 and 7 turn to Vietnam. They probe the North Vietnamese leadership's efforts to understand America in the years preceding the war's escalation. While we know a great deal about what American leaders thought about Vietnam during the war, far less has been written on what the North Vietnamese leaders thought about the United States. Few Americans even realize that the man largely running North Vietnam just prior to and during the war was not Ho Chi Minh but rather a shadowy figure named Le Duan. These chapters try to gain a sense of how Le Duan struggled to grasp America's drivers and constraints.

The first two of these historical cases (the chapters on Gandhi and Stresemann) provide examples of talented strategic empaths. The case of Stalin presents an example of empathic failure. In the case regarding Vietnam's Le Duan, the record is mixed. In each case I show that understanding pattern breaks provided an essential heuristic for achieving strategic empathy.

Chapter 8 steps back from particular case studies to consider several notable efforts to assess an enemy in the twentieth century. As a useful comparison, I consider the thinking behind the opposite of the pattern-break heuristic—what I refer to as the "continuity heuristic." By using past behavior as a guide, leaders and their advisors have often missed the mark. Finally, chapter 9 examines a present-day trend: a troubled love affair with quantitative analysis as the basis for predicting enemy behavior.

In an afterword I briefly describe how this book fits into the existing history and political science literature on enemy assessments, while I also spotlight some of the theories and concepts from other fields, which help illuminate our task. I then discuss my basic approach: the methodology I employ for tackling the questions surrounding the history of war and peace.

Most of the cases I consider in this book involve states in militarily and economically weaker positions with respect to their chief opponents. All nations need strategic empathy, but for the weaker states in any conflict, strategic empathy can be necessary for survival. If the

United States is entering a period in which its relative power is declining, the lessons from past strategic empaths will only rise in value. And even if this were not the case, America, or any nation in the stronger position, can always profit from a clearer sense of its enemies.

The Aim

My primary aim in this book is to write a history of international conflict through an alternative lens. In essence, I am conducting a meta-exercise: to think about how leaders thought about their enemies. Historians typically try to reconstruct the past through the eyes of history's key actors. We do this mainly by attempting to see the world as those people saw it. In the pages that follow, however, I am attempting to enter the minds of certain leaders, to see how they in turn tried to enter the minds of others.

Because this book is a work of history, it is more descriptive than prescriptive. It asks not what statesmen should have done but rather what they actually did, how they thought, and what they believed about their opponents. That said, the book has a secondary aim. This study may hold value for present-day analysts by highlighting ways of thinking about the problem of prediction.

I have still a third aim with this study. As with each of my previous books, I want to allow history to illuminate how we think. While the cognitive sciences, from psychology to behavioral economics and the like, are steadily advancing our knowledge of how the mind works, those fields suffer from a serious constraint. Their conclusions are based on carefully controlled laboratory experiments. As a result, it is much harder to say how people would behave under actual conditions. History, however, provides us with precisely that. It enables us to reconstruct how people thought and made decisions in real life, under the complex, uncontrolled, and uncontrollable conditions of their realities. This book, then, is also a study of historical decision-making.

The chapters that follow provide an alternative way of thinking about modern international affairs. Together they tell the story of how pivotal moments in history resulted from the ways that leaders identified their enemies' underlying drivers and constraints. I do not assume that strategic empathy is the sole cause of foreign policy successes. Multiple factors invariably combine to shape outcomes. Contingency and chance are always at play. A statesman's strategic empathy is only one factor in success, though I argue it is often a crucial one. How leaders came to think like their opponents is a telling and too often overlooked aspect of international conflict. If we can deepen our understanding of how key figures thought, we will better comprehend why wars are fought, lost, and won. And if we could actually apply those insights, we might just take one step closer to making war no more.

Before we can begin the exploration of the past century's greatest struggles, we first need to understand a bit about how we mentalize— meaning how we all try to enter into someone else's head—and we need to know about heuristics—the decision-making shortcuts we all employ. One powerful example of each can be found in the story of an eighteen-year-old orphan who had a chance to win a fortune. With the spot-lights on and cameras rolling, the young man had to mentalize about a stranger. Riches were in reach. All he had to do was to penetrate the mind of the enigmatic TV host who was offering a cryptic clue.

Slumdog Strategist

Jamal was on the spot. He had just two options left. If he chose wisely, he would win 10 million rupees and advance to the final round. If he chose poorly, he would lose it all. The entire Indian nation was watching. The problem was that Jamal did not know the answer. He had no choice but to guess.

In the blockbuster film *Slumdog Millionaire*, a young man from the Mumbai slums lands a spot on a popular game show. By an amazing run of good luck, despite his lack of formal education, Jamal is asked a series of questions to which he always knows the answers. The show's host, however, continues to belittle Jamal's success, demeaning him as a mere tea server from the slums. By the penultimate round the stakes have grown exceedingly high, and Jamal is stuck. Which cricketer has scored the most first-class centuries in history? His options are reduced to B or D. A commercial break allows the tension to stretch out. It also presents Jamal with a strategic conundrum.

During the break, Jamal and the host meet in the men's room. Jamal admits that he is clueless and will lose. To our surprise, the host encourages Jamal, telling him that if he selects the right answer, he will become the most fortunate slum dweller in India, the only person other than the host himself to have risen from extreme poverty to riches and fame. The host tells him not to lose heart. Before exiting the men's room, the host cryptically suggests: "Perhaps it is written." Jamal then sees that in the steam on the bathroom mirror the host has traced the letter B.

Jamal now needs to think strategically. If he trusts the host and believes he is giving him the correct answer, he can choose B with confidence. But if he thinks there is a chance that the host could be lying, wanting him to lose, then Jamal's situation becomes infinitely more complex. He cannot simply choose D, the cricketer Jack Hobbs, and be sure that this is correct. He must instead assess his enemy on two counts: how clever is the host, and how clever does the host think Jamal is.

The host might be setting a trap. The correct answer might in fact be B, but the host could be psyching Jamal out, giving him the right answer but expecting that Jamal will choose D just because it is the opposite of what the host advised. Of course, if Jamal thinks that the host expects him to expect this trap, then Jamal should instead choose D. At this point, Jamal could fall into an impossibly complicated loop of "if he thinks that I think that he thinks," ad infinitum.

But does anyone really think this way?[10] In fact, we almost never do. Instead, we all rely on heuristics—shortcuts for decision-making. Because no one can keep track of so many levels of second-guessing, heuristics help us to simplify strategic decisions with rules of thumb.

Jamal chose D, the cricketer Jack Hobbs, and he was right. The host had fed him the wrong answer in the mirror. Obviously, we cannot know for certain what Jamal, a fictional character, used for a shortcut to reach his decision, but the film does give us a number of clues. Up to this point we have witnessed flashbacks of key moments in Jamal's life, and they have been painful to watch. As a young boy he lost his mother to rampaging Hindu nationalists. He was nearly blinded by a cruel orphanage operator who drugged the children and scooped out their eyes with a spoon, then used them to beg for money on street corners. And his own brother separated him from the woman he loved. Given the information we have about Jamal, it is likely that he employed a simple heuristic: Trust no one.

Like Jamal, leaders also use heuristics in the game of international affairs, even though they have vastly more to lose than in a quiz show. Sometimes national leaders formulate their heuristics as maxims: The enemy of my enemy is my friend. Sometimes their heuristics are analogies: If aggressors are appeased, they will become as aggressive as Hitler after Munich. However dubious they might be, heuristics ease decision-making by simplifying the thinking process. Jamal's experience spotlights a hidden truth: When the stakes are high, we all need shortcuts for predicting our enemy's moves.

While Jamal's story gives us a hint of how we all try to strategize in high-stakes situations, that fictional tale can only take us so far. It's time to examine a true Indian hero, upon whom the eyes of every Indian, and indeed the entire world, were fixed. Mahatma Gandhi holds special interest in a study of strategic empathy precisely because he managed to win his nation's freedom without ever firing a single shot.

I

The Conscience of an Empire
Gandhi and the British Character

GENERAL REGINALD E. DYER thought he would teach the natives a lesson. On April 13, 1919, approximately 25,000 Punjabis assembled in the Jallianwala Bagh, a public square in Amritsar, for a festival celebration. The square, a mostly barren ground roughly 200 yards long and about as wide, had at its center a large well nearly twenty feet wide. The square was surrounded by the high walls of houses and apartments. There were just five narrow entryways to the grounds, some with locked gates, making it almost impossible to escape. Dyer positioned his troops to block the main exit. On a raised platform, the editor of an Amritsar newspaper was gesticulating, decrying the recent actions of colonial authorities. The silent crowd, absorbed in the speaker's words, had no reason to expect what happened next.

Dyer ordered his troops to open fire, directly into the heart of the assembled mass. As people screamed and fled to the sides of the square, Dyer directed his soldiers to aim at the walls and corners where they were concentrated. He instructed his men to continue firing until their ammunition was spent: all 1,650 rounds. The terror lasted between ten and fifteen minutes. Some died instantly; others were trampled to death in the frenzied scramble for cover. People piled atop one another, ten or twelve bodies deep, suffocating those beneath them. More than 100 others, desperate to avoid the bullets, leapt to their deaths down the well. From the rooftops and windows of the surrounding homes, residents looked down in horror.[1] When the killing spree at last abated, nearly 400 were dead, including a six-week-old baby. Dyer and his troops withdrew, leaving more than 1,000 wounded to fend for themselves. Astonishingly, Dyer did not stop there. Still intent on preventing rebellion from spreading, he instituted a crawling order, requiring any Indian who passed through the street where a British schoolteacher had been attacked to slither on his belly through the muck. There were no exceptions. Over the following weeks, hundreds were beaten, tortured, arrested, and imprisoned, nearly all without trial or evidence against them.[2]

Mahatma Gandhi faced a conundrum. In order to lead his nation to freedom, he had to adopt effective, long-term strategies of resistance to colonial authority. But to accomplish that, he needed to read the British correctly. Amritsar presented an opportunity. The massacre was a definite break in the pattern of British rule. Though colonial forces had often employed brutality, nothing this extreme had occurred since 1857, when British troops savagely crushed an Indian mutiny. Since then, lower levels of repression had remained the norm. But now General Dyer's attack marked a dramatic spike in the level of violence. In its wake Gandhi had to decide whether the majority of British leaders supported or opposed General Dyer's form of control. If it were the former—if Britain were a country governed by leaders who would not hesitate to gun down unarmed civilians in cold blood—then nonviolent disobedience had little chance to succeed.

Amritsar and its aftermath formed a pattern break, one that revealed much about the British as an enemy. Pattern breaks are teachable moments. They are the times when one side in a conflict reveals what it values most, hinting strongly at what it plans to do. What makes the Amritsar pattern break so compelling is that Gandhi actually determined that the majority of British leaders were not, in fact, supportive of harsh repression, yet he repeatedly said the opposite.

One popular image of Gandhi is of a man devoted to truth, simplicity, and love, a gentle soul peacefully spinning his yarn while defying an empire. And while he was indeed these things, Gandhi was also a British-trained lawyer, possessed of a clever mind and a potent dose of strategic empathy, which he had developed in part through years of immersion in British culture.[3] Because he had studied British patterns of behavior, he was therefore more attuned to their behavior at pattern breaks. Although Gandhi was appalled by what Dyer had done, he soon grasped the incident's enormous value for opposing British colonial rule, and he skillfully employed the massacre to serve multiple strategic ends. In Gandhi's rhetoric, Amritsar became a rallying point for Indian independence, a source of Hindu–Muslim unity, and a weapon in his battle for British hearts and minds. In 1920, referring to the British response to the massacre, Mahatma Gandhi called the Empire's representatives "dishonest and unscrupulous," proclaiming that he could "no longer retain affection for a Government so evilly manned as it is nowadays."[4] As chief author of the Indian National Congress's investigative report into Dyer's actions, he labeled the massacre a crime against humanity. In speeches across India, Gandhi rallied his countrymen by demanding redress for the events in the Punjab,[5] and in his 1927 autobiography, he reiterated the same scathing words, asserting that the Congress report "will enable the reader to see to what lengths the British Government is capable of going, and what inhumanities and barbarities it is capable of perpetrating in order to maintain its power."[6] Gandhi stuck to that line for as long as he could. As late as 1931, when the American journalist William Shirer asked Gandhi if he still had faith in British promises, the Mahatma replied: "I had faith in them—until 1919. But the Amritsar Massacre and the other atrocities in the Punjab changed my heart. And nothing has happened since to make me regain my faith."[7]

By repeatedly stoking Indian anger over Amritsar, Gandhi simultaneously fueled the self-rule movement while elevating himself and his cause to international prominence.[8] In fact, in the very same document in which he charged the British government as being "evilly manned," Gandhi also remarked that his speeches were "intended to create disaffection" in order that the Indian people would feel ashamed if they cooperated with the government.[9] Throughout the 1920s, Gandhi heaped his criticism of the British upon the pyres of Indian nationalism, hoping to inflame Indian opinion. The massacre, coupled with the perceived injustice over Dyer's light punishment, could hardly have been better suited to the task.

Gandhi also strove to keep the memory of Amritsar alive in order to foster Hindu–Muslim unity, since members of both religions had been killed there.[10] In this way, he used General Dyer's atrocity to serve the cause of independence. Building and maintaining amity between India's two largest religious groups remained one of Gandhi's prime objectives throughout his long drive for independence. He understood that a country riven by internal hatreds could not and would not survive intact, and he was determined to prevent the fracturing of India along religious lines. By encouraging all Indians to contribute money to a Jallianwala Bagh memorial, Gandhi believed he could construct a monument to religious harmony that would be a symbol of joint suffering at the hands of a common foe. In February 1920, Gandhi wrote: "In visiting the Bagh, our purpose is not to remind ourselves of General Dyer's cruelty. Men have always made mistakes. We do not want to keep alive the memory of General Dyer's wrong and thereby feed our hatred." Instead he saw it as a chance to raise the nation to a higher cause. And then he added: "Maybe we cannot bring about such a miraculous result from the slaughter of the innocent people in the Jallianwala Bagh; the event, however, will always be recognized as a potent influence in uniting Hindus and Muslims and in creating an awakening throughout the land." On February 18, 1920, Gandhi reiterated that the massacre must serve Hindu–Muslim unity. This, he insisted, was the primary meaning of the memorial. He reminded his readers that the blood of the Mohammedan had mixed with that of the Hindu, signifying their shared sacrifice. "The memorial," he opined, "should be a national emblem of an honest and sustained effort to achieve Hindu–Muslim unity."[11]

General Dyer had meant to quash a rebellion, but instead he fueled a movement that would eventually bring down the Raj. Gandhi deployed the massacre's memory to sting the British conscience over the injustice of colonial rule—and it worked.[12] Yet despite all his assertions of British evil and injustice, the Mahatma knew that most British leaders were repelled by what Dyer had done. Having had many years of exposure to British society, both from studying law in London and through interactions with British administrators in South Africa, Gandhi had developed a familiarity with various strands of British thinking about liberalism and empire. The question he now faced was which strand would prove stronger in the Dyer debate.

By early December 1919, Gandhi had concluded that British officials were repenting for Amritsar. "They may not do so in public, and General Dyer may say what he likes," Gandhi observed, but "they do feel ashamed, none the less. They dimly realize that they have made a mistake and, I am certain that, if we go about our task in a clean way, the time will come when they will repent openly."[13] On December 31, referring to the Queen's 1858 Proclamation granting Indians equality under the law, Gandhi made his point about British leaders explicit. The proclamation, he declared, "gives one an insight into the true British character." Gandhi saw Dyer as an aberration, a "man becoming devil under fear." In contrast, he viewed the royal decree, along with the Montagu Reforms of 1917, as evidence of British leaders' intention to do justice to India. Gandhi even made a point of calling the Secretary of State for India, Edwin Montagu, a "true friend to India" and someone who had earned the gratitude of all Indians.[14]

Gandhi had read his enemy correctly. The Amritsar pattern break showed not that the British were evil but that they suffered deep remorse. In the massacre's aftermath a sizeable segment of the British public and its leaders ardently opposed Dyer's form of repression. Edwin Montagu found the cold-blooded killings so objectionable that he launched an inquiry into the entire affair and spoke passionately before the House of Commons against the atrocity. Though the subsequent report of Lord Hunter's committee largely exonerated General Dyer—which rightly outraged most Indians—it did lay bare much of the "frightfulness" of his deeds in grim detail. As for the humiliating crawling order, no one above Dyer in the military chain of command saw any need for such excess. Even the Lieutenant Governor of the Punjab, who supported Dyer to the end, rescinded the order once he learned of it.[15]

As reports of the atrocity filtered back to London, reaction was extreme. A vocal segment of conservatives hailed Dyer as a hero, dubbing him the man who saved India. A campaign spearheaded by the *Morning Post* raised a stunning 28,000 pounds for the General, making him suddenly a wealthy man.[16] But a more significant part of the public felt sickened by the affair. Both the left-of-center *Manchester Guardian* and the right-of-center *Times of London* harshly criticized the General's actions.[17]

Britain's political leaders proved no less ardent in their views. In June, at the Labour Party's annual conference, the delegates boldly demonstrated their opinion by unanimously resolving that the officers in Punjab be recalled and tried and all repressive legislation be repealed. As for the governing Liberal Party, it too could not stomach what Dyer had done. It sought to sack the General at once, but the conservatives demanded a debate in Parliament. It was in this protracted session that British leaders exposed their true convictions. Most could not condone Dyer's brutal ways.

Gandhi's collected writings during this time evidence that he stayed abreast of debates in the House of Commons. They do not appear to indicate a direct reference to these debates on General Dyer, but it is highly doubtful that Gandhi would have ignored them. Anyone interested in gauging the British leaders' sentiments and predicting their likely responses to future protests would have found in those speeches valuable nuggets of information. However, even if he had not read the newspaper synopses of those speeches, by 1920 Gandhi had already decided to use the Jallianwala Bagh atrocity to further his cause. The knowledge of what was said in Parliament would not have altered his course; it would only have further substantiated his convictions regarding the British character.

On July 8, 1920, the House of Commons met in a caustic and incendiary session to determine General Dyer's fate. The General was present in the chamber, along with Sir Michael O'Dwyer, the Lieutenant Governor for the Punjab. The debate began with a speech by Edwin Montagu, the Secretary of State for India, who lambasted Dyer. Conservatives shouted him down, interrupting, badgering, and bullying him at every turn. The Conservatives who taunted Montagu despised him on multiple counts. They resented his 1917 reforms, which they saw as lessening the power of the British Raj and weakening the empire as a whole. They also disliked him on racial grounds. Montagu was Jewish, and those Conservatives loathed the idea that a gallant Brigadier could be skewered by a "crooked Jew."[18]

Despite the Conservatives' verbal battering, Montagu spoke forcefully against what Dyer had done. He put the matter bluntly, equating support for Dyer's actions with support for terrorism. "Are you going to keep your hold upon India by terrorism, racial humiliation and subordination, and frightfulness," the Secretary asked, "or are you going to rest it upon the goodwill, and the growing goodwill, of the people of your Indian Empire?"[19]

The deadly trap with a policy of terrorism, Montagu explained, is that it compels the wielders to apply ever more force against ever-growing opposition. There can be no end to it, he continued, until the Indian people rise up and terminate your rule. Montagu maintained that the only viable alternative was for Britain to enable India to become a completely free partner in the Commonwealth. He implored the House to say to Indians: "We hold British lives sacred, but we hold Indian lives sacred, too."[20]

Naturally, those who supported General Dyer did not appreciate being likened to terrorists. Those who spoke on the General's behalf argued that he was defending the civilian population by putting down a rebellion. Had he not acted with decisiveness, many more lives would have been lost. The English population, especially the women, were deeply grateful to Dyer for safeguarding their lives and their honor. The Sikhs, whose Golden Temple sits in Amritsar and who had long comprised a reliable part of the British military, offered to make Dyer an honorary Sikh in gratitude for his preservation of law and order. It was unfair, Dyer's supporters charged, for those who sat comfortably in London, thousands of miles from the scene and more than a year after the event, to judge the General for doing what he deemed necessary under the circumstances. It was wrong, they insisted, to break a man after thirty-four years of exemplary service for having committed an error of judgment.

Labour members took a rather different stand. Mr. B. G. Spoor asserted that until we "recognise the sacredness of Indian life as on a par with the sacredness of European life . . . our policy in that country will be a failure." He called for the government to go beyond mere censuring of General Dyer and to hold all of those involved in the massacre accountable. Spoor said that Britain must eradicate the "pre-historic mental outlook" that was driving Indian unrest, and he cited the noncooperation movement that had recently awakened Indians to their plight. Spoor hoped one day to see all Indians truly free.

Also speaking for Labour, Colonel Josiah Wedgwood went even further in support of justice. He observed that because every word said in the House that day would be read by Indians, every speech should attempt to show them that the English people unequivocally condemned the Amritsar murders.[21]

The ruling Liberal government found itself besieged by both the Left and Right. Labour felt the government had not gone far enough in punishing all those involved, while Conservatives believed it had gone too far by persecuting a gallant General. Although leading Liberals such as former Prime Minister Herbert Asquith had backed Montagu, calling Amritsar "one of the worst outrages in our whole history," the government continued to fall under furious Conservative attacks throughout the session. In hope of salvaging the government's position, it sent to the floor one of its most articulate orators, a man known for his unshakable support of the empire, a man who himself had fought and fired on native peoples. Who better to counter charges of being soft on military matters than the current Secretary of State for War?

Winston Churchill marched defiantly out of the nineteenth century, both hands clenched upon the jewel in the empire's crown. From his early years in Parliament to the end of his days, Churchill never accepted the notion that Indians could rule themselves without Britain's civilizing lead. As late as 1935, still viewing Indians as children, Churchill led a final desperate charge against the Government of India bill, which guaranteed a path to independence. His backward-looking vision met with total defeat.[22] Yet even this dogmatic champion of empire broke ranks in 1920 to speak against General Dyer.

Stunning the Commons not with his usual rhetorical pomposity but rather with a chilling account of the facts, Churchill laid out the gruesome details of precisely how Dyer's troops slaughtered Indian civilians. He stressed that the Amritsar assembly was neither armed nor attacking—facts that made Dyer's decision an act of murder, not an act of self-defense, and therefore thoroughly indefensible. The massacre, he declared, was unparalleled in the history of the British Empire; it was "a monstrous event, an event which stands in singular and sinister isolation." "We have to make it absolutely clear, some way or another," he implored, "that this is not the British way of doing business."[23]

The Empire had never, and indeed could never, rely on force alone, he averred. In every part of the Empire, he continued, the British have always aimed at "close and effectual cooperation" with the native peoples. General Dyer should not simply have been censured, Churchill concluded, but disciplined and forced to retire. While his speech in no way signaled a softening of his intention to maintain British dominion over India, it demonstrated his core conviction that abject brutality could not be tolerated. In the end, Churchill's and the government's position triumphed. Both of the motions to reduce Montagu's salary—symbolic gestures meant to register opposition to the government's forced retiring of Dyer—were overwhelmingly defeated. The vote totals themselves indicated how the mainstream of British leaders stood, since the Conservatives held the vast majority of seats. Only the diehard fringe supported Dyer's deeds. General Dyer left the Commons with his reputation in ruins. He would forever be remembered as the "Butcher of Amritsar."

Churchill's principled stand came at some personal cost, making it all the more remarkable. Still hoping to resurrect his political career following his disastrous Gallipoli campaign of World War I, he could ill afford to lose more credibility. A neutral position on Dyer might have been politically expedient and would at least have spared him the inevitable hostile critiques. Charles Frederick Palmer, a member of Parliament speaking in Dyer's defense, denigrated Churchill for having cost more lives than anyone sitting in the chamber.[24] The *Morning Post* seized on Palmer's remarks, comparing the 379 Indian lives taken at Dyer's hands to the more than 41,000 killed and captured at Gallipoli.[25] The words stung, but Churchill understood the distinction between military debacles and mass murder. He hoped that the bulk of the British people would grasp it as well.

Anyone who hoped to gauge the likely success of nonviolence as a strategy for defeating the British Empire could have learned much from Amritsar and its aftermath, particularly when contrasted with a previous atrocity of comparable magnitude. The savage British suppression of the 1857 mutiny was not followed by any public soul searching. There were no government-sponsored reparations to the victims' dependents, no calls by opposition parties for the trial of those officers responsible, and certainly no debates in the House of Commons describing the British acts as monstrous events. Times had changed, and a dispassionate observer could have sensed the shift.

Amritsar was a pattern-break moment. Rather than revealing an evil empire, the episode exposed a growing British queasiness with repression. To fire on unarmed crowds had become abhorrent. A significant segment of the British public and its leaders simply no longer accepted the traditional harsh-handed response to protest. If even a stalwart imperialist like Churchill opposed the slaughter of unarmed natives, the implications for how to beat the British were profound. It meant that colonial authorities would not dare fire on great masses of peaceful protestors flouting British laws. It meant that a strategy of aggressive nonviolence could work.

As Gandhi was absorbing the lessons of Amritsar, other Indians reacted viscerally to Britain's meager punishment of Dyer. When Motilal Nehru, a leader of the Indian National Congress and father of the future first Indian Prime Minister, learned of the Hunter Committee's inadequate treatment of Dyer, he famously threw every article of European clothing and furniture on a bonfire and burned it. It marked the turning point after which he became a convert to Gandhi's point of view. Nehru was not alone. Many more Indians reacted angrily to the sense of injustice and joined the noncooperation movement with a vengeance. It was precisely what Gandhi had hoped for, and he did not hesitate to stoke the flames of indignation by pointing out that justice was not served. Although the punishment of General Dyer was far less than he deserved, the remorse surrounding the affair was greater than what that punishment suggested. It was clear to Gandhi that British remorse was real and that another Amritsar was unlikely to occur. If it did, the British and the international condemnation could only work to the ultimate benefit of independence. When Gandhi led his famous salt march to the sea in 1930 in direct defiance of British law, he did so armed with only his walking staff. The thousands of Indians who followed him stood equally unarmed in the face of colonial police. Yet not a shot was fired. Gandhi had gauged his enemy correctly.

Gandhi understood that Indians would never receive justice or freedom without agitating for it. Yet because he viewed most British leaders as honorable, he cooperated with them when prudent, as he did most notably in 1931 on the Gandhi-Irwin Pact. The slow pace of reforms never made him lose heart in British liberalism. He could not have pursued nonviolence for decades without an unshakable faith in the British conscience.[26]

In the end, Gandhi's movement triggered even more than his nation's freedom. It sparked a wave of decolonization that ended the age of empire and transformed the world. His nonviolent methods inspired national liberation leaders from Ghana to South Africa and beyond. His ideals empowered those fighting for equality in America as well, from César Chávez to Martin Luther King Jr.[27] Although these global repercussions could not have been foreseen, the success of Gandhian nonviolence for India was, in fact, foreseeable, given what this episode revealed about Churchill in particular and the British leadership as a whole. If, in 1920, you had wanted to predict whether nonviolence could help win India's independence, the Amritsar pattern break contained some vital clues.

If the years immediately following World War I proved turbulent for India, in Europe they were bringing even more unrest. Our next leader of interest must be considered a remarkable man because of the complex and dangerous relations he navigated while in office. After the horrors of World War I, when the guns of August had fallen still, it soon became apparent that Europe was again at risk. Revolutions and political violence became the norm, and international antagonisms threatened the shaky peace. In the wake of such a devastating global conflict, the premium on properly assessing one's opponents rose substantially. Amid extreme upheavals, a German statesman emerged who helped set his nation back on course toward stability and strength. Had he lived long enough to combat the Nazis who eventually replaced him, modern history might have taken a dramatically different turn. Unlike Gandhi, who had lived for several years in Britain and gained a firsthand sense of the people and their politics, Gustav Stresemann had far less familiarity with the new and violent Soviet regime. Yet he could hardly afford to misread it, for at the same time that Russia's rulers were supposedly cooperating, they were also working to overthrow him.

2

Arming Your Enemy
Stresemann's Maneuver, Act I

FROM FLAPPERS AND THE Charleston, to speakeasies and the Wall Street boom, America's roaring twenties are remembered as a time of exuberance and hope. Having emerged from World War I as the world's largest creditor nation, the United States enjoyed a decade of economic growth. But Europe's 1920s stood in shocking contrast. Devastated by the Great War, Britain and France had lost a generation of young men. The Russian Revolution had unleashed fears of contagious unrest. And nowhere on the continent was the situation more unstable than in Germany. The decade's early years brought invasion, hyperinflation, political assassinations, and revolts across the nation. Throughout the tumult, one of the few steady hands was Dr. Gustav Stresemann.

Squat and stocky, a lover of good food and wine, Stresemann never saw fit to exercise. He consumed his work like his meals, spending long hours and late nights at his desk. There was an intensity to his manner, whether opining on high literature or dissecting political alignments. So much of his passion shone through in his face. His personal secretary once described his boss's "watery and bloated skin" as merely the frame around his piercing eyes.[1] Born in 1878 to a lower-middle-class beer distributor in Berlin, Stresemann developed into something of a *Wunderkind*. By the age of twenty-one, he had already earned a doctorate in economics, writing his dissertation on the bottled beer industry. He landed his first job in Dresden, representing the organization of chocolate manufacturers for the state of Saxony. As a lobbyist for industry, he became closely tied to politics. In 1906, he won a seat on the town council, and the following year he stood for and won a seat in the German Parliament as a member of the National Liberal Party. When World War I came, a weak heart left him unable to serve. Later he would suffer from kidney disease. His overall ill health condemned him to die in office, much too young and far too soon to check the spread of extremism.

After the war, Stresemann emerged as a leader in the right-of-center German People's Party, serving a mere 100 days as Chancellor, then assuming the role of foreign minister, a post he would retain until his death in 1929. Within a few years of taking office, Stresemann came to be seen by Western publics as a sensible statesman intent on establishing his country as a cornerstone of European stability. Coming to terms with Britain and France at a meeting in Locarno, Switzerland, in 1925, Stresemann pledged Germany to join the League of Nations, settle its disputes with eastern neighbors, and preserve the current arrangements in the West. In recognition of Locarno, he was awarded the Nobel Prize for Peace.[2] Albert Einstein later praised Stresemann as a great leader, asserting that his finest achievement was "to induce a number of large political groups, against their own political instincts, to give their support to a comprehensive campaign of European reconciliation." Einstein concluded that Stresemann was a "man of mind and bearer of an idea. . . . as different from politicians of the usual stamp as a genius differs from an expert."[3]

The Locarno Agreement has been called the hinge on which the interwar era turned. It marked the true end of the First World War, and its collapse eased the way for the Second to occur. Despite its ultimate failure, the "spirit of Locarno" stabilized Germany's international relations and reestablished Germany as an equal among the European powers.[4] Given the series of crises that the Weimar government confronted following the war, maneuvering Germany back to strength was a remarkable feat, one that only a masterful strategic empath could pull off.

How did Stresemann do it? How did he succeed in sensing his rivals' drivers and thereby help reclaim his country's greatness? One way to answer that question is by focusing on Stresemann's reading of the Russians: the pattern of Soviet behavior and their behavior at pattern breaks.

In order to restore his nation's position among the great powers, Stresemann needed to balance dangerously delicate relations with Britain and France on the one hand and with Soviet Russia on the other. He had to manage this while simultaneously safeguarding his own position atop the Foreign Ministry. The keystones of his Western strategy were twofold: fulfill the terms of the Versailles Treaty (a policy dubbed "fulfill-ment") and normalize relations with Britain and France. To bolster his bargaining position with the Western powers, he needed to foster ties to the Soviet Union through overt accords and covert deals. It was a daring strategy. Any moves too far into one camp or the other risked upending the entire endeavor. To advance along such a tenuous tightrope, Strese-mann had to assess the drivers and constraints of his adversaries both East and West. While the drivers of Western statesmen were not always completely transparent, they were far simpler to assess than those of the Soviets. Gauging whether the Soviets wanted to ally with the German government or to overthrow it formed a crucial test of Stresemann's stra-tegic empathy. Fortunately, he possessed a true knack for learning how the other side thought and felt.

One of Stresemann's contemporaries, Antonina Vallentin, tried to encapsulate the great statesman's diplomatic aplomb:

> The moment he sat down opposite a man, he was no longer confined within his own personality, he felt himself into the other man's mind and feelings with such amazing accuracy that he could follow the most unusual trains of thought as quickly as if he had been familiar with them for years. He could thus forestall objections, and so startle his interlocutor by his intuition, that the latter found himself strangely disposed to reach agreement. . . . His sudden flashes of capacity for self-transference into another's mind gave him moments of uncanny clarity of vision such as scarcely any statesman has possessed before him.[5]

Stresemann's empathic gifts undeniably aided his sense of what drove others around him. Yet the traits that Vallentin described were not the only factors fueling Stresemann's success. The Foreign Minister also possessed an acute capacity for recognizing the constraints upon his rivals. From the moment he assumed the Chancellorship through his long tenure as Foreign Minister, he would need every drop of strategic empathy he could muster when dealing with the Soviets. The Russians played diplomatic hardball, and Lenin had skillfully selected the man to represent the Bolshevik regime.

Georgi Chicherin stood in striking contrast to his German counterpart. Unlike Stresemann, whose father was a lower-middle-class beer distributor, Chicherin was heir to the refined traditions of Russia's landed aristocracy. Tall and heavy-set, with a moustache and thin beard, Chicherin walked hunched over, as if weighted down by the knowledge contained in his capacious mind. Conversant in English, French, German, Italian, Serbian, and Polish, he could dictate cables in multiple languages simultaneously. He played piano expertly and studied the works of the composers he adored: Mozart, Beethoven, and Wagner. Like Stresemann, Chicherin never exercised, typically working at his desk until early morning, and his health suffered as a result. Intensely introverted, his preference for books over people left him with long hours to absorb seemingly endless facts and figures.[6] Riveted by history, he consumed volumes about the wider world. In 1904, he adopted Marxism, and with it came the zeal of the converted. His commitment to the movement had a passion that rivaled even Lenin's. He gave all that he possessed—wealth, time, energy, and talent—to furthering the cause. Intent on renouncing the outward ostentation of his class, he lived in spartan accommodations and wore only a single yellow-brown tweed suit, never varying his attire. Chicherin's convictions, coupled with his extraordinary breadth of knowledge and his aristocratic erudition, made him a brilliant choice by Lenin to lead the Soviet Foreign Ministry. The statesmen of Europe could not begrudge him their respect. He was, in short, a daunting opponent in diplomatic affairs.

One of Chicherin's earliest impressions on the world stage came at the economic conference in Genoa, Italy, in 1922, when he stunned his Western interlocutors. The Bolsheviks had not only frightened Western states by threatening to spread revolution throughout the world; they had also earned Western ire by repudiating the Tsarist debts. Britain and France in particular had invested enormous sums into prewar Russia, and they fully intended to recoup those funds. The Bolsheviks maintained that the corrupt Romanov dynasty did not represent the Russian people's will, and therefore the new communist regime was not bound to honor Tsarist commitments. At Genoa, Britain and France pressed their case with the Soviet delegation. Chicherin responded by presenting the Allies with the Soviet Union's counter-claims—to the staggering tune of 35 billion gold marks, a figure even greater than what the Allies claimed was owed to them.

To justify these counter-claims, Chicherin, along with his deputy Maxim Litvinov, conjured up an obscure precedent of international law. Chicherin drew British attention to the Alabama Claims Case, which followed the American Civil War. During that conflict in the 1860s, Britain had supported the South, even funding the building of southern warships, one of which was called the *Alabama*. After the U.S. Civil War concluded and the North prevailed, the American federal government sued Great Britain for damages inflicted on the North by those British-built ships. The United States won the case, and Britain paid. Chicherin then drew the obvious analogy. During the Bolshevik struggle for power against the conservative White Russian armies, Britain and her allies had supported the Whites, thereby prolonging the conflict. Chicherin asserted that Britain and her allies therefore owed the Bolshevik regime for damages inflicted during the Russian Civil War. The Soviets, rather conveniently, estimated those damages at an amount even greater than what the Tsarist government owed the West.

Britain's Prime Minister, David Lloyd George, was, in a word, flabbergasted. He retorted that Britain had never billed France for its support of the British monarchy during the English Civil War, and France had not billed Britain for its support of the Bourbons in the French Revolution.[7] Lloyd George's protestations notwithstanding, the fact remained that the Allies had actively intervened against the Bolshevik government, backing anti-Bolshevik Russian armies, and even deploying forces of their own. The analogy remained, and negotiations stood at an impasse.

Although Chicherin had the capacity to rival Stresemann in diplomatic skill, Chicherin was hamstrung by the Politburo, the key decision-making body of which he was not even a member. Unlike Stresemann, who had tremendous latitude over German foreign policy, the Soviet Foreign Minister was forced to execute the wishes of his superiors. In fact, if Chicherin had had his way, the Soviet Union would have honored the Tsarist debts. He urged Lenin to do so, but Lenin was adamant. On May 2, 1922, Lenin sent a telegram to the Soviet delegation essentially ordering his foreign minister not to grant any concessions to the West. The Soviet government would not even return any private property it had seized since the revolution. If Chicherin vacillated, Lenin threatened, he would be publicly disavowed. Before the message was sent, the Politburo removed the language about discrediting its foreign minister, but it retained the stern warnings not to compromise.[8] There was nothing Chicherin could do.

Using his formidable knowledge of history and world affairs, Chicherin fell into line, toughened the Soviet position, and dispatched an armada of arguments like the Alabama Claims case. As with so many legal wranglings, the move was extremely clever and thoroughly unwise. The talks eventually disbanded without agreement. Constructive diplomatic relations between Russia and Britain would not resume for years. Later in the conference, the Soviet delegation met secretly with German representatives at the nearby town of Rapallo. There, the then German Foreign Minister Walther Rathenau signed the treaty renouncing all debts between the Russian government and his own, and the two countries embarked on a troubled alliance that would shape the decade to come.

Struggling for Stability

We cannot comprehend the full challenge Stresemann confronted in reading the Russians without first recognizing the dangerous environment in which he had to function. Stresemann had to develop his strategic empathy in the crucible of nationwide upheaval. He and most of Germany's prominent politicians in the immediate postwar years risked much more than merely their careers. In a very real sense, they had reason to fear for their lives. With the stakes this high, knowing one's enemy could literally be vital.

In January 1919, both of the German Communist Party's (KPD) most prominent spokesmen, the fiery Jewish intellectual Rosa Luxemburg and the rash Karl Liebknecht, were murdered by right-wing Free Corps units, paramilitary bands that had sprung up across the nation. Another left-wing leader, Bavaria's Jewish Minister-President Kurt Eisener, was shot and killed in Munich. Immediately thereafter, Bavaria declared itself a Soviet Republic. Within one month, that government was overthrown by Reichswehr (the German military) and Free Corps forces who killed more than 1,000 government supporters during the struggle. The following year, Free Corps units under the leadership of Wolfgang Kapp marched on Berlin, forcing officials of the federal government to flee to Stuttgart. Though militarily proficient, Kapp and his men failed to forge the political alliances needed to govern. A general strike quickly brought them down, and the Social Democratic government returned to power.

The year 1921 saw workers' strikes and revolts flare up across the country. In the wake of Rosa Luxemburg's assassination, Ruth Fischer, a fervent Marxist who had helped found the Austrian Communist Party before moving to Berlin, assumed an increasing leadership role within the KPD. Yet neither she nor her comrades were able to inspire enough of the German working class, the majority of whom still supported the more moderate Social Democratic Party. The KPD attempted to spark a revolution, but the unrest was met with force and quelled.

Political violence touched even some of the government's highest officials. In 1922, Weimar's first Chancellor, Philipp Scheidemann, who had resigned in protest over the Versailles Treaty, went strolling in the woods. His daughter, along with her eight-year-old niece, walked at his side. From behind a large tree, an assailant rushed toward the ex-Chancellor and sprayed acid at his face. The chemicals missed his head, burning instead his arms and legs. Prudently, given the climate of political violence at the time, Scheidemann was armed. Pulling a revolver from his pocket, he managed to fire two shots before he collapsed. The perpetrator and his accomplice escaped.[9] Years later, Scheidemann's assailants were captured and tried. In their defense they claimed that their actions had been inspired by the right-wing media.

One of the first to contact Scheidemann to congratulate him on his escape was the German Jewish Foreign Minister, Walther Rathenau. A few weeks later, when Rathenau was driving to work at the Foreign Ministry, armed gunmen drove up beside him, fired machine guns, and lobbed a hand grenade into his car. It was Rathenau who had signed the Rapallo Treaty with Russia, normalizing relations with the communist regime, an extraordinary diplomatic move but one that the far right-wing could not abide.

As turbulent as the political scene had become, it was about to grow worse. In January of 1923, French and Belgian armies invaded. Frustrated over Germany's refusal to pay the exceedingly high reparations imposed at Versailles, France and Belgium seized the coal-producing Ruhr region of western Germany. The plan was ill-conceived from the start. Militarily, Germany had no means of response. Unwilling to accept a violation of its sovereignty, the German government organized a general strike in the region. Without German workers to mine and extract the coal, France had no ability to remove what it had seized. A popular cartoon of the day depicted a French general telegraphing to Paris that the military operations had gone exactly to plan, but the soldiers were freezing, so please send some coal.

Just as Kapp's plans had succeeded militarily but foundered politically, defeated by a general strike, the French and Belgian efforts met a similar result. Force could not accomplish what only a political solution could achieve. Yet the strike took a painful toll on the German populace. In order to maintain their defiant action, the federal government continued to pay workers in the Ruhr not to work. This decision, combined with the printing of money in order to purposely inflate the Reichsmark and thereby render reparation payments worthless, led to hyperinflation. The political costs of extreme economic dysfunction left the country primed for revolution.

It was in this troubled context that Gustav Stresemann assumed the Chancellorship in August of 1923. Although he served as Chancellor for a scant three months, it proved a breathtakingly tense period. Facing the fallout from domestic hyperinflation and foreign invasion would have challenged any new regime. On the economic front, Stresemann's introduction of the Rentenmark dramatically reduced inflation.[10] On the political front, however, instability was still deadly. On September 26, Stresemann called off resistance to the Ruhr occupation, realizing that it only inflamed the situation and hindered Germany's hopes of normalizing relations with the West. Continued truculence could not raise the nation up from its supine posture. He believed that a certain degree of compliance with the West was the only feasible method of getting Germany back on its feet and restoring its strength. The danger in his fulfillment policy was that the far right viewed it as unforgivable: nothing less than subservience to the victors. Unbeknownst to

Stresemann, scarcely more than one month into his Chancellorship, Hugo Stinnes, an extremely wealthy Ruhr industrialist, was plotting a coup. Stinnes approached American Ambassador Alinson B. Houghton to feel out whether he could obtain American support. In place of Stresemann, Stinnes himself, along with the head of the Reichswehr, Hans von Seeckt, and the former chief of the Krupp corporation would rule Germany, presumably ensuring order and economic growth. This in turn would enhance Germany's ability to repay its reparations to the United States and others. American Secretary of State Charles Evans Hughes was not impressed, and the plot never materialized.[11]

But this was merely the first bullet that Stresemann luckily escaped. Another came from within a rogue band of the German military. Hans von Seeckt, head of the Reichswehr and a staunch monarchist, had no fondness for the Weimar Republic. He served the state in order to rebuild the military. His eventual hope was to destroy Poland and restore German borders to their prewar frontiers. Although in 1920 he had refused to move the Reichswehr against the Kapp putsch, leaving the Weimar government in the lurch, he did act decisively to crush a putsch attempt on the night of September 29, 1923. For several years, a clandestine group within the military known as the Black Reichswehr had been murdering Germans who cooperated with the Inter-Allied Military Control Commission, a body established by the victors in World War I to inspect and oversee German disarmament. Now a Black Reichswehr leader, Major Bruno Buchrucker, captured several forts on the outskirts of Berlin, the first step toward a coup d'état. Seeckt ordered the official Reichswehr to put down the attempt. Buchrucker capitulated after only two days. He was tried, fined, and sentenced to prison.[12] General Seeckt used this opportunity to disband the Black Reichswehr, rather than lose control of it.

Where the Russians Stood

The Reichswehr's intrigues proved minor in comparison to the two large-scale violent uprisings that Stresemann next confronted. One came from the Right, when Adolf Hitler launched his notorious Beer Hall Putsch. The other emerged from the Left, when the Soviet Union's leadership instigated what it hoped would be a communist seizure of power.

Moscow's attempt to topple Stresemann's regime and spark a revolution across Germany left Stresemann in a bind. For the remainder of his time in office, he would need to maintain extreme vigilance against a repeated Soviet threat while at the same time cooperating with the Russians to help gain leverage against Britain and France. His most immediate concern in 1923, however, was simply to survive.

On August 23, 1923, the Politburo met to discuss opportunities for fomenting a German revolution. Leon Trotsky was the most enthusiastic, believing that Germany's time was imminent. Grigory Zinoviev was only slightly less optimistic, assuming that the revolution might still be months away. Their expectations resulted in part from the popular German resistance to the French invasion of the Ruhr earlier in the year. Stalin, in contrast, doubted that a revolution would succeed, but he had not yet consolidated his power within the group. Years later, he would use the fact that he had been right to discredit his rivals. But in the fall of 1923, Trotsky and Zinoviev held greater sway. Karl Radek, the Communist International (Comintern) member most knowledgeable about Germany, also believed that the German masses were not yet prepared to take the requisite action in support of a revolution, but he did not express his full concerns at the Politburo meeting. Heinrich Brandler, who led the KPD, tried to resist the push for immediate uprisings, but during a series of meetings in Moscow, his reluctance withered. Under pressure, Brandler consented to the ill-conceived plot.[13]

On paper, the scheme must have seemed plausible. Using the Soviet embassy in Berlin as cover, Moscow smuggled money and advisors into Germany to help organize the coming assaults. The Politburo charged the Soviet Ambassador to Germany, Nikolai Krestinski, with overseeing the secret funds.[14] The Soviets covertly shipped weapons from Petrograd to Hamburg, which were then off-loaded by Communist Party longshoremen. These party members stored the weapons in areas under their control. The entire operation was to be overseen by Radek. Meanwhile, Brandler was instructed to ally with Social Democrats of Saxony and organize 50,000 to 60,000 workers to serve essentially as armed paramilitary units, warding off the expected attacks from the Right. Brandler asked Moscow to send an appropriate expert to coordinate the revolution's military aspects. Peter Skoblevsky, who served as a general during the Russian Civil War, arrived to take charge of all armed operations.

Spotting the signs of increased agitation, the Prussian police began cracking down on the KPD in late August. They raided the office of the communist newspaper, the *Rote Fahne* (Red Flag), and soon thereafter raided the Party's headquarters. They had a warrant for Ruth Fischer's arrest, but she was not to be found. Fischer, along with Brandler and other top communists, were already in (or heading toward) Moscow, making plans for the coming seizure of power. Trotsky distrusted Fischer and preferred that she remain in Moscow during the revolution, but Zinoviev opposed him on this point. As a compromise, Fischer was permitted to return to Germany, while her colleague Arkady Maslow was forced to stay behind and endure an investigation of his past performance within the Party.

Soviet Russia's dual policy of conducting traditional diplomacy on the one hand while supporting foreign revolutions on the other left diplomats and statesmen both frustrated and perplexed. The German Ambassador in Moscow, Count Ulrich von Brockdorff-Rantzau, reported on his conversations with Soviet Foreign Minister Chicherin. The Soviets were anxious over the possibility of a Franco–German alliance that would leave Russia isolated. This fear would haunt Moscow throughout the interwar era. Yet if this were truly a Soviet concern, then Russian policy seemed contradictory. In the wake of ongoing Soviet support for communist upheavals in Germany, Brockdorff-Rantzau expressed the same confusion occurring across Western capitals. Just who was making Russian foreign policy: the government or the communist party?[15]

Diplomacy is full of duplicity, and the Ambassador's conversations with Karl Radek illustrate this well. On September 27, Brockdorff-Rantzau complained to Radek about an article in the German Communist newspaper *Rote Fahne* in which Leon Trotsky called for a widening of revolutionary activity. Radek explained that Trotsky was merely referring to activity in Bulgaria. There was no reason for concern. Radek expressed confidence in the possibilities for greater German–Soviet cooperation.[16] In actuality, Radek was not only aware of the imminent German communist uprising, he was in the midst of organizing it.

Fortunately for Stresemann, the October revolution was a total failure. German communists lacked both the popular support and the military sophistication to replicate 1917. Unable to obtain the support of German Social Democrats, Brandler called off the uprisings before they ever switched into high gear. Reichswehr forces moved into Saxony and thwarted any insurrection. Word of the cancellation could not reach Hamburg in time, where revolutionaries were crushed by police. Adding insult to injury, even the revolution's military head, General Skoblevsky, was captured and imprisoned. Shortly after the communist uprising was aborted, Adolf Hitler set a right-wing coup in motion in Bavaria. Stresemann immediately issued a report to the heads of all German states. Hitler's act of high treason would be countered with the full energy of the government. Stresemann survived both challenges, thanks in both cases to strong police and military actions, as well as his own decisive response. The lessons were clear. Stability was essential if a politically moderate government in Berlin hoped to continue.

Within such a tempestuous domestic and international scene, Germany needed stability abroad as much as at home. Soviet Russia represented one essential part of the foreign policy puzzle. Unfortunately for Stresemann, the Russian piece was exceedingly hard to fit into place. This was partly because Stresemann could not forget the Bolshevik attempt to overthrow him. He would remain conscious of the dangers Moscow posed even as he dealt secretly with that same regime.

Inconsistent Ally

Stresemann faced a conundrum. How could he deal with a Soviet Union that wanted to cooperate militarily on the one hand yet overthrow him on the other? He was well aware that the recently failed communist revolution had been funded with Russian gold. In a letter to Brockdorf-Rantzau on December 1, 1923, Stresemann, now serving as foreign minister, admitted that this covert financial support to revolution was the worrisome aspect of their relations with Russia.[17] The Foreign Minister described how the Russians, under cover of their embassy in Berlin, had clumsily attempted to purchase weapons from a local arms dealer, but the dealer immediately informed the police. The buyer was a counselor in the Soviet Embassy, a Frenchman using the pseudonym Petrov. The entire episode underscored Soviet untrustworthiness and Germany's current weakness. Yet Stresemann assured Brockdorff-Rantzau that Germany's present state was merely temporary. Like a fever, it would soon pass and the nation would return to strength.

He urged the Ambassador that, at such challenging times, it was crucial for him not to be merely a "diplomatist like Chicherin, but a German Count," whose powerful personality could represent his nation well. Such pep talks did nothing to resolve the basic tension. To avoid isolation, Germany had to preserve diplomatic relations with an aggressive communist regime.

Stresemann's deputy, Carl von Schubert, emphasized this point in a meeting with Soviet Ambassador Krestinski, even though the Ambassador himself was known to be involved in the failed October uprisings. When the Prussian police raided Ruth Fischer's apartment, they discovered a cache of letters between her and Zinoviev in Moscow, along with documents linking her to Petrov, Radek, and the entire misbegotten plot.[18] The Soviet regime had been caught red-handed, yet the German Foreign Ministry knew that its larger foreign policy objectives depended on preserving the semblance of alliance.

In time, Stresemann came to see that the Soviets were changing and could be encouraged to change in a direction beneficial to German interests. Sobered by its debacle in Germany, the Kremlin leadership increasingly sought to focus on normalizing relations with continental powers in order to avoid a concerted bloc of hostile states to its west. To that end, relations with Germany assumed a growing importance. Stresemann, however, had to be wary. What Soviet leaders said mattered far less than what they did, but their actions were often contradictory. Even as Stresemann felt embattled by Soviet efforts to overthrow the Weimar regime, he recognized that Russia also sought German technical assistance in building up the Red Army.

Secretly, and in stark violation of Versailles, the German military, along with German industry, was conducting a covert rearmament plan in collaboration with the Russian government. Beneath the Soviet Union's cloak, German industrial giants such as the Junker aircraft manufacturer established satellite factories inside Russia. German companies built munitions, arms, and poison gas there and quietly shipped their illegal war materiel back to Germany. Though Stresemann repeatedly denied these activities, he was not only well aware of them but took considerable risks to help them continue.

Ambassador Brockdorff-Rantzau had been cabling from Moscow with periodic updates. On September 10, 1923, the Ambassador attempted to fill Stresemann in on the secret dealings between the Reichswehr and the Red Army. Brockdorff-Rantzau complained that the military had been keeping him in the dark about their efforts. The previous year, he told Stresemann, a six-member military mission traveled to Moscow for talks, but these conversations failed to produce concrete agreements. A second mission resulted in equally little success. The third high-level conversation occurred when a Russian representative visited Berlin on July 30, 1923, and met with Stresemann's predecessor, Chancellor Wilhelm Cuno. Brockdorff-Rantzau expressed relief that in the event of an indiscretion, Germany would at least not appear as culpable as it would if German military representatives were discovered in Moscow. He worried that these secret Reichswehr dealings could be exposed, having damaging effects on Germany's international position.[19]

The signs from Moscow throughout 1924 continued to be mixed. Brockdorff-Rantzau urged the continuation of relations and argued that all Western nations must deal with Russia's dual policy.[20] In April, the Ambassador informed Stresemann of difficulties delivering funds to the Junker factory inside Russia, evidencing signs of growing cooperation between both governments over the production of war materiel.[21] Yet by May, another source of tension emerged when the Prussian police raided the Soviet trade delegation in Berlin. The Soviets were outraged. The German Interior Ministry, which had overseen the raid, thought it was doing its job. But the affair put Stresemann and the Foreign Ministry in a bind. Stresemann took the Interior Minister to task for failing to consult with him beforehand. The raid, coupled with Stresemann's efforts to improve relations with the West, made the Soviets increasingly anxious.[22] Their nervousness did not stop them, however, from escalating their demands both for compensation and full extraterritoriality for the trade delegation. Stresemann attempted to placate the Soviets, but by the month's end he had reached the outer limit of what he was willing to do.[23] Then came a signal that the tensions would be, if not exactly forgotten, then at least surmountable.

At 9:30 on the evening of June 10, Trotsky received Brockdorff-Rantzau in the War Commissariat. Looking fully recovered from his recent illness, Trotsky vigorously insisted that positive relations with Germany were paramount. The Ambassador worried that the raid had severely damaged relations, but Trotsky fervently objected. He assured the German Ambassador that the problem would be solved. The positive and important military cooperation they had already begun, he declared, must continue.[24]

Following Lenin's death in January 1924, Trotsky appeared to many outsiders as Lenin's most likely heir. Stalin had yet to consolidate his power and destroy his rivals.[25] Since Chicherin was not even a Politburo member, he could not be considered a true shaper of Soviet foreign policy. Trotsky's pronouncements, in sharp contrast, had to be taken seriously. For Brockdorff-Rantzau, meeting with Trotsky at night in the War Commissariat and hearing him passionately assert that the German–Soviet military agreement must continue, was a break in the normal routine. Whether it was a meaningful break remained to be seen.

Tension flared again when Joachim Pieper, head of the Soviet Trade Mission in Berlin, made scarcely veiled threats to expose the two countries' secret military cooperation unless the Germans accepted the Russian demands. Now it was Stresemann's turn to be incensed. Brockdorff-Rantzau tried to obtain Chicherin's written confirmation that the Soviet government would not permit its officials to blackmail Germany. Chicherin received the Ambassador at half past midnight on July 2, but their conversation did not resolve the matter. The following night at 10:00, Trotsky himself came to see the Ambassador. Brockdorff-Rantzau had been attempting to reach him for several days, but Trotsky had been in the countryside. Having only just returned and learned the news, Trotsky tried to calm the situation down. Russia and Germany, he insisted, had exactly the same interest in keeping their military relationship secret. If Pieper were to make any moves to expose relations, Trotsky assured the Ambassador that he personally would, in the name of the Soviet regime, denounce Pieper and throw him out.[26] Not entirely satisfied by Trotsky's promises, the Ambassador still attempted to obtain a written statement of the Soviet government's stand on Pieper's threats.

For Stresemann, the ongoing anxiety over the possible exposing of military cooperation only worsened as his Western policy progressed. On September 24, a Soviet Embassy advisor in Berlin came to see Stresemann to voice concern over Germany's plan to join the League of Nations.[27] Stresemann's tightrope dance now stepped up in earnest. Soviet fears of being isolated waxed. So too did their threats to expose Germany's Versailles violations. Stresemann had to keep both the

Russians and the Western powers satisfied that Germany was not fully committed to one camp or the other. All the while, Stresemann also faced the threat of Soviet-inspired agitation via the Comintern, which served largely as a tool of the Soviet regime. Chicherin maintained the party line, much to the annoyance of Western statesmen, that Comintern activities had no connection to the government in Moscow. On September 26, the Russian newspaper *Izvestya* reported on Chicherin's meeting with American Secretary of State Hughes, in which Chicherin stressed that a sharp dividing line separated the Comintern from the regime. In the margin of this translated article in Stresemann's collected papers is the handwritten note: "This hypocrisy is revolting."[28]

The great complication in German–Soviet relations continued to be the threat of Soviet-inspired revolution inside Germany and more broadly Soviet meddling in German domestic affairs. In October 1924, Britain's ruling Labour Party was defeated in general elections, partly because of the now infamous "Zinoviev Letter." Although the document was probably forged by White Russian expatriates, the conservative British newspaper *The Daily Mail* published a letter from Moscow's Comintern to the British communist party calling for revolutionary incitement in Britain. The letter was allegedly signed by Zinoviev, who forcefully denied having anything to do with it. Real or not, its effects were potent enough to concern Stresemann. Having already survived a communist revolution the previous year, the Foreign Minister had no intention of allowing a similar Zinoviev Letter to weaken his own government. At the close of October, Stresemann met with Soviet Ambassador Krestinski to warn him that a Zinoviev Letter episode in Germany could have a deeply damaging impact. Naturally, Krestinski fell back on the standard Soviet defense that would irritate diplomats across the continent: Zinoviev was not a member of the Soviet government but instead of the Comintern. The government thus had no control over his actions. Nevertheless, Krestinski agreed to pass along Stresemann's concerns to Moscow.[29]

Meanwhile, power within the Bolshevik hierarchy was shifting, signaling a change relevant to Germany. In December 1924, Stalin declared that building socialism in one country represented a legitimate interpretation of Leninism. This enabled him to distance himself from the failed October revolution from the previous year and to begin undercutting Trotsky, Kamenev, and Zinoviev. But Stalin's pronouncement was hardly a guarantee that Stresemann could take seriously.

By the start of 1925, Stresemann was still frustrated with the Comintern. On January 2, the Foreign Minister sent a sternly worded note to Krestinski, demanding that the Soviet government cease interfering in German domestic affairs. The Soviets continued to insist that they had no control over Comintern calls for worldwide revolution, but no one took this claim seriously. Stresemann reiterated that he viewed the Comintern and Soviet regime as intimately intertwined.[30]

By June, Stresemann's fears of Soviet interference had increased. Writing to American Ambassador Houghton, Stresemann expressed deep anxiety over Soviet meddling in Bulgaria, believing that Moscow was behind a recent political assassination and saying, "These events demonstrate in shocking manner the methods they use." They show, he told Houghton, that the Soviets remain wedded to world revolution.[31] Stresemann also assured Houghton that the communists were not likely to make much headway in Germany if the German economy remained stable. Naturally, the Foreign Minister was playing on the Americans' concerns of a communist takeover in order to keep up pressure on the Western powers to reduce German reparations and ensure American loans to Germany. Despite this, Stresemann's comments reflected his consistent worry over Moscow's machinations.

The following week Stresemann held a two-and-a-half-hour discussion of the Russian problem with Brockdorff-Rantzau and two days later discussed the situation with Ambassador Krestinski. On June 11, Stresemann made plain his deep distrust of the Soviets and their attempts at worldwide revolution. Entering into an alliance with the Soviets was like "going to bed with the murderer of one's own people." There could be no illusions that the Soviet regime genuinely sought friendly relations with Germany, he declared, while it simultaneously used the Comintern to undermine Germany.[32]

The complexities of Stresemann's policies were substantial. On the one hand he feared Soviet-led revolutions and on the other he facilitated secret military cooperation. Though initiated by the Reichswehr, Stresemann knew of the initial attempts at military collaboration as early as September 1923, thanks to Brockdorff-Rantzau's reports. Stresemann undeniably understood the details of the relationship at least as early as June 18, 1924, when he forwarded to General Seeckt a report from Brockdorff-Rantzau detailing some of the arrangements.[33] He denied the existence of this relationship just six months later. On December 30, 1924, Stresemann told foreign journalists:

> If there had really been any serious derelictions by Germany in the matter of disarmament, the leading French journals would long since have raised an outcry, and if, as is maintained, the German liaison officers had pursued a policy of deliberate obstruction, the German Government would long since have received a Note from the Allies . . . we possess no gas-masks, no aeroplanes, no artillery, and no tanks.[34]

Cooperation with the Soviets was intended to address precisely this deficiency. In the same address to reporters, Stresemann masterfully refuted Allied objections to the militarization of German police by invoking Stresemann's own use of police to put down Hitler's Munich Putsch in 1923. "What could I then have done if I had not had a couple of thousand police at my disposal, who could, in the event of danger, have protected the Wilhelmstrasse?"

There is no question that early in his tenure as foreign minister Stresemann knew about the Reichswehr's cooperation with the Red Army. Brockdorff-Rantzau even informed him that the Reichswehr intended to cultivate the military relationship by funding factories inside Russia to produce tanks and poison gas. At the same time, he saw hints that the Soviets were just as anxious as the Germans to keep the matter under wraps. The Russian War Minister allegedly feared loose lips on the part of German generals.[35] This and similar signals helped Stresemann to see that Soviet threats to expose their covert deals were probably mere bluffs. He could not be certain until matters reached a turning point.

Yet all the while that Stresemann followed, and indeed actively participated in, these covert military arrangements, he understood that Germany's secret rearmament in Russia risked derailing the Western-oriented Locarno policy, on which he had staked his reputation and career.[36] The aim of fulfillment was to reassure the West that Germany was committed to forging a cooperative peace. A pivotal part of that peace process required no provocative military measures by Germany.

The Versailles Treaty stipulated that Germany could not possess an air force or a navy, and its army could not exceed 100,000 men. The covert rearmament, therefore, placed Stresemann's very public policy in jeopardy.

From periodic embassy reports and through his own discussions with Soviet representatives, Stresemann could see that the Russians were clearly nervous too. Over the next two years, Stresemann would receive conflicting information. On the one hand, there were signs that the Soviets, just like the Germans, feared having their secret military connection exposed. On the other hand, the Soviets repeatedly threatened to expose that relationship themselves. Stresemann's challenge was to determine what the key Soviet decision-makers actually desired most: military cooperation or the ability to extract concessions by threatening to disclose it. Was there a true signal amidst the noise, and, if so, how could he detect it?

Threats or Bluffs?

As Stresemann strove to stabilize relations with the West, the Soviets grew increasingly fearful of being isolated. If Germany drew too close to Britain and France, then Russia would be facing a hostile coalition of great powers across the continent. The Soviets' fear of this scenario drove their behavior. If they could not prevent Germany from joining the League of Nations, it was essential that they gain at least some form of security agreement with Berlin. For the moment, they sought to disrupt Stresemann's Western strategy by any means at their disposal. One tactic they employed was to threaten to expose their two countries' covert military arrangements. In essence, they had the power to blackmail the Weimar regime.

Soviet pressure had been gradually increasing as German relations with the West improved. Moscow had no wish to see Germany join the League of Nations, which would tie Germany tighter to the West. To forestall German entry, the Soviets employed both carrots and sticks. American military intelligence had been following Russo–German relations and managed to penetrate the Serbian representative[37] in Berlin, who in turn had close contact with Soviet Ambassador Krestinski. According to an unnamed source, sometime prior to July 15,

1925, Krestinski wielded the stick. He threatened to expose the secret clauses of the Soviet–German agreement, which provided for "a camouflaged development of German armament on Russian territory." The best carrot he could muster, however, proved insufficiently enticing. If Germany remained apart from the League of Nations, the Ambassador promised Soviet assistance in undoing the Polish Corridor as well as Polish occupation of Danzig. The Americans subsequently learned that the Germans would continue their military cooperation with the Soviet Union.[38] The report continued by detailing German naval and aircraft developments inside Russia, as well as their work on poison gas. Although American officials knew at least some details surrounding Russo–German military cooperation, Stresemann and the Reichswehr could not know exactly how much the Western powers knew, and they were not eager to have any aspect of the relationship publicly revealed.

In the lead up to Locarno, Soviet Foreign Minister Chicherin intensified his efforts to block Stresemann's cooperation with the West. Just prior to Stresemann's departure for Locarno in October 1925, Chicherin, along with Ambassador Krestinski, visited Stresemann in Berlin, seeking reassurances that Russo–German military cooperation would continue. Specifically, Chicherin wanted to know that Germany remained committed to dismantling the Polish borders created at Versailles. Implicit in both Chicherin's comments and the timing of his visit was a not so subtle threat: the Soviets could expose their two countries' collaboration at any time.

A Russian indiscretion would be more than just an awkward moment. Coming on the eve of Stresemann's coveted summit with Britain and France, it could wreck his Western strategy. Though Stresemann was not willing to break off talks with the Western powers, he tried to mollify Chicherin by assuring him that the secret military arrangements between their two countries would continue and that there would be no guarantees of Polish borders.[39]

The conversation was tense. The German Foreign Minister not only needed to keep quiet on the extent of German–Soviet military relations, but also had to combat Soviet-inspired efforts to spark communist activities inside Germany. Stresemann had not forgotten Moscow's attempts to overthrow his government in 1923. He reminded Chicherin of Zinoviev's duplicity during that affair and pointed out that Zinoviev continued to agitate for revolution in a recently published speech in *Rote Fahne*. Soviet meddling forced him to assume that the German labor unions were being infiltrated and dominated by communists. The unions, he complained, did not shy from expressing their intention to change the leadership of German parties. They boldly called for continuing the struggle for world revolution.[40]

Chicherin played the standard Soviet card. Zinoviev was merely the mayor of Leningrad, not a high-ranking member of the government. He could not be controlled. Stresemann retorted that he would object just as much if the mayor of London called for revolution inside Germany. How would you feel, Stresemann asked, if the mayor of Munich called for anti-revolution inside Russia?

As Stresemann and Chicherin battled back and forth, the meeting, which had begun at 11 in the evening, dragged on until 1:30. Ambassador Krestinski, exhausted by the discussions and the late hour, occasionally nodded off. Talk turned to Poland, and Stresemann refused to agree to any anti-Polish alliance. At mention of the League of Nations, Stresemann had to pacify Chicherin that Germany had no intention of forging a secret alliance with the West against Russia.[41] Eventually, the meeting adjourned. The fear, threats, and innuendos that had charged the air had dissipated, but only slightly. The following day, as Stresemann prepared to leave for Locarno, Stresemann rejected Chicherin's attempts to agree on a formal secret alliance.[42]

Stresemann did not succumb to Chicherin's carrots, though he did take seriously the sticks. He pursued cooperation with the West, brought Germany into the League of Nations, and deflected Soviet threats by continuing talks on a separate Russo–German agreement. The historian Peter Krüger has argued that caution, above all else, characterized Stresemann's foreign policy. While this may be true on the whole, with respect to the secret rearmament, Stresemann proved more risk-accepting than some of his colleagues.[43] The Foreign Minister believed that he could extract more concessions from Britain and France by preserving the threat of closer cooperation with Russia. If this policy succeeded, it offered a means for restoring Germany's place among the great powers. By dealing with both Russia and the West, Germany could revise both the military as well as the economic aspects of Versailles. Stresemann therefore had to continually balance relations precisely. He resisted

Soviet pressure to keep Germany apart from the League, yet he maintained military collaboration for as long as he thought the West would permit it, even as his deputy, Karl Schubert, grew increasingly uneasy about the risks.

At this stage just prior to Locarno, it was useful to keep the extent of Russo–German cooperation ambiguous. Britain, France, and America all had intelligence reports on the nature of Germany's covert rearmament, but they lacked a complete picture. As it turned out, those secret dealings with the Soviets did not greatly trouble any of those three Western powers. They were willing to ignore it in the hope that they could prevent future German aggression by binding it to the evolving security agreements such as Locarno and the League. What made the possible exposure of Russo–German rearmament matter, of course, is that Stresemann did not know for certain that the Western powers would look the other way. This was something he had to learn over time as he developed a sense of his Western counterparts.

What Stresemann understood was that the Soviets needed German assistance even more than Germany required Soviet ties. For Germany, the actual military advantages were small, though the relationship with the Red Army did help to placate the Reichswehr. Politically, however, threat of closer cooperation with Russia enhanced its leverage with the West. Stresemann perceived a second political benefit to the relationship. Maintaining ties, active communication, and some cooperation with the Soviet regime helped the Wilhelmstrasse to keep a more careful watch on Soviet efforts at domestic German agitation. Schubert stated this view frankly to the American Ambassador, Jacob Gould Schurman, on April 7, 1926. Germany, he explained to Schurman, had a far better chance of combating communism at home if it had good relations with Russia abroad.[44]

For Russia, in contrast, its collaboration with Germany provided two crucial advantages. First, the collaboration meant access to German technical know-how, which Stalin hoped would help to modernize Russia's tank and tractor industry, as well as develop the Red Army.[45] Second, cooperation with Germany staved off Russia's political isolation.

More than this, Stresemann also recognized a crucial caveat in the Soviet Union's dual policy of fostering traditional international relations on the one hand while exporting revolution on the other. He saw that the Soviet leaders' commitment to revolutions was context dependent, not fundamental to their nature. It could change as circumstances necessitated. The Soviets were not to be trusted, but they could be allies of a kind. Unlike Winston Churchill, who railed against the Bolshevik disease and urged against British dealings with Moscow throughout the 1920s, Stresemann adopted a more flexible view. Each new interaction reinforced his sense that Soviet behavior was not consistently revolutionary. Toward the close of December 1925, Chicherin seemed changed. He visited Stresemann in Berlin for a two-hour conversation. Chicherin explained that when he arrived in Berlin, nearly 100 representatives of the Berlin labor councils were waiting to greet him. He gave a short speech because he knew he had to. Chicherin emphasized that he had not come to Berlin to meddle in German domestic affairs. He said not to place any significance on this event. He had not planned it and had made efforts to keep it out of the press. All of this gave Stresemann the impression that Chicherin was sincere. There was a relaxed feeling in their discussions, and Stresemann concluded that the Soviet representative might now be less fearful of German policy.[46] That same month, Leon Trotsky was ousted from the Politburo. Perhaps a shift was underway, one that augured well for the coming year.

Throughout 1926, Stresemann was receiving signs that Kremlin leaders valued cooperation with the German government more than they wanted to overthrow it. Zinoviev was sacked as head of the Leningrad Soviet, and by July he too would be removed from the Politburo. In October, there was a new head of the Comintern.[47] Again, Kremlinologists inside the Wilhelmstrasse could not be certain what these signs meant with respect to Russo–German relations, especially since they did not prevent Moscow from continuing to threaten exposing their two countries' military dealings.

One irony of the covert cooperation was that by 1926 an arrangement was in place that strikingly resembled the plot of 1923. Arms were illicitly shipped from Russia to Germany and advisors were secretly being exchanged. This time, however, Russian arms were sent not to communist revolutionaries but to their nemesis—the very Reichswehr that had crushed the 1923 plot. The reversal from arming revolution to arming the Reichswehr represented a meaningful break in the pattern of Soviet behavior. Although the Comintern remained active, national interests were superseding ideology in Moscow's relations with Berlin. Stresemann understood that this arrangement was not just mutually beneficial; it could also only be pursued and maintained by a Soviet government that was more concerned with its own survival than with the violent spread of its ideology. He further grasped that neither side in the arrangement desired that their dealings be fully exposed.

Stresemann's deputy, Karl von Schubert, however, was growing increasingly anxious. During the Soviet-inspired uprisings of October 1923, a Russian general, Peter Skoblevsky, had been arrested and imprisoned. By May 1926, his trial had still not been held. Soviet officials offered to release more than forty Germans currently in Russian jails in exchange for General Skoblevsky's freedom. One of the German prisoners, an engineer for the Junker corporation, had been engaged in the illegal production of war materiel inside Russia. The Soviets used this to pressure Berlin into giving up Skoblevsky. If Berlin refused, the implicit threat meant that the German engineer's trial would publicly reveal what the Junker Corporation was manufacturing. The threat caused consternation inside the Foreign Ministry. Brockdorff-Rantzau urged the release of Skoblevsky.[48] Shubert was eager to keep the Russians from exposing the secret arrangements. He was beginning to doubt the value of continued military cooperation in light of the risks. The Foreign Ministry agreed to release Skoblevsky, but Stresemann was not ready to end the arrangements with Moscow. Having Skoblevsky tried was an issue of no consequence to the Wilhelmstrasse. His release cost the Ministry nothing. There would have been no point in calling the Soviets' bluff over this one case. Yet Schubert's fears steadily mounted.

On July 9, Schubert strongly advised against Reichswehr participation in Soviet military maneuvers inside Russia. Such actions, he believed, could only raise unwanted suspicions in the West.[49] On July 23, Schubert's fears reached a tremulous pitch. The situation was dire, he wrote. The Western powers suspected that Germany was involved in a secret military alliance with the Soviets. He denied any such allegations. But if the truth emerged, he pleaded, "our entire strenuously constructed policy could be ruined."[50]

Although Schubert was correct that their business with Russia was getting riskier, Stresemann held firm. In full knowledge of the dangers, he allowed and facilitated the transfer of weapons from Russia into

Germany, in flagrant violation of his own assurances to the West that Germany was disarmed. On August 11, he noted that Brockdorff-Rantzau had informed him that 400,000 Russian-produced grenades were stockpiled on the sparsely populated Bear Island (*Bäreninsel*), soon due to be moved. Brockdorff-Rantzau expressed concern that if this shipment of weapons became known, it could severely compromise German foreign policy. The Reichswehr assured him that the chartered ships would be so carefully selected that no one would suspect a thing.[51] Nothing could possibly go wrong.

As weapon shipments began to flow, so too did rumors. By year's end, an event occurred that could easily have severed the two countries' covert cooperation. It very likely would have, but Stresemann's strategic empathy for his adversaries enabled him to keep a steady hand.

Despite Stresemann's best efforts, the details of German rearmament could no longer remain secret. Remarkably, the disclosure came not from the Soviet government, as had often been threatened, but from within Germany itself. On December 16, 1926, Philipp Scheidemann, the ex-Chancellor and now head of the Social Democratic Party, stepped forth and delivered a stunning speech to the assembled Reichstag. In full view of foreign dignitaries, including American Ambassador Jacob Gould Schurman, Scheidemann detailed Germany's covert activities inside the Soviet Union. His speech exposed the ways that Germany was violating the Treaty of Versailles—in stark contrast with Foreign Minister Stresemann's prominent policy of fulfillment.[52] The revelations would unleash dissension, bring down the government, and call German foreign policy into question. Yet unbeknownst to Scheidemann, it would also create a pattern break, one which Stresemann could use to his advantage.

3

Steady on the Tightrope
Stresemann's Maneuver, Act II

Revelations

When Philipp Scheidemann took the floor, he plunged the Parliament into mayhem. Within minutes of his speech, the parties on the Right exploded in anger. "Traitor!" they shouted. "Treason!" Using their greater numbers, the Socialists tried to shout their opponents back down but to no effect. Communists shrieked in disbelief at Scheidemann's allegations, unable to believe what they were hearing about this unwholesome union between Mother Russia and the Fatherland. Reichstag President Paul Löbe repeatedly rang his bell, fruitlessly calling the assembly back to order. At one point, a parliamentarian on the Right leapt up and, pointing to the American Ambassador seated in the gallery, cried, "Why reveal these things to our enemies?"[1] In the end, Scheidemann's speech, just days before Christmas 1926, would bring down the Weimar government and force a new coalition into being.

Scheidemann asserted that it was not only their right but their responsibility to speak out in order to keep Germany on the democratic path and the path of peace. An armed force that pursues its own political agenda that is opposed to democracy and peace, he continued, cannot be maintained. Citing a recent speech by General Wilhelm Heye (Chief of the *Truppenamt*[2]), in which the General called the army an obedient instrument of the state, Scheidemann remarked that this is a goal that had not yet been reached. Instead, he charged, the Reichswehr had become a state within a state.[3]

Given his stature, Scheidemann's revelations could not simply be dismissed. He was, after all, the very man who had proclaimed the German Republic. Standing on the Reichstag balcony in 1918 at the war's close, Scheidemann addressed a mob of Berliners and declared that rule by monarchs had ended. He did this in part to stave off an impending revolution, but no vote had ever been cast on the matter. He was acting on his own authority. In February 1919, he became the Republic's first Chancellor. That summer he resigned, refusing to sign the Versailles Treaty once its harsh terms were announced. Despite his act of nationalistic protest, as a leading German socialist Scheidemann remained the target of right-wing furor, even being attacked with acid by extremists. His historical significance aside, as the Social Democratic Party head, he presently controlled a substantial bloc of votes in parliament. Thus, in December of 1926, when the ex-Chancellor rose to speak, he commanded considerable attention.

Turning to the delegates on the Right and addressing them directly, Scheidemann announced: "Do not pretend that what we discuss here today is a surprise to other nations. I know and expect this comment. If you are honest, you must admit that probably all countries in the world know exactly what is happening here." The German people, he explained, knew the least about what the Reichswehr was doing.[4]

Although German resistance to disarmament and Allied occupation had been widely suspected, Scheidemann was referring specifically to a recent exposé in the December 6 *Manchester Guardian*. The newspaper—probably working from leads given to them by the Social Democratic Party—described some of the details surrounding the Reichswehr's secret rearmament inside Soviet Russia. Because he could not obtain satisfactory assurances from the government that these activities would cease, Scheidemann decided to reveal the full story (or as much of it as he could) to the public through his Reichstag address. His speech has often been depicted as a purely political maneuver, intended to discredit the government and force a reorganization, but when one actually examines the text of his remarks, it is clear that deeper issues were also at stake.

Scheidemann's address covered three distinct acts of subterfuge: financial improprieties, covert military training, and the production of war materiel. First, he described how money from the federal budget was being diverted to fund illegal rearmament in Russia. He outlined the scheme of withdrawing cash from a bank account and covering up the money trail. When he told the assembly that German officers and generals had been traveling to Russia under fake names and false passports, the Right erupted. One parliamentarian from Mecklenburg, Herr von Graefe, shouted, "What would happen to you in Paris if you said these things about the French?"[5] His point was that no nation would tolerate the public disclosure of state secrets.

The effect of von Graefe's words was electrifying. The entire room descended into cries from the Right and counter-charges from the Left. Reichstag President Löbe called for silence. Scheidemann tried to continue. "I have only the wish—" before being drowned out by shouts of "Traitor!" President Löbe fecklessly rang his bell for order.

When Scheidemann at last resumed, he described in overpowering detail how the Reichswehr was in league with right-wing organizations across Germany to secretly drill future soldiers under the guise of athletic training. The military, he alleged, was providing weapons and funds to train civilians in military functions. It was employing former officers as so-called sports instructors—all in violation of Versailles.

In the final section of his address, Scheidemann discussed the rearmament currently underway inside Russia, to the great embarrassment of Communists present. Seeing no need to rehash the details reported by the *Manchester Guardian*, he instead supplemented the case with additional allegations. According to his sources, airplanes, bombs, and poison gas were all being built beneath the Soviet cloak. As recently as late September to early October 1926, four ships had traveled from Leningrad to Stettin, a port city then part of Germany. Three of these ships—the *Gottenburg, Artushof,* and *Kolberg*—reached Germany, though the fourth had sunk. The workers unloading the cargo were sworn to secrecy. The contents were innocuously labeled "Aluminum" and "*Rundeisen"* (a type of steel). In reality it was thousands of tons of war materiel. Finally, Scheidemann described a collaboration between Reichswehr financing, a chemical company in Hamburg, and the plant in Russia producing gas grenades. This time, the Communists were outraged. Though publicly pledged to supporting Communist movements throughout the world, here was evidence that Soviet Russia was aiding the harshest opponents of Communism inside Germany. Nothing was making sense.

Turning to address the Communist delegates, Scheidemann admonished that they should be opposed to what Russia was doing because it was only pushing the country further to the Right. "We want to be Moscow's friend, but we don't want to be its fool." Scheidemann called it a mistake that Germany forged an agreement with Russia just after making peace, but it would be far worse if such dealings were continuing even after Locarno and Germany's entry into the League. Becoming ever bolder, he proclaimed, "Enough with these dirty dealings. No more munitions from Russia for German weapons." The Communists let loose a cacophony, but Scheidemann was not cowed. "You want to drown me out with your shouts, so I will repeat it. No more munitions from Russia for German weapons."[6]

To some, Scheidemann's Reichstag speech was a flagrant act of high treason. To others, it was a profile in courage. Toward the close of his remarks, Scheidemann delivered a powerful and prescient defense of his position. He declared that secret armament was a grave danger. It irresponsibly damaged foreign policy. It compelled the nation to lies and hypocrisy. One day, he warned, we will be caught, and then the world will say that Germany is dishonest. "This cannot serve our Republic. We want to be seen in the world as an upstanding people that fulfills its obligations." Finally, Scheidemann announced that his Party would withdraw its support for the government in order to trigger the formation of a new one.[7] But neither Scheidemann's words nor his Party's actions could alter the course toward rearmament.

Throughout the whole of his speech, Scheidemann restricted his attacks to the military alone. In one of his only references to the Foreign Minister, he portrayed Stresemann as embattled by the Reichswehr's actions. He insisted that Germany's opponents abroad referred continuously to Germany's lack of disarmament, saying that Germany gave only the appearance of disarming. He implied that, unfortunately, they were correct. "If you don't know this, ask Herr Stresemann, who must overcome these difficulties."[8] In essence, he was giving the Foreign Minister a free pass.

Reactions

Scheidemann's speech created a pattern break moment. It forced the issue of German rearmament into the open, enabling Stresemann to observe reactions from East and West. Would the British and French demand an end to German–Soviet relations? Would the Soviets call off the military cooperation? Or could Germany continue with business as usual, preserving ties to both sides and thereby extract concessions from both?

The Soviet response was telling. Having frequently threatened to expose the secret arrangements, once they were already partly revealed, the Soviets now showed themselves eager to cover up the rest and keep the agreements intact, just as Stresemann had suspected. What Stalin had declared at the start of 1926, that the Soviet Union should build socialism in one country, appeared to be his genuine position. Stresemann had grasped that Stalin's greater aim, at least for the time being, was not fomenting revolution inside Germany but instead revitalizing Soviet military and economic strength.

Stresemann also did not expect the West to retaliate against Germany, and after the speech he received ample signals that his assessment was correct. Scheidemann's allegations created a sensation across the Western press. The story ran prominently in all the major papers. Under the headline "German Royalists Accused of Raising Huge Secret Army," the *Washington Post* detailed the stormy Reichstag session and the key points of Scheidemann's speech, including, at the article's start, the covert shipment of arms from Russia to Germany.[9] The following day, the *Post*'s page-one headline declared "Germany's Cabinet, Defeated, Resigns in Face of Charges."[10] Evidencing the general respect for Stresemann's leadership in foreign affairs, the *Post* piece ended by observing that Stresemann had not been seriously attacked at any time during the past two days of bitter Reichstag debate, and therefore German foreign policy would likely remain unchanged. *The New York Times* also featured the story, while *Time* referenced it within an article on Weimar's unstable coalitions.[11]

In Britain, *The Manchester Guardian*, having first broken the story, continued to run articles on the unfolding events. The newspaper reported that the issue had become the primary topic of discussion in the press and Parliament. It added that "big sums" from the German taxpayer have been secretly diverted to fund illegal dealings in Russia and at home.[12] The next day, *The Guardian* ran a piece on German gun-running, filled with speculation about possible Reichswehr plans to acquire large quantities of arms from Russia, including rifles, field guns, howitzers, and antitank guns.[13] The paper followed up the reports on December 21 with a piece titled "The Exposure of German Militarists," noting that French Socialist leader Leon Blum had requested an inquiry into the issues that Scheidemann had raised.[14]

Unlike the left-leaning *Guardian*, the conservative newspaper *The London Times* downplayed the significance of Scheidemann's disclosures, claiming that they were all well-known abroad. The *Times* itself had noted the rumored dealings between German and Soviet militaries back in 1922, shortly after the two nations signed their infamous Rapallo agreement, which was putatively restricted to diplomatic and trade issues, not military ones.[15] The *Times* now painted the German Socialists as having launched a fierce but undeserved attack on the German army. It reported almost none of the details contained within Scheidemann's speech. Instead, it portrayed the Socialists as paranoids: "The more recent revelations of negotiations between Reichswehr officers and the Soviet Government with regard to the manufacture of arms, with all their schoolboy paraphernalia of false names and forged passports, made the Socialists still more suspicious . . ." The paper then described the Chancellor's defense, that most of the allegations were either untrue or under investigation. Strongly suggesting support for the German Right, the article's final sentence cited a Nationalist Deputy, Herr von der Schulenburg, who declared that ". . . if the assertions of Herr Scheidemann were true, his speech fulfilled all the requirements of an act of treason."[16]

Scheidemann's speech was an embarrassment for Stresemann. He had repeatedly vowed that Germany would disarm, as this condition was central to the withdrawal of Allied troops from German soil. To make matters worse, just six days earlier he had received the Nobel Prize for Peace, owing to his accommodating fulfillment policy. If Scheidemann's allegations were found to be true, then Stresemann would appear a hypocrite, and his Locarno success could be in jeopardy.

Stresemann's deputy, Schubert, urged yet again that the relationship with Moscow be brought to an end, as the risks had become too great.[17] Stresemann disagreed. Instead, he waited to gauge both Soviet and Western reactions. He had good reason to think that Britain and France would be reluctant to pressure him into terminating the covert rearmament. As embarrassed as the German government might be by Scheidemann's revelations, the British and French Foreign Ministers might be even more so, thanks in large part to the Nobel Foundation.

The timing of Scheidemann's speech could hardly have been more awkward for Britain and France, nor more providential for Stresemann. *The Manchester Guardian* story appeared just as the French and British Foreign Ministers, Aristide Briand and Austen Chamberlain, were finalizing the withdrawal of the Inter-Allied Military Control Commission (IMCC), even though the Commission's report stated that Germany had not met the disarmament conditions.[18] Four days later, the Foundation announced not only that Dr. Stresemann would receive the Peace Prize for his handling of European disputes but that Briand and Chamberlain, along with American Vice-President Dawes, would share the award for their roles in ushering in the spirit of Locarno. For the British, French, or American foreign ministries to have loudly protested German violations at the very moment when they were basking in their Nobel glory would have been an unmitigated embarrassment. It could have called into question the entire Locarno undertaking, the trustworthiness of Stresemann, and the credibility of the statesmen themselves. Instead of drawing attention to German rearmament, the Nobel laureates voiced their genuine hopes for future peace.

Upon learning that he had won the Nobel Prize, Austen Chamberlain declared: "I feel greatly honored by the award, because it sets the seal of international approbation on the work of peace accomplished at Locarno."[19] French Foreign Minister Briand enthused over the announcement with equal relish:

> Of course, I am delighted; but my ambition is that, ten years hence, the people will say that we deserved this award. Sir Austen Chamberlain, Dr. Stresemann and myself have worked together for the last two years in perfect harmony, with only one object in view. That object was the peace of the world. We have done our best, and will continue

in the same spirit. Today we have the distinguished honor of receiving the Nobel prize. But history will say whether we deserved it. For the sake of humanity I sincerely hope that it will.[20]

Commenting on Stresemann's receipt of the honor, *The New York Times* reflected the popular view of him at the time. The newspaper called Stresemann "sincere in his tribute to the new spirit of the international accord." The profile credited the Foreign Minister with changing German attitudes toward the once-detested League of Nations. Affirming the general perception, *The New York Times* proclaimed: "Stresemann has held firm to the major principle that for Germany the soundest policy is loyal cooperation with her former enemies."[21]

The Peace Prize was a windfall for Stresemann, as it constrained the French and British foreign ministers' reactions. They could not raise objections to Germany's covert rearmament without tarnishing the luster on their award.

Around the same time as the Nobel Prize awards, Stresemann was receiving many more signals that Britain and France were not prepared to make an issue of German violations. The official British response to Scheidemann's revelations proved remarkably muted. The episode had no effect on the government's impressions of Stresemann. It appears not even to have triggered an investigation into the extent of Stresemann's knowledge of the Reichswehr's activities. Instead, Foreign Secretary Austen Chamberlain remained exceedingly deferential to his German counterpart throughout the episode.[22] At a Cabinet meeting on December 1, 1926, Chamberlain described how well he, Briand, and Stresemann had cooperated at a recent meeting in Geneva. Relations were so congenial that they envisioned the withdrawal of Allied forces from Germany in the very near future in exchange for a financial payment from Germany. Chamberlain hoped for another conference similar to Locarno, but he feared that the sensitive state of European public opinion was not yet ready for such an affair.[23] Obviously, Stresemann did not know the details of this particular Cabinet meeting, but British and French compliance with German demands continued to be forthcoming.

At the following Cabinet meeting on December 15, just one day before Scheidemann's speech but a week after *The Manchester Guardian*'s exposé, Chamberlain reported that the IMCC would at last be fully withdrawn from German territory, thanks to Briand's acceptance of German goodwill.[24] The planned withdrawal date had been set for February 1, 1927, but in deference to Stresemann they reset the date to January 31, as this was the anniversary of the evacuation of Allied troops from Cologne and held symbolic value for the Germans.[25]

Chamberlain went on to assert that 99 of the 101 outstanding points not settled at Locarno had each been resolved. The remaining two issues involved what would today be called "dual use materials" and the disarmament of the Königsberg fortress. Both the British and French War Offices recognized the danger from the accumulation of large quantities of jigs and gauges. These devices could be used for commercial purposes, but they could also be used in weapons. As the minutes reveal, Stresemann's word sufficed to allay any concerns. "Dr. Stresemann had, however, given an emphatic undertaking that there should be no accumulations."[26]

The question of disarming the fortress proved more complicated. The Versailles Treaty stated in Article 180 that Germany's system of fortified works along its southern and eastern frontiers should be maintained in its existing state. The British assumed that this referred to the state the fortresses were in at the war's end. But the Germans devised a novel interpretation, insisting that the article meant that Germany could keep them up to date. Presumably the fortresses had the latest weaponry in 1918, and the Germans wanted them to have the latest weaponry now, in 1926. Though Chamberlain initially insisted on the British interpretation, General Paweltz, who was the German liaison officer to the IMCC, vehemently refused to agree. The talks might have foundered on this point, but then "Dr. Stresemann had insisted that the Germans had no offensive ideas and only contemplated the fortresses in their defensive capacity."[27] Again, Stresemann's assurances were enough, and this provided the basis for renewed negotiations. In point after point, Germany was getting its way.

The day after Chamberlain informed the British Cabinet that the IMCC's mission would soon end, Scheidemann delivered his stunning Reichstag address. But owing to the Christmas holiday, the British Cabinet did not reconvene until January. When it next met, the entire agenda was consumed by a single item: a crisis in China regarding the seizure of a British concession. In fact, each weekly Cabinet meeting that month centered almost exclusively on the China issue. Unlike normal meetings at which a variety of domestic and foreign affairs were discussed, the China crisis absorbed the Cabinet's near-complete attention.

If the secret rearmament in Russia had been well-known to the British, then why did they not seize this opportunity to protest it? Governments are often hamstrung in their ability to object to a country's actions when their objections are based on covert intelligence reports. No government wants to risk exposing its spies, sources, or methods. But once a public disclosure occurs, governments are free to make diplomatic protests at no risk. Scheidemann's speech handed the British a perfect chance to do this. Chamberlain, for one, could have expressed Her Majesty's Government's deep disapproval of Germany's violations and demanded they cease. Instead, the British said nothing.[28]

From the British perspective, German rearmament was rather modest at this stage. Knowing that some German rearmament was inevitable, the British were willing to ignore these relatively minor violations. However, Britain's lack of response only hastened the pace of Russo–German cooperation. As the incisive German diplomat in Russia, Gustav Hilger, observed in his post–World War II memoirs, after the Scheidemann affair German activities inside Russia rapidly expanded. More German officers than ever before came to Moscow, Hilger wrote, though greater efforts were taken to camouflage their identity.[29]

Some limited German rearmament was viewed as a positive development given concerns over a potentially resurgent Russia and the growing communist movement. But if the British truly feared a Russian resurgence, then the last thing they would have wanted was German aid to the Red Army. The Reichswehr was actively training Russian officers, teaching pilots, and establishing a school for instruction in tank warfare. German industrial plants agreed in some cases to give the Red Army one-third of the planes produced on Soviet territory. For Britain, however, a moderately rearmed Germany might also one day serve as a counterweight to France.

The British Foreign Office pursued a parallel policy of tacit acceptance toward internal as well as external German violations. Cabling from Berlin, British Ambassador Ronald Lindsay offered a lengthy assessment of the many militaristic *Bunds* operating inside Germany, the groups to which Scheidemann had referred in his Reichstag address. Lindsay attributed a fundamental nature to the Germans, who, when assembled in a group of more than one, adopt a "combative nature." He asserted that the German ". . . becomes peculiarly aggressive in combination with others, and that he cannot conceive of co-operation except as directed against something or somebody." Despite these putative national characteristics, Lindsay concluded that the upsurge in militarism and covert training of young men by ex-officers should not be a cause for concern. He argued that the only reasonable course available was to ". . . secure a promise from the German Government that they will observe the clear stipulations of the Treaty of Versailles on this point."[30] In other words, trust the German government and hope that rearmament would not lead to aggression.

In fact, there was little that Britain and France could do to prevent German rearmament. If Britain had come down hard on German violations, the Germans might have proceeded with rearmament at full speed and Britain would have likely been unable to halt it. This in turn would have revealed Allied weakness.

Britain and France also feared jeopardizing Germany's payment of reparations. If the Allies raised too much fuss over disarmament violations, then Germany might refuse to continue its payments, the subject of greatest concern to Allied statesmen throughout the 1920s. Establishing how to extract those payments from Germany consumed more time and effort than any other issue of postwar politics. By 1926, it seemed as though a system, and a leadership, at last existed for the smooth transfer of money from Berlin to Allied capitals. One rather obvious clue to the French attitude came on September 17, when Stresemann met secretly with French Foreign Minister Briand in the town of Thoiry. The two ministers hoped to strike a deal: the return of French-occupied German territory in exchange for a one-time payment to France. At one point in their discussions Briand admitted that when his military intelligence officers presented him with documents detailing German violations of Versailles, he had casually tossed the files in a corner and ignored them.[31] Although Briand was concerned about some of Germany's attempts to rearm and remilitarize, those qualms were secondary to his desire for German reparations.

Given the limited scope for British and French action, their policy of tacit consent for rearmament was grounded in the hope that German behavior could be changed over time—a not unreasonable ambition. The timing of Scheidemann's speech, the hopes invested in Stresemann as a peacemaker, and the West's limited ability to impose meaningful penalties all combined to constrain British and French responses. Those constraints led to a tacit overlooking of Germany's transgressions and Stresemann's possible role therein. And Stresemann had every reason to expect that his Western counterparts were sufficiently constrained. He soberly judged their reactions while also observing the signals emerging from the East.

In contrast to the British, the Soviets were outraged, and for good reason. One of their best bargaining chips had just been whittled down. Though they could still conceivably threaten further exposures, two important changes had occurred in the wake of Scheidemann's address. First, now that at least some of the secret arrangement had been made public, Soviet threats of exposing more details were unlikely to have a significant impact on Germany's relations with the West. Second, the Soviets themselves revealed that they wanted military cooperation to continue without obstruction. The immediate reaction among some in Moscow was to abandon military cooperation with Germany altogether, but this was of course impractical. The relationship held too much value for both technological progress and international relations.

The day after Scheidemann's speech, Schubert met with Krestinski. The Soviet Ambassador was in a highly agitated state. He wanted to know what the German Foreign Ministry intended to do about Scheidemann's revelations. Schubert assured him that the Ministry had no intention of saying anything about it unless compelled to do so by the French press. In that event, they would make a partial admission and say that the whole affair simply belonged to a previous era. Krestinski was scarcely pacified. He felt that the best approach was to deny everything.[32]

The Soviet bluff had finally been called. Yet instead of retreating from the secret military relations, as they had threatened to do, they sought assurance that the arrangements would remain in place. At the start of the new year, Stresemann received the clearest signal yet that Moscow wanted to cooperate with the German government far more than it wanted to overthrow it. On January 5, 1927, Krestinski met with

Stresemann and raised the issue of Scheidemann's indiscretion. Although the scandal had faded from the news, Krestinski feared that it could be resurrected. The Soviet Ambassador understood from his conversations with Schubert and Herbert von Dirksen, head of the Foreign Ministry's East European division, that if the German government were compelled to clarify the matter in public, it planned to claim that the arms shipments were from long ago and did not reflect any current military cooperation between the two countries. Krestinski explained that this would place the Soviet regime in a very uncomfortable position, as it had been denying the deal entirely. The Ambassador expressed the wish of his government that the German government consider the Soviet position as well as its own.

Stresemann tried to reassure Krestinski by declaring it unlikely that the Social Democrats would pursue the issue. Krestinski was not mollified. He said that the Second International (a worldwide association of socialist parties and trade unions) might draw attention to the scandal. In the end, he expressed the Soviet wish that both governments remain in contact regarding their mutual tactics for handling the matter.[33]

In effect, the Soviets were pleading with the Germans not to expose their duplicity. The Russians were scared of the consequences, and Stresemann knew it. The long pattern of Soviet threats to expose their secret arms deal had finally broken, and the Russians blinked. The fact that they were now intent on covering up the affair had to mean that the Kremlin valued German military and technical assistance more than it valued fomenting a German revolution. This in turn meant that Schubert was wrong. The costs of cooperation to Germany were indeed minimal, as Stresemann had surmised. The arrangement could continue without risk to Locarno and Germany's broader Western policy. At a pattern break moment, the Soviets revealed their underlying drivers: the restoration of Russian might. It would clearly take years before Russia's resurgence could rival Western power, and no one could know what that would eventually produce. But for now, that day was still far in the future. For at least the short and medium term, Stresemann had a pretty clear sense of his enemy's drivers and constraints.

Although attacks and disinformation about Germany persisted in the Russian press over the early part of 1927, they did not seriously derail relations. Meanwhile, within the German parliament, the

Social Democrats formed an investigative committee and the government attempted a cover-up. Schubert cabled Brockdorff-Rantzau that although the head of the Reichswehr did not want to make any admissions, Schubert thought that some statement would be necessary.[34] Brockdorff-Rantzau wired back advising the Foreign Ministry not to admit to anything in the hearings, as that would embarrass key individuals in Moscow who were clinging to their denials. Chicherin was even charging that the allegations were British provocations.[35]

Eager to ensure that no further disclosures would occur, Chicherin's deputy, Litvinov, contacted the German Foreign Office about continued military cooperation. The Soviets wanted to obtain a clear understanding on the furnishing of the training school in Kazan, which Germany had been financing by cooking the books. In May of 1927, Stresemann, along with General Heye and War Minister Gessler, met in the Foreign Ministry to discuss the Soviet request. With only some qualifications, Stresemann endorsed the arrangement. By August, Stresemann cabled the embassy in Moscow about the presence of Germans at the training school in Kazan. As far as Stresemann was concerned, "We have no concerns about the continuation of this program."[36] With Stresemann's blessing, Russo–German military cooperation henceforth intensified.

Stresemann's Own Drivers

If Stresemann recognized the Soviets' underlying drivers and constraints by scrutinizing their behavior during pattern breaks, then could his foreign counterparts have done the same to him? What did Stresemann actually want? His pursuit of rearmament has left historians without a consensus on his underlying motivations. Some historians conclude that Stresemann's policies of overt cooperation and covert defiance of Versailles demonstrated an aggressive inclination, one that inadvertently helped lay the groundwork for Hitler's later war.[37] More recent historians take the opposite view, insisting that Stresemann actively strove for European amity. They assert that his support of covert rearmament was merely a political necessity.[38] In the view of these scholars, Stresemann actually sought to check or restrain the Reichswehr's rearmament plans. Henry Kissinger once called the problem of divining Stresemann's true intentions "one of history's unsolved riddles."[39] Historians are still divided in their judgment, and if historians cannot agree on how to assess this important figure, what chance did Stresemann's contemporaries have of accurately assessing him?

Stresemann was a controversial figure in his own time. He may be even more of one today. The earliest interpretations of Stresemann, those written in the years shortly after his death in 1929 and those just after World War II, depicted the foreign minister as a cooperative, sober-minded statesman, working toward peaceful resolution of post–World War I conflicts.[40] Within a decade following the end of World War II, however, some historians, Hans Gatzke most prominently among them, fervently challenged the more positive prior interpretations.[41] Gatzke saw the foreign minister as a cool, calculating nationalist, bent on German revanchism. Other works then echoed this view. Recently that interpretation has been challenged in a probing biography by the Oxford scholar Jonathan Wright.[42] In Wright's account, Stresemann sought to revise Versailles but to do it peacefully. Four years later, Wright's view was complemented by Patrick Cohrs, whose impressively researched study of 1920s European diplomacy cast the Foreign Minister in a similar light.[43]

Naturally, this revision of Stresemann's reputation has not gone unchallenged. Writing in the *Journal of American History*, Stephen Schuker argued that Stresemann's intentions are best reflected in a letter he wrote to the German Crown Prince shortly before Locarno. In that missive, the Foreign Minister rather bluntly outlined his foreign policy objectives. These included (as cited by Schuker):

> . . . freedom from Allied occupation; a reparations solution tolerable to Germany; the protection of the ten to twelve million ethnic Germans living under a foreign yoke; readjustment of the eastern frontiers; union with German Austria; exploitation of disarmament, Danzig, and the Saar questions at the League of Nations; and, in the background, though postponed until a future generation, the recovery of Alsace-Lorraine.[44]

Schuker questioned whether such robust ambitions could plausibly reflect a peaceful plan.[45]

Both Wright and Cohrs see this letter in a less incriminating light. Cohrs believes that Stresemann never sought revision through military means. "Crucially, Stresemann only envisaged territorial changes if they could be achieved in 'agreement' with Germany's neighbours and did not jeopardize its accommodation with the Western powers."[46] Wright asserts, "All the evidence suggests that Stresemann remained committed to peaceful revision . . ."[47]

For Gatzke and Schuker the letter reveals Stresemann's true colors, but for Wright and Cohrs it merely indicates a nonviolent intention to restore Germany's rightful place among the great powers of Europe while highlighting his political acumen for playing to his audience. Stresemann's policies were therefore not two-faced but two-sided: win over the West through fulfillment and placate the German Right with modest bows to rearmament.

Still, Stresemann's letter to the Crown Prince is not the only inconvenient evidence against his pacific intentions. More problematic is his reluctance to oppose rearmament. Stresemann's biographer, Jonathan Wright, concludes that while the Foreign Minister believed in the utility of military force he objected to the Reichswehr's pursuit of an independent policy and wanted to rein in the Reichswehr's activities. But Stresemann never did so. Wright speculates that this was either because he did not feel strong enough to oppose them or because he was held back by his innate respect for the military and did not want to damage its morale. Wright notes that Stresemann was constantly worried that the rearmament would be exposed, and only after he saw the West's minimal reaction to Scheidemann's speech did he agree to continue the program in Russia. "Perhaps because of this lack of reaction," Wright explains, "when General Heye asked for political authorization for continued cooperation with the Red Army in the training of pilots, a tank school, and gas warfare, Stresemann agreed."[48]

By this point in 1927, Stresemann had succeeded in exerting some control over Reichswehr activities. Military officials were requesting his consent. They were not pursuing a wholly independent policy. Yet Stresemann did not use his position to check Reichswehr rearmament. He exerted influence over the program simply because he understood that knowledge is power and ignorance can cause a politician's demise. The Foreign Minister wanted to ensure that he was kept in the know about Reichswehr programs. He does not appear to have had any interest in obstructing them.

Stresemann's contemporaries, as well as subsequent historians, could have looked to the great statesman's behavior at a critical pattern break. If Stresemann had truly been opposed to the Reichswehr's secret program, Scheidemann's speech represented the ideal moment to end it. The Foreign Minister could have insisted that the risks to Germany's image abroad were simply too great. He could then have sought to placate the Reichswehr and industrial concerns by other means. Stresemann's German People's Party drew much of its support from German industry, and if anyone knew how to curry favor with industrialists, it was Stresemann. He might have used his considerable influence to persuade the industrialists who were profiting from rearmament that their interests would be better served by looking West. He could have appeased the industrialists with promises to seek more favorable trade agreements. He could have pointed out that the scale of American loans dwarfed the financial benefits flowing from covert rearmament. The industrialists would never have wanted those to be placed in jeopardy. He could easily have argued that the financial benefits from rearmament could not possibly outweigh the risk of further revelations similar to Scheidemann's. Given Stresemann's close working relationship with Chamberlain and Briand, he could also have quietly urged his counterparts to raise a ruckus against the Reichswehr's activities, if he had really wished to dissuade the military from proceeding. Instead, he did none of these things. He accurately sensed that Britain and France were unlikely to object and that the Soviets were desperate to preserve the arrangement. Once his assessments proved correct, he supported the program's continuation.[49]

Diplomats must often lie for their country, and Stresemann was no different in that respect. After Scheidemann's revelations, Stresemann denied knowledge of the rearmament program. He continued to deny it thereafter. The fact that he did this so skillfully shows his effectiveness as a diplomat. In a speech before the Reichstag in February 1928, he went so far as to proclaim that ". . . no state has contributed more or even as much to the solution of the security question as Germany." He categorically announced, "Germany is disarmed."[50] This statement was not entirely truthful. Although the IMCC had succeeded in destroying considerable quantities of munitions, German violations were many, and Stresemann was well aware of them.

Like most clever politicians, Stresemann said many different things to different audiences. One can find evidence to support claims of his aggressive intentions and counterevidence in defense of his pacific ways. Speaking about the far-off future, he once remarked to the State President of Wurtemburg, in response to the State President's assertion that there could be no peaceful solution to Germany's situation:

> I fervently hope that if it comes to that—and I believe that in the final analysis these great questions will always be decided by the sword—the moment may be put off as long as possible. I can only foresee the downfall of our people so long as we do not have the sword—that much is certain. If we look forward to a time when the German people will again be strong enough to play a more significant role, then we must first give the German people the necessary foundation . . . To Create this foundation is the most urgent challenge facing us.[51]

If Stresemann had one underlying driver, it was to restore German greatness by any reasonable means. It was his responsibility to the nation to keep rearmament moving forward so that Germany's sword would one day be ready. However, being a consummate diplomat, he recognized that the implicit threat of force, not its actual use, can often be sufficient to achieve one's ends. To that end, cooperation with the Western powers and the Soviet Union made perfect sense. *Schaukelpolitik*, the policy of balancing between East and West, held that Germany could extract the most concessions from each side by preserving ties to both. The riskiness of this strategy was that it required a sensitive estimation of how far Germany could go. Stresemann witnessed Moscow's transformation from arming German revolutionaries to arming the Reichswehr. That break in Moscow's pattern of behavior helped him to sense just how much the Soviets needed German cooperation. This in turn enabled him to gauge how much German closeness to the West that the Soviets could accept. Conversely, by accurately assessing the constraints on British and French statesmen, Stresemann gained a sense of how much military cooperation with Russia the West could tolerate. One measure of Stresemann's strategic empathy is that he never pushed either relationship beyond a point that the other side could bear.

Of Many Minds

There is yet another way of thinking about how Stresemann thought. His behavior at the pattern break moment strongly suggests an underlying driver: the desire to restore German greatness. But we do not need to conclude from this that the Foreign Minister possessed a definite long-term plan, one that he assiduously and consistently pursued. He could easily have held to a consistent desire for German great power status while varying his behavior over time. In other words, his specific actions at any given moment need not have been consistent with aggressive rearmament or peaceful conciliation. He might easily have been of many minds.

The evolutionary psychologist Robert Kurzban not only argues that most of us are awash in conflicting beliefs, but insists that it does not even make sense to say that a person holds consistent beliefs at all. At least when it comes to preferences, psychologists have argued that we do not hold fixed preferences, as rational choice advocates have long maintained. In just one of many studies, for example, people were asked to choose between receiving six dollars or a fancy pen. Roughly one-third of the subjects chose the pen. But when the choice was presented between receiving six dollars, a fancy pen, and a clearly inferior pen, the number of people who chose the fancy pen rose to nearly 50 percent. Other studies have shown how people reverse their preferences when the context changes. The evidence has been mounting that preferences are context-dependent.

In Kurzban's view, and that of other evolutionary psychologists, the mind evolved bit by bit and not toward a state of rational perfection. Whereas psychologists such as Daniel Kahnemann see the mind as divided into two systems—one fast and emotional, the other slow and calculating—Kurzban asserts that our minds are constructed of many modules, each performing different functions. Those modules can be thought of as subroutines in a computer program. Sometimes they work in concert, but often they clash. This is why people sometimes hold contradictory beliefs. Different modules in the brain are engaged at different moments. This does not mean, of course, that we never believe anything or that we cannot maintain certain beliefs over a long period. It means instead that context can shape our desires, and it can activate a variety of conflicting beliefs. Kurzban puts it this way:

If the context one's in, or the state one's in, turns certain modules on, then the preferences in those modules will drive one's performance. In a different context, the very same options will be evaluated by different modules, leading to the possibility of a different choice being made.[52]

These findings can offer us an alternative way of understanding Stresemann's seemingly inconsistent behavior. Surely the choice between six dollars and a pen cannot be analogous to a statesman's choices between passivity and aggression. This is true enough, but the massive body of research on rational decision-making, heuristics, and biases illustrates that, at least on small-scale decisions, we are frequently inconsistent and affected by context.[53] Indeed, on larger-scale matters, there is also evidence that we compartmentalize our views. We need only consider the many professional scientists who hold deeply religious beliefs to realize that sophisticated thinkers often adhere to seemingly contradictory ideas. Seen in this light, the debate about Stresemann (and by extension the debates over the motives of other complex historical figures) has been too narrow.

Historians who depict the Foreign Minister as ceaselessly bent on a forcible revision of Versailles force him into an unnatural box. Such interpretations take a static and far too consistently rational view of individuals. These historians point to Stresemann's ferocious support for unrestricted submarine warfare against the West during World War I, followed by his ongoing attempts to evade disarmament, and above all the aggressive aims outlined in his letter to the Crown Prince. In these acts, and many more, they see a man whose aims were unaltered throughout the course of his political life. By imposing upon him a long-term, single-minded consistency, they rob Stresemann of any true complexity.

The revisionists, however, who portray Stresemann's views as having either transformed or evolved toward greater cooperation with the West appear overly optimistic about his unwavering commitment to peace. His support of rearmament during the Scheidemann affair, and indeed his failure to oppose it at such an opportune moment, suggests at the very least that he desired greater military might, not merely that he wished to placate the Reichswehr and industrialists. Stresemann lent his support to rearmament knowing that the Reichswehr leadership sought military strength in order to use it. Whether he would have subsequently supported forceful territorial annexations can never be proved. His decisions would have depended on the future context. But the notion that he was compelled to follow the Reichswehr's lead on rearmament is not substantiated by his behavior.

More than merely keeping his options open, he may have genuinely held both intentions at different times and sometimes simultaneously. It is not hard to imagine that at various points, such as when writing to the Crown Prince or when supporting covert rearmament, he longed for German greatness and even the satisfaction that comes from military conquest, especially the kind motivated by revenge and the desire to take back what was once in German hands. Yet at other times, at other moments, he may have felt it not only necessary but virtuous to construct the foundations for a stable peace with his former enemies. It is entirely possible to hold multiple and conflicting desires over time. Stresemann's behavior need only remain an unsolved riddle if we insist on perceiving him as *either* a peacemaker *or* an aggressive nationalist. A view that accounts for the contradictory evidence would see him as a man caught amidst a stream of conflicting desires. This view would not diminish his political acumen or strategic savvy. On the contrary, it would be commensurate with the sophisticated thinker and passionate German that he was.

Stresemann's conflicting behavior aside, his behavior at the pattern break indicates his genuine support for rearmament. His overall pattern of behavior, along with his actions at the pattern break, suggests an underlying desire to resurrect German greatness by any plausible means, namely skillful diplomacy combined with military restoration.

Conclusion

From the time that Stresemann assumed the Chancellorship in 1923 to his death in 1929, Germany transitioned from a country wracked by revolution, hyperinflation, and foreign occupation to a nation of growing economic strength and international power. These extraordinary achievements resulted in no small part from Stresemann's strategic empathy, enabling his clever playing of the Russian card. Domestically, cooperation with Moscow placated the Reichswehr, satisfied the industrialists who profited from the arrangement, and further secured Stresemann's own position within the government, lending the Weimar Republic an invaluable degree of stability amidst frequently shifting governing coalitions. Internationally, the ongoing Soviet ties helped to wrest concessions from Britain and France and facilitate Germany's entry into Western security arrangements from Locarno to the League. The ties, mainly the secret military cooperation, also helped the German government to maintain close communication with Moscow, providing a useful channel for Stresemann to voice objections to communist agitation. Despite the frequent tensions over Soviet meddling in German affairs, when a major pattern break occurred—Scheidemann's revelations—Stresemann could recognize how much the Soviets valued their two nations' military engagement.

Stresemann's sense of precisely how far he could push rearmament proved astute. Against the wishes of his deputy, Schubert, who argued for terminating the arrangement, Stresemann correctly assessed both the drivers and constraints on his opponents. He saw that the Soviets had changed since their failed attempt to spark a German revolution in 1923. By 1926, the Soviet pattern of putting ideology first in foreign affairs had reversed. By the close of 1926, at least with respect to Germany, matters of national interest took precedence. The Kremlin was more concerned with avoiding international isolation and modernizing its military. Cooperation with Germany offered the best means of accomplishing both those ends. By May 1927, it was even more apparent that the Soviets wanted that relationship to persist, especially as Soviet efforts to forge agreements with Poland and France had not produced benefits comparable to cooperation with the Reichswehr.

Stresemann gained an equally clear sense for British and French drivers and constraints. The Nobel Peace Prize made it highly unlikely that Chamberlain or Briand would raise objections to Germany's Versailles violations. Their continued acquiescence to German demands over the withdrawal of Allied troops from German territory only reinforced his conviction that Britain and France were not willing to pressure Germany to halt rearmament.

Following Stresemann's death in 1929, Germany's domestic instability increased in the wake of the Great Depression and the rise of the

Nazi Party. As Chancellor, Hitler oversaw the general course of German foreign policy, though he was often greatly influenced by the irrational organization of overlapping ministries that he created.[54] Throughout the 1930s and beyond, statesmen would again struggle to determine the relative primacy of ideology in foreign policy. National leaders needed to know Hitler's underlying drivers—something that in retrospect seems painfully clear but at the time was far more murky. By 1941, Stalin faced this same difficulty when deciding how to deal with the Nazi invasion that he knew would eventually come. Part of the reason why he failed to heed the warning signs lies in the patterns he perceived and the pattern breaks he could not grasp.

4

Stalin the Simulator

The Problem of Projected Rationality

BY THE SUMMER OF 1941, 3 million soldiers were preparing for the largest invasion in history. For months German aircraft had been flying reconnaissance over Soviet airspace, noting the position of Russian planes and military installations. German troops had been boarding trains headed east and not returning. Soviet spies were sending back to Moscow a steady stream of warning signs that attack was soon to come. Then, just five days before the assault, the head of Soviet foreign intelligence delivered a report from a source inside Hermann Göring's Air Ministry. All preparations for the invasion of Russia were complete. The strike was imminent. Yet when Stalin received the intelligence, he scratched across it: "You can send your source from the headquarters of German aviation to his fucking mother." The Soviet leader simply refused to believe what was obvious to everyone else.

In fact, Stalin had been receiving reliable intelligence, and lots of it, since 1939. It increased after December 1940, when Hitler issued Directive Number 21, ordering his generals to prepare to conquer Russia. On May 19, 1941, Richard Sorge, the posthumously famous German who spied for the USSR from Japan, reported that a massive German invasion would happen by month's end. Sorge's network had penetrated the Japanese General Staff as well as the high-ranking German officials in Tokyo, and his information was typically reliable. Yet Stalin dismissed the reports as disinformation, calling Sorge "a little shit who has set himself up with some factories and brothels in Japan."[1]

When war came, Russia was utterly unprepared. The initial German onslaught, dubbed Operation Barbarossa, was so effective it almost seemed as though the entire campaign would be over in weeks. Much of the Soviet Air Force was destroyed before its planes ever left the ground. The poorly led troops on the western borders were slaughtered by the thousands. Stalin's purges, which had cut deep into his officer corps, left the nation vulnerable, just as Hitler had expected. Eventually, the Russians would regroup, reorganize, and retaliate without mercy, though they would lose an estimated 20 million citizens before the war was won.

Why did Stalin fail so spectacularly to recognize that Hitler planned to invade Russia in June 1941? Numerous scholars have attempted to fathom Stalin's seemingly inscrutable behavior on the eve of war. Gabriel Gorodetsky,[2] David Murphy,[3] Dmitri Volkogonov,[4] Geoffrey Roberts,[5] and David Holloway,[6] to name only a few, have all combed the historical record for clues. This chapter does not attempt to unearth new archival findings that will definitively settle the mystery. Instead, it reexamines the question of Stalin's failure in order to further illuminate this book's two key questions: what produces strategic empathy, and how has its presence, or absence, affected international history.

Much of the scholarship on Operation Barbarossa has centered on Stalin's intelligence before the attack. Some have argued that the Soviet leader received all the information he needed to make defensive preparations and that his failure to do so leaves him squarely to blame for the debacle. Others have countered that no body of intelligence is ever pure. All accurate reports arrive amid a background of noise—inaccurate information, rumor, and speculation—that makes it impossible or extremely difficult to discern the true signals from the false. Still others have pointed out that, beyond mere noise, Stalin also received intentionally false signals as part of the German disinformation campaign. The Germans hoped to convince Stalin that their military buildup in the east was intended for use against Great Britain. Their disinformation campaign rested on the notion that Eastern Europe provided a safe haven where Nazi forces could be assembled, free from British bombing raids. Stalin's failure therefore lies less in his personal behavior and more in the craftiness of German counterintelligence.

Each of these interpretations emphasizes what Stalin actually knew. The problem with this approach is that it downplays the fact that statesmen must typically choose between divergent interpretations of intelligence reports. In this case, Stalin had to choose to believe in one of two conflicting sets of views: namely that the German forces on Russia's border were preparing to attack Britain or, alternatively, that they were preparing to attack Russia. What Stalin knew, therefore, is important, but it is far less crucial than what he believed. If we want to understand why Stalin so stunningly lacked strategic empathy for Hitler on this crucial occasion, we have no choice but to explore how he developed a sense of his enemies.

What Drove Stalin

The international historian John Lewis Gaddis has observed that history is largely about the process of getting into and back out of another person's mind, "and then arguing among ourselves about what we saw there."[7] Gaddis's reflections on how we discern a historical figure's character are useful springboards to a discussion of how the historical figures themselves assessed their opponents. Gaddis observes that historians typically seek patterns of behavior across scale. For example, in one anecdote about the Soviet leader, Stalin removed his pet parrot from its cage and remorselessly crushed the bird's skull. Some see Stalin's brutal treatment of Ukrainians as merely the extension of his ruthless character. In the micro and the macro, many historians perceive a consistent streak of cruelty toward others.

While we can easily conclude the obvious about Stalin's character—that his emotional empathy was commensurate with that of a psychopath—we can also say that in many respects he also lacked strategic empathy. Like the Slumdog Strategist from the Introduction, Stalin employed Jamal's heuristic "trust no one," but to very ill effect. He decimated his officer corps and Party faithful, consistently misperceiving threats from those around him, especially, of course, when it mattered most, in the summer of 1941.

Stalin's lack of both emotional empathy and strategic empathy dramatically affected his behavior, yet those traits do not suffice to explain his underlying drivers. These traits were prominent aspects of his character; they were not motivating forces in and of themselves. His Marxist ideology did indeed shape his actions, yet neither was it at the root. Despite his early adoption of Marxism, his years of bank robbing and imprisonment in the name of the cause, and all the ideological rhetoric he espoused, Stalin was a fair-weather fanatic. By this admittedly provocative statement I do not mean that Stalin was not a devoted Marxist. Although he may have been a true believer, many of his actions while in power suggest that fulfilling Marxist ideological aims proved secondary to his primary goal of preserving his own power.

Like all individuals, Stalin held multiple, fluid identities. Changing contexts brought one or another to the fore. Also like many notable leaders, Stalin possessed a single underlying driver of greater salience than his other traits. He sought power, for himself and for his nation.

Throughout his career, many of Stalin's excesses were committed to protect or enhance his own power. His early purges of Party rivals were not designed to achieve any ideological purity within the Party ranks. They were primarily to eliminate threats to his own advancement. The same was true of his purges of the military, which cut deep into his own officer corps. Those soldiers were victims of Stalin's fear of losing power in a coup d'etat. Their murders had nothing to do with dogma. Even the mass murders of the Great Terror from 1937–1938 can be seen rooted in power considerations, not ideological ones. The historian Norman Naimark makes this point, concluding that although Stalin used the threat of sabotage by internal traitors to justify the killings, the ultimate aim was to preserve his position as dictator.[8] Naimark wisely observes that multiple factors combined to produce Stalin's genocides, and ideological convictions were just one factor among many.[9]

The historian Geoffrey Roberts put it well when he wrote that Stalin was "blinkered by his ideology, but not blinded by it."[10] Though Roberts was commenting on the Russo-Finnish War of 1940, his point was that Stalin's military leadership style was not driven exclusively or even primarily by Marxist doctrine. This was equally true of his domestic and foreign policy. Early evidence of this came when Stalin began to consolidate his power soon after Lenin's death.

Trotsky's yearning for worldwide revolution demonstrated his unyielding devotion to Marxist dogma. After Lenin named him foreign minister, Trotsky infamously quipped that he merely intended to issue a few proclamations and close up shop. Lenin's replacement of Trotsky with Chicherin evidenced the need for precisely the traditional diplomatic niceties that Trotsky's worldview abjured.

Following the Trotsky–Zinoviev push for a German revolution in 1923, and the revolution's dramatic failure, Stalin was able to oppose a policy of global revolution and instead argue for socialism in one country. This had the benefit of distinguishing him from his chief rivals for power atop the Soviet hierarchy. Stalin subsequently supported the growing cooperation with the German military, arming forces on the German Right, not the Left. Of course he believed in the historical inevitability of a worldwide communist victory, but because he was exceedingly patient and clung to no timetable of events, he never needed to behave recklessly by advancing ideological ends to the detriment of his own power. Advancing his own position always came first. Marxist dogma lingered ever-present in the background, and often rose to the foreground, but never supplanted his hunger for power.

Hitler, like Stalin, had multiple, competing motivations, and, like Stalin, he could compromise his views when it proved expedient. But unlike Stalin, Hitler was not driven ultimately by a thirst for power. Instead, he strove to achieve power in order to fulfill his perceived mission—even if the attempt to achieve his ideological ends would cost him his power and his life. The aim was simple: to ensure the German people their rightful place atop a hierarchy of world races. The means to achieve this were more complicated. Based on a social Darwinistic notion of competition, the German people would need to test their mettle in battle. If victorious, their place atop the pyramid of races would have been earned. If they failed, then, just as Hitler wrote in his final testament, the German people were not ready. Along the course of this epic struggle, it would be necessary to exterminate as many of the *Untermenschen* as possible. The war in Russia was not solely a war of expansion; it was a war of extinction, designed to obliterate the Slavs and Jews. As cruel as Stalin had been, it is not hard to grasp why the Russian people supported him during the Nazi invasion: Their alternative was even worse.

One of the clearest signs of Hitler's devotion to dogma can be seen in his relentless pursuit of the Jews, both within and beyond German borders. At a time of war, it was not efficient to divert resources away from military objectives and channel them into extermination campaigns. The ongoing operation of concentration camps as well as the use of *Einsatzgruppen*—those units designated for killing noncombatant Jewish men, women, and children in occupied territories—strongly suggests that the Führer's ideology superceded his other objectives. Stalin, for all his barbarity, would not have focused on killing Ukrainians, for example, if by doing so it risked a possible loss of his power. Hitler was naturally concerned with attaining and protecting his power but primarily as a means of fulfilling his racist mission.

Stalin, like many others at the time, recognized a pattern in Hitler's behavior whereby his pragmatism trumped his ideology. Hitler had repeatedly indicated that, despite his racist rhetoric, in foreign affairs realism came first. In 1934, Hitler violated his oft-stated hatred of the Poles by forming a nonaggression pact with Poland.[11] In 1939, Hitler showed that he could easily discard his anti-Slavic, anti-Bolshevik pronouncements by forging an accord with Soviet Russia. The Führer again overrode Nazi racial dogma in 1940 by forming an alliance with the Japanese because the Tripartite Pact would cripple Britain's access to raw materials in the Far East. Stalin observed this pattern, misread Hitler's key driver—his ideology—and failed to scrutinize the pattern breaks.

Without recognizing Hitler's key driver, it was impossible for Stalin to predict the Führer's actions in June 1941. But prior to the invasion, how could Stalin have grasped that Hitler was willing to take extraordinary risks in order to accomplish his racist mission? There were, in fact, some clues. They were to be found among the pattern breaks.

For more than a decade following his membership in the German Nazi Party, Hitler had been building up the *Sturmabteilung*, a paramilitary band of thugs variously known as the SA or Brown Shirts. Atop this rapidly expanding organization of ex-World War I soldiers and unemployed young men stood one of Hitler's few close friends, Ernst Röhm.

Röhm possessed two salient traits. He exuded an aggressive toughness, exemplified by the scar he bore on his right cheek, the remnant of an earlier fencing duel. Hitler saw in his friend a reliable machismo, a quality essential for building the Nazi movement. Both men believed that strength should be tested in battle and that the worthy would always prevail. Röhm's other notable trait was his flagrant homosexuality. The fact that Hitler overlooked this behavior evidenced the degree to which Hitler depended on his SA chief. But by the fall of 1933, Röhm had grown overconfident in his newfound power.

Having assembled such a massive paramilitary force, Röhm expected that he could subsume the small German military within the SA's ranks. The Reichswehr naturally resisted. Though the bulk of the professional officer corps were not Nazi Party members, they possessed the skills and training that Röhm's brown-shirted bullies thoroughly lacked. Reichswehr commanders complained that former soldiers who had been dishonorably discharged now held prominent positions in the SA. Seeing no other option, War Minister von Blomberg decreed on September 19, 1933, that all Reichswehr members must offer the Nazi salute when encountering SA men. Soon thereafter, a Reichswehr lieutenant in Giessen failed to salute an SA flag. The stormtroopers attacked him. Rather than coming to his lieutenant's defense, General von Blomberg confined the young officer to three days of room arrest.

On December 1, Hitler elevated Röhm to a Cabinet position, which only exacerbated Röhm's sense of self-importance. The following month Röhm pushed the issue too far. He wrote to Blomberg: "I regard the *Reichswehr* now only as a training school for the German people. The conduct of war, and therefore of mobilization as well, in future is the task of the SA."[12]

Tensions between the SA and the military had reached a breaking point. The Reichswehr could not abide Röhm's high-handed attempts to subvert them. Hitler would have to make a choice. He could continue to back the Nazi paramilitary force that had helped bring him to power, or he could support the non-Nazi professional military. In an episode known as the Night of the Long Knives, Hitler chose the Reichswehr. On June 30, 1934, Hitler ordered Röhm arrested. He had hoped that Röhm would commit suicide with a pistol left in his cell. When Röhm refused, a guard shot him dead.

In the bloodbath that followed, Hitler, with the aid of Himmler's SS and Göring's police force, rounded up all of the leading SA officials and had them shot. Hitler replaced Röhm with Röhm's own deputy, the squeaky-voiced Viktor Lutze, a man unlikely to intimidate anyone, and the SA never again played a meaningful decision-making role in the Nazi regime. It was Lutze who had informed Hitler that Röhm had insulted the Führer and was plotting a coup against him. The government portrayed the mass killings as a necessary countermeasure to crush a plot against the regime. However much of Lutze's report was fabricated for his own benefit, the tension between the SA and the Reichswehr was undeniable. Hitler could not escape a choice between the increasingly uncontrollable Nazi Brown Shirts and the disciplined officer corps.

Hitler's liquidation of his old friend, and his demotion of the SA from a position of influence, represented a meaningful break in his behavior pattern. By choosing the vastly smaller, non-Nazi Reichswehr, Hitler revealed that he was committed to a long-term plan, one that required the skills of a professional military. It meant that he intended to use that military, and soon. If foreigners wanted to gauge Hitler's underlying drivers, this episode should have caught their attention.

Correctly interpreting the Röhm purge presented a legitimate challenge to any foreign observer. On its surface, the events seemed to represent a choice for realism over racism. Hitler sided with the non-Nazi Reichswehr and against his ideological compatriots. It looked as though Hitler had acted to crush a potential threat to his power—nothing more. That is, in fact, precisely how Stalin understood the affair.

Stalin was watching. He learned about Hitler's actions and spoke of them in admiring tones. "Some fellow that Hitler. Splendid," Stalin remarked to his close colleague, Anastas Mikoyan. "That's a deed of some skill."[13] Stalin no doubt saw himself in Hitler, or at least some aspects of himself. Despite their dramatically opposing ideologies, Stalin viewed Hitler's violent power play as a mirror of his own behavior. The Night of the Long Knives was merely a small-scale version of the deep and wide mass murders that Stalin himself would soon unleash upon his country. There was, however, a crucial difference between Hitler's and Stalin's actions. Stalin's purge of the Soviet officer corps reflected a madly paranoid desire to protect his own power. Hitler's purge of the SA, in contrast, was motivated by a long-range ideological plan. Hitler recognized that the SA could never substitute for a highly trained, professional military, and such a disciplined military would be essential for executing his ideological agenda: the acquisition of *Lebensraum* (living space) for the German people and the extermination of subhuman, inferior peoples from the Reich. Hitler was dependent on his military to bring his racist plans to fruition. The tensions between the two organizations impelled him to choose one over the other. Tellingly, after the coup, Hitler did not elevate Röhm's replacement to the Cabinet, and he confined the SA to less consequential matters, not the decisive affairs of party or state. Had Hitler acted solely to prevent a putsch, he could have simply eliminated Röhm and his supporters but kept the SA in a position of high influence as rivals to the Reichswehr. Instead, Hitler backed the non-Nazi military because it was essential to his future plans.

Two questions immediately arise from this analysis. First, could Stalin have read Hitler's drivers correctly at the time, without the benefit of hindsight? The answer is almost certainly no, given Stalin's particular proclivity for projecting his own reasoning processes onto others. Second, how did Stalin try to enter Hitler's mind? By what means did he attempt to understand the German chancellor?

The Great Simulator

In the Introduction I briefly mentioned that cognitive psychologists have developed theories about how all of us try to understand how others think. The scientists in this field have coined the term "mentalizing" as shorthand for the act of placing ourselves into someone else's head. Much of this vein of exploration centers on the theory of mind. Within the theory of mind literature, two principal theories stand out. The first of these is called, rather awkwardly, theory-theory. It holds that we construct a theory about what another person believes, based on what we know about that person's attitudes and experiences. We then use that theory to predict his behavior. For example, if you believe that John is driven mainly by greed, then in a situation where he would be able to steal money and get away with it, you would expect him to steal.

The second prominent theory of how we get into another person's head is called simulation theory. It suggests that we ask ourselves, "What would I do if I were she?" Simulation theory suggests that we imagine ourselves in the other person's position. It is, unfortunately, the worst approach to empathy because it assumes that others will think and act as we do, and too often they don't. Simulation theory essentially says that we project our own motivations onto someone else, assuming that her motivations will resemble our own.[14]

Although psychologists and cognitive neuroscientists debate which approach is more common, most likely we all engage in both types of thinking at different times. Stalin, however, may well have been different. He appears to have engaged in simulation theory most of the time. Viewing Stalin's thinking in this light makes his behavior far more comprehensible.

Stalin typically asked himself what he would do if he were in another's shoes, and being a distrustful, violent person with no regard for the feelings of others, he naturally assumed that others were likely to behave in disloyal, violent ways. This explains Stalin's destruction of his own officer corps in the Great Terror of 1937–1938 and the subsequent murders of his intelligence officials. Stalin believed that others were more than merely against him. He was certain that they would depose or destroy him. He believed this about his officer corps not simply because they had the weapons, the organization, and therefore the power to remove him. He believed they were a threat because he asked himself what he would do in their position. Since Stalin himself would have sought to overthrow the leader and install himself atop the hierarchy, that is what he assumed his officers would do. This is, in fact, what Stalin did do after Lenin's death. He consolidated his power base, isolated his rivals, and ruthlessly destroyed them. In fact, immediately after the Nazi invasion, when it was plain to all that his judgment had utterly failed and now imperiled the Soviet Union's existence, Stalin despondently awaited his colleagues from his home. When they arrived, he appears to have assumed that they had come to arrest and depose him. Only gradually could they convince him that they actually sought his leadership.[15] That his subordinates did not, in fact, arrest him at this moment is a testament to Stalin's strategic empathy toward those he knew best. Attuned to the greed, corruptibility, and fear in others, Stalin managed for decades to manipulate his colleagues with exceptional aplomb. But this skill betrayed him when it came to reading Hitler.

From 1940 through June 1941, Stalin confronted two contradictory bodies of intelligence. The first indicated a German invasion of Russia; the second suggested a German invasion of the British Isles. Stalin's generals, and his competent intelligence officers, recognized that a German invasion of Russia was likely. They suggested to Stalin that they make all reasonable preparations. But Stalin refused to let them prepare.

He insisted that this might provoke a war, believing that a split existed within the German leadership between those who favored war with Russia and those who wanted to conquer England. Stalin feared that by putting Russia on a war footing, the Germans could interpret this as justification for launching preemptive strikes, making war inevitable.

Stalin interpreted all incoming information about the German buildup through this filter. When in April 1941 he received a direct communication from Churchill warning him of the coming invasion, Stalin had to dismiss it as a British provocation. After reading the letter, Stalin smiled and declared that Churchill would benefit if they entered the war as soon as possible, but it would benefit them to remain on the sidelines.[16] When the Soviet Ambassador to Germany, Vladimir Dekanozov, provided intelligence on Germany's intensifying preparation for a Soviet invasion, Stalin remarked that Dekanozov was not clever enough to recognize that he was being fed disinformation. Even when Germany's own ambassador to Moscow, Werner von der Schulenburg (who would later be hanged for his part in a plot to assassinate Hitler), informed Dekanozov that Hitler was preparing to invade, Stalin still could not accept the truth. No matter the source, be it a British ally, a Soviet colleague, or a German anti-Nazi ambassador, Stalin assumed a trap. He did so not simply because he trusted no one. It is obvious that Stalin was paranoid, but that is irrelevant in this case. His paranoia could just as easily have led him to conclude that Hitler was indeed planning to invade, despite Hitler's repeated assurances to the contrary. Stalin's distrustful nature cannot explain his interpretation of the evidence surrounding Barbarossa. Instead, the explanation must be found in Stalin's particular reasoning process, namely his projected rationality.

As a consummate simulator, Stalin would have asked himself what he would do in Hitler's place. Stalin's own underlying driver, the force that ruled him above all others, was power—the desire to attain it and the fear of losing it. Had he been in Germany's position, with Britain still undefeated and the Americans drawing closer to the British war effort via Lend-Lease, he never would have risked fighting a two-front war. Stalin was a realist not out of some philosophical conviction that pragmatism was the sine qua non of sensible statecraft. It was much simpler than that. Stalin was a realist because adventurism abroad could jeopardize his power. From Stalin's perspective, the sensible move for Hitler in 1941 would have been to finish off Britain before turning on Russia.

The problem, of course, was that Hitler never thought this way. Hitler's underlying driver was to accomplish his mission, the one he believed fate had enabled him to achieve. That mission was the destruction of Jewish Bolshevism and the conquest of Russian lands to provide living space for Germans. Conquering Britain was never part of his vision. Quite the opposite—Hitler consistently desired an alliance with Britain, and he wrote about this in *Mein Kampf.*

Stalin did try to understand Hitler's main drivers by reading a translated edition of *Mein Kampf.* The Nazi leader was, if nothing else, unsubtle; Hitler stated plainly that the primary aim of German foreign policy had to be the acquisition of land and soil. National borders, he insisted, could always be changed. According to Hitler, a nation's existence depended on sufficient living space, not merely for the production of food but also for military and political needs. As a nation grows, its need for land follows. From Hitler's perspective, the acquisition of territory was inextricably bound to great power status: "Germany will either be a world power, or there will be no Germany. And for world power she needs that magnitude which will give her the position she needs in the present period and life to her citizens."[17]

Regarding Russia, Hitler made his views equally plain. He wrote,

> The Russian state was not formed by the Slavs, but by the German element within Russia. Today Russia is dominated by Jews. The giant empire in the east is ripe for collapse. And the end of Jewish rule in Russia will also be the end of Russia as a state. We have been chosen by fate as witnesses of a catastrophe which will be the mightiest confirmation of the soundness of the Volkisch theory.[18]

As for his opinion of Soviet leaders, Hitler characteristically pulled no punches:

> Never forget that the rulers of present-day Russia are common, blood-stained criminals, that they are the scum of humanity, which, favored by circumstances, overran a great state in a tragic hour, slaughtered

and wiped out thousands of her leading intelligentsia in wild blood lust. And now for almost ten years have been carrying on the most cruel and tyrannical regime of all time. Furthermore, do not forget that these rulers belong to a race which combines in a rare mixture of bestial cruelty and an inconceivable gift for lying, and which today more than ever is conscious of a mission to impose its bloody oppression on the whole world.[19]

For Hitler, Russia represented the perfect enemy. Ruled by Marxist Jews, it sought to impose its ideology upon whomever it could control. Germany, he believed, was its prime target: "Do not forget that the international Jew, who completely dominates Russia today, regards Germany not as an ally, but as a state destined to the same fate."[20] Germany, therefore, had a mission to save itself by simultaneously destroying Jewish Bolshevism and liberating the Russian soil for use by the German race.

Stalin read these declarations by Hitler and discussed *Mein Kampf* with his close colleague, Andrei Zhdanov, but the knowledge that Hitler dreamt of conquering Russia's vast lands could not override Stalin's simulation process.[21] A realist simply would not invade Russia when a two-front war would ensue.

Stalin's Foreign Minister and close colleague, Vyachaslav Molotov, also tried to read his way into Hitler's mind. One source he engaged was Hermann Rauschning's best-selling study, *Hitler Speaks*.[22] Unfortunately for Molotov, the book was mostly fabrication. Rauschning claimed to have spoken with Hitler on 100 occasions. In fact, postwar scholarship determined that they had only met four times. Most historians today consider Rauschning's book a largely illegitimate source.

To his credit, Stalin did employ multiple methods for getting into Hitler's head. In addition to reading Hitler's own words, he fell back on his favorite pastime: consuming histories and searching for lessons. He found one main principle and latched onto it. It was never wise for Germany to fight a two-front war, and the fear of this scenario haunted German generals and statesmen alike. Unfortunately for Stalin, he assumed that Hitler would be constrained by the weight of historical precedence. He projected a rational, realist worldview onto Hitler, imagining that the Führer would not violate this cardinal rule of German military strategy.[23]

Stalin saw clearly that Hitler wanted war. He expected a German attack at some future time and hoped to forestall it as long as possible. But by the close of 1940, Stalin still did not yet have a clear sense of Hitler's more immediate plans or timeframe. Reading histories only offered general lessons. There were no guarantees that the Führer would obey them. *Mein Kampf*, for its part, revealed a racist worldview, the dogma of a fanatic, and, at points, the thinking of a realist. The underlying driver lay somewhere therein. *Mein Kampf* presented Stalin with the classic problem of a great mass of information. It seemed impossible to determine from its rambling tracts and turgid prose precisely what Hitler's underlying motivations were. Looking back, it seems all too clear that acquisition of living space and extermination of Slavs and Jews were paramount. But at the time it could also have been read as the demagogic rants of a man bent on seizing power. Stalin needed a heuristic for determining whether racism or realism was Hitler's prime driver.

Despite confidence in his own analysis of the enemy, Stalin still harbored some qualms about Hitler's intentions prior to Barbarossa. To uncover the riddle wrapped in a mystery, Stalin would enlist one other method. He would send his colleague, Foreign Minister Molotov, to meet with Hitler and attempt to glean his thoughts.

The time was right for another high-level meeting between Soviet and German officials. With Japan's entry into the Axis on September 27, 1940, the Soviets could easily be encircled if the Germans and Japanese should jointly attack. For the time being, the Japanese had been deterred thanks to Marshall Zhukov's skillful leadership during clashes with the Japanese army at Nomonhan in Mongolia. With their noses bloodied, the Japanese turned southward for expansion. As for the Germans, the Nazi–Soviet pact kept Stalin's western front safe only as long as Hitler intended to honor it. Molotov therefore needed to gain some sense of Hitler's intentions, or better still, a sense of the Chancellor's key drivers.

Before we examine Molotov's mission, we need to explore a similar attempt to read Hitler's mind. Across the Atlantic a rather different type of world leader was about to attempt the same method of dispatching a personal envoy to probe Hitler's plans. President Roosevelt possessed a firm grasp of Hitler's basic character and the nature of the Nazi regime. Despite this understanding, FDR did not know Hitler's intentions regarding the Soviet Union or the course of the war. By the early months of 1940, with Germany occupying part of Poland and at war with England and France, Roosevelt would not have been so naïve as to suspect that a peace initiative could succeed.[24] Nonetheless, the President enlisted his most trusted foreign policy advisor, Sumner Welles, to hold talks with the highest-ranking German officials, including an audience with the Führer himself.

5

A Rendezvous With Evil

How Roosevelt Read Hitler

STALIN'S EFFORTS TO UNDERSTAND and predict Hitler's actions stood in contrast to President Roosevelt's approach most notably in three distinct ways. First, Stalin tried to read his way into Hitler's mind by studying *Mein Kampf* along with German military histories. He tended to dismiss or disparage the information sent to him by his Soviet representatives in Berlin. Roosevelt, conversely, placed stock in the information he received from American officials in Germany. He took pains to establish back-door channels through which information would flow directly to him from his chosen representatives. Second, whereas Stalin simulated what he would do in Hitler's place, Roosevelt mentalized by asking what Hitler would do based on a theory of what made Hitler tick. Third, Stalin assumed that the behavior of past German leaders could serve as a useful guide to predicting the current German leader's actions. FDR may not have used the pattern break heuristic precisely, but it is clear that his image of the Führer was shaped in part by the information he obtained during pattern-break moments. By examining the data that Roosevelt received, we can gain a glimpse into how the American President formed a picture of Hitler's mind, and we can contrast that with Stalin's approach.

Franklin Roosevelt came to office in 1933 facing an extraordinary economic crisis. The widespread unemployment, hunger, and privation across the nation made revolution seem like a genuine possibility. As a result, we would not expect foreign affairs to have been foremost in

FDR's thoughts during his first term. Nonetheless, Roosevelt took care to stay informed of German and European developments. Hitler's more violent actions certainly caught the President's attention.

Although Stalin praised Hitler's first pattern break, the mass shootings of SA leaders in 1934, Franklin Roosevelt was less sanguine about the affair. It is unclear precisely what Roosevelt thought about the Night of the Long Knives, though he clearly found it disturbing. One day after the mass murders occurred, in a private correspondence to his personal secretaries who were traveling to Europe, FDR warned them not to go to Germany and to avoid riots and revolutions. "The U.S.A. needs you," he added affectionately, "and so do I."[1] Nevertheless, he did not consider the killings sufficiently distressing to warrant remaining in Washington. That evening, FDR departed for a previously scheduled summer vacation, though he continued to request information on the unfolding events. In fact, he steadily sought out both official and back-door channels to gauge the nature of Hitler's young regime.

At Secretary of State Cordell Hull's request, the American Ambassador to Germany, William E. Dodd, telegrammed his analysis of the rapidly changing situation in Berlin. Given the confusion, fear, and propaganda surrounding the purge, it is understandable that the Ambassador could not report with full accuracy. He did, however, grasp that the SA was finished as a military organization. Lutze, who replaced Röhm as SA chief, was not appointed to the Cabinet as Röhm had been. Dodd correctly concluded that the Reichswehr's power had been greatly enhanced as a result of what occurred on June 30.[2]

On July 12, the director of America's National Recovery Administration, retired Army General Hugh S. Johnson, delivered bold, honest, and obviously inflammatory remarks on the purge. General Johnson's role atop that organization made him a well-known public figure. He had been Time's "Man of the Year" in 1933. Given his status, Johnson's comments naturally garnered attention. In a public statement, General Johnson declared that the events of June 30 had made him physically ill: "The idea that adult, responsible men can be taken from their homes, stood up against a wall, backs to the rifles and shot to death is beyond expression." Then Johnson remarked that he had witnessed such savagery in Mexico by semicivilized drunks, but he could not comprehend how such barbarity could happen in a supposedly civilized and cultured nation like Germany. Naturally, the German Charge d'Affaires visited Hull to make an official protest. Hull took the standard diplomatic line: General Johnson was speaking as an individual citizen and not in any official capacity as a representative of the U.S. government. It was to be regretted that his remarks were misconstrued as an official U.S. position.

The following day Hull cabled all of this information to FDR, who was traveling aboard the *USS Houston*. Hull stated that he hoped the President approved of his actions. Roosevelt replied simply, "Cordially approved."[3]

Germany was not FDR's primary concern in the summer of 1934. Recovering from the Depression and furthering the New Deal occupied more of his attention at that time. Yet the Röhm purge helped to form Roosevelt's early impressions of Hitler and his regime. Hitler's brutality was evident. Less obvious were the German Chancellor's longer-term objectives in elevating the Reichswehr over the SA. Though the purge signaled a meaningful pattern break, it is doubtful that Roosevelt recognized this at the time. Nonetheless, in sharp contrast to Stalin, FDR could not identify himself with Hitler's actions. When mentalizing about Hitler, it would be necessary for Roosevelt to construct a theory of how the Führer thought. FDR could not readily project himself into Hitler's head, especially because the Nazi regime increasingly revealed itself to be bent on racist ends

FDR frequently circumvented the standard diplomatic chain of command by engaging in direct communications with key ambassadors, undoubtedly to the annoyance of Hull and other Foreign Service officials. On August 15, 1934, Ambassador Dodd wrote directly to the President, summarizing his impressions of the German situation. Dodd observed that displays of militarism were increasing across the country, despite Hitler's protestations of peaceful intentions. He reported that in an audience with Hitler, the Chancellor had assured him that Germany would never go to war. The only way a war could be triggered, Hitler insisted, would be if violent SA men acted against his commands. Yet Dodd could not help noticing that Hitler's assurances were frequently contradicted by his government's actions. In particular, Dodd had sought to assure Jews in the United States that they were not threatened by the Nazi regime. Soon thereafter Dodd read a speech by Propaganda

Minister Joseph Goebbels calling Jews "the syphilis of all European peoples."

Even at this early point in Dodd's time in Berlin, the Ambassador was recognizing Hitler's deceitfulness. Dodd wrote the President: "I am sorry to have to say this of a man who proclaims himself the savior of his country and assumes on occasion the powers of President, the legislature, and the supreme court. But you know all this side of the matter: June 30 and July 25!"[4] Dodd was referring to Hitler's failed attempt to annex Austria on July 25, 1934. Obviously, Dodd understood that FDR grasped at least some of the significance of Hitler's June 30 purge as well as the Führer's aggressive intentions abroad. Ten days later, Roosevelt took the time to reply to Dodd's letter. The President agreed that the "drift in Germany was definitely downward." He expected something to break within the next six months to a year. FDR concurred with Dodd's pessimism about Europe, but he stressed that he looked for any ray of hope, though he saw no signs of it at present.[5]

By September, the President was fully aware of the growing police state that Hitler had erected. At a press conference in Hyde Park, FDR commented on a report from Dodd that the many secret services—those obedient to Hitler, Goebbels, Goering, and the Reichswehr—were all following each other around. The President wryly remarked that in order to retain their power, someone would probably have to march on some border. At that point, the only way to know which border it would be was to toss a coin.[6]

In November, Dodd again summarized his impressions of rising German militarism in a cable to Assistant Secretary of State R. Walton Moore, which Moore forwarded to the President. Dodd observed that Hitler Youth and SA men were marching in every town he visited. In Bayreuth the Ambassador could not sleep because the marching and singing kept him awake all night.[7] Dodd noted intense smokestack activity, suggesting that poison gas and weapons were being manufactured at full speed. A great many German men were being trained to fly, far more than would normally be needed. Dodd's overall impression was that the German public was becoming exceedingly militarized: "The result of all this, if allowed to go through, will of course mean annexations and predominance of the whole of Europe." Dodd qualified his conclusion by stressing that he was not predicting that this would definitely occur, only that the signs clearly pointed in that direction.[8]

By May of 1935, Dodd's direct reports to Roosevelt were assuming a more alarming pitch. Germany now possessed, he stated, more than a million young men expertly trained in everything except the handling of the most modern guns. Its airfields were expansive, modern, and equipped by underground storage areas. The manufacture of arms, tanks, and poison gas was continuing day and night. When Dodd asked one admiral what Germany would do in two years' time when it possessed the greatest military in Europe, the admiral bluntly said, "Go to war." Dodd further observed that although Hitler constantly reiterated his peaceful aims, he had placed well-drilled police units along the Rhine's demilitarized zone. Dodd frankly informed the President: "While I do not think the Chancellor will wish to make a war before May 1937 or '38, I believe I am right in saying that it is a fixed purpose. Such is the view of every leading diplomat here."[9]

In mid-September of 1935, the Nazi Party held a mass rally at Nuremberg. It was there that the regime outlined what came to be known as the Nuremberg Laws, a set of anti-Jewish legal codes that formalized discrimination. Ambassador Dodd cabled Hull with summaries of the speeches delivered by Hitler and other Party leaders. Roosevelt wanted to know more. On September 23, Dodd hosted a luncheon in the American embassy for a handful of guests. Among the invitees was Dr. Hjalmar Schacht, Minister of Economics and a prominent conservative economist of the old school. Schacht had helped steer Germany back to financial health in the 1920s when Gustav Stresemann was working to restore German strength through its foreign relations. At one point during the luncheon, Dodd took Schacht aside with a special request. President Roosevelt desired that Schacht speak privately with American representative S. R. Fuller, Jr. Via Fuller, FDR wanted to glean Schacht's views on Europe's and especially Germany's trajectory, yet the subjects they discussed were not limited to economics.

Fuller invited Schacht to speak freely. Presumably they were safe from surveillance in the library of the American embassy. Schacht did not hold back. He praised Hitler for his moral courage and his achievements uniting the German people. Schacht insisted that Hitler did not seek dictatorship but instead was pursuing policies through democratic means. And then Schacht himself brough the conversation to the Jews, explaining to Fuller that the Jews and Roman Catholics historically had been a domestic problem for many states in Europe.

Fuller observed that Germany's treatment of the Jews was resented in many countries. The new Nuremberg Laws, he noted, deprived the Jews of their citizenship. Schacht conceded this, but he defended the laws, stating that the Jews were fully protected as any other minority. Fuller pressed the point. "And their positions by these laws is an inferior one to the Germans?" Fuller asked. "Yes," Schacht replied, "that must always be."[10] Fuller then asked what would happen if the Jewish people refused to accept their inferior status. Schacht simply shrugged his shoulders and replied that he did not know what would result.

The discussion turned to economic matters for a time, before touching again on politics. Schacht declared that Hitler stood closely with the army and that the army supported Hitler unreservedly, seeing Hitler as a necessity for them and for the nation. When Fuller asked at last what part of their discussion he wished Fuller to share with President Roosevelt, Schacht emphatically responded, "Everything. You can tell the President everything I have said."[11]

Clearly, by late 1935, in the wake of the Nuremberg Laws, FDR felt it necessary to understand the German Chancellor. Roosevelt's private, back-door channel to Schacht offered the President a further glimpse into the racist mood within Germany, as well as the surprising degree of support for Hitler's agenda, even from an old-school conservative like Schacht. And yet, the President understood that Nazi control over German media and society severely inhibited both free speech and free thought. At the start of December, he wrote Dodd that while he could not guarantee that America could save civilization, he at least hoped that the United States could, by example, encourage freedom of thought. "The trouble is," FDR added woefully, "that the people of Germany, Italy and Japan are not given the privilege of thinking."[12]

Kristallnacht, the Night of Broken Glass, marked another pattern break in which Hitler imposed costs upon himself and thereby revealed something about his underlying aims. Spearheaded by Propaganda Minister Joseph Goebbels in close collaboration with Hitler, the sudden surge in anti-Jewish violence on November 9, 1938, shocked observers within and beyond German borders. Perhaps the most unsettling aspect was the episode's medieval character: rampaging mobs bent on mayhem, brutality, and murder. More than 100 Jews died during the savagery, while many more tried to commit suicide as an escape. Gangs broke into Jewish homes, stabbed the occupants to death, and looted at will. More than 8,000 Jewish-owned businesses were vandalized, more than 100 synagogues were destroyed, and hundreds more were burned. Jewish-owned property lined the streets, smashed, torn, and shattered. The estimated cost of this one night ranged in the hundreds of millions of marks.[13]

The horror of Kristallnacht made an unalloyed impression on FDR. Roosevelt felt it necessary to make a public statement in response to these events. Hull provided a draft of the official remarks, which Roosevelt used almost verbatim. There was one notable addition, which affords a glimpse into how FDR had come to view Hitler and the Nazi regime. In his own hand, the President inserted the words: "I myself could scarcely believe that such things could occur in a twentieth century civilization."[14] FDR recalled the American Ambassador from Berlin to provide him with a firsthand account of events across Germany. If there had been any question before this point as to the nature of Nazi rule, there could be little doubt thereafter. Five days later, on November 14, Roosevelt and senior administration officials, including George Marshall, met in the White House to discuss the dramatic expansion of American air power. At that time, the Army's Air Corps possessed a mere 160 warplanes and 50 bombers. The officials debated the merits of constructing 10,000 new warplanes.[15] Kristallnacht was not the cause of this proposed expansion—an accurate assessment of Hitler's aggressive nature was.[16]

The historian Ian Kershaw has argued that Hitler's anti-Jewish mania was linked to his ambition for war. "If international finance Jewry inside and outside Europe should succeed once more in plunging the nations into a world war," Hitler declared, "the result will be not the Bolshevism of earth and thereby the victory of Jewry, but the annihilation of the Jewish race in Europe."[17] *Mein Kampf* revealed Hitler's intimate intertwining of Jews and Bolshevism. What Kristallnacht revealed was Hitler's inability to restrain his anti-Jewish, anti-Bolshevist obsession, even at a time when he sought international acquiescence to his plans for territorial expansion. The Munich Agreement had been concluded merely one month earlier. Hitler still hoped to persuade foreign leaders of his peaceful and just intentions, yet Kristallnacht undermined that aim. A hardened realist would never have permitted Kristallnacht to occur at so sensitive a time. On November 9, Hitler's racism collided with his realism, and his realism was momentarily pushed aside.[18]

Once war came in September 1939, American entry became a British objective and the isolationists' nightmare. By early 1940, Roosevelt needed to gain a clearer sense of Hitler's aims. The President also had to prepare to win a third term. To accomplish both these ends, FDR dispatched his most trusted advisor in the Department of State, Sumner Welles, to Berlin. Welles's mission was to gauge Hitler's more immediate intentions as well as the Führer's longer-term goals.

Although FDR did not expect to broker a peace deal at this late date, he did hope to buy England and France a bit more time. If Welles could draw Hitler into negotiations, this could at least allow for more supplies to reach the British Isles. But Hitler was far too clever and determined to allow himself to be ensnared. On February 29, 1940, he issued a memorandum to all officials scheduled to meet with Welles. Under no circumstances were they to give Welles the impression that Germany was interested in discussing peace.[19] For Welles's part, he imagined that he might create a wedge between the Duce and the Führer and thereby prevent a world war, but this too had little chance of succeeding.

At noon on March 1, Welles first met with Joachim von Ribbentrop, a former champagne salesman who possessed disturbingly little aptitude for diplomacy. After years of wrangling with his predecessor, in 1938 Ribbentrop finally displaced Konstantin Freiherr von Neurath as German Foreign Minister. Although he managed to alienate most traditional diplomats, he did succeed in negotiating the now infamous Molotov-Ribbentrop Pact, forging an alliance with Soviet Russia and enabling the Second World War to begin. Still, even the Soviets who had dealt with him had a hard time taking him seriously. "Those hips," Andrei Zhdanov had exclaimed once the pact was sealed. "He's got the biggest and broadest pair of hips in all of Europe."[20] Welles would find nothing to joke about. He saw the Foreign Minister as an utterly distasteful presence. Given Ribbentrop's icy reception, that was no surprise.

Welles was immediately struck by the Wilhelmstrasse's untraditional atmosphere. Every Foreign Ministry official dressed in military uniform.

Nazi stormtroopers guarded the halls, just past the two sphinxes outside the Foreign Minister's office, the eerie remnants of Bismarck's era.

Ribbentrop held forth for two hours straight, pausing occasionally to allow the interpreter to translate. He spoke with eyes closed while he lectured on about the aggression of England and the unlikelihood of peace. Welles thought the Foreign Minister imagined himself some kind of Delphic Oracle. Welles let FDR know exactly what he thought of Ribbentrop, describing him as "saturated with hate for England," "clearly without background in international affairs," and "guilty of a hundred inaccuracies in his presentation of German policy during recent years." Welles concluded that he had rarely met anyone he disliked more.

The conversation did touch briefly on human rights. Welles raised the issue of humanitarian conditions, clearly with the plight of the Jews in mind. Ribbentrop suggested that Welles should spend a little time in Germany; then he would see for himself just how good the German people had it. Germany had become a nation of "enthusiastic, happy human beings. . . ." This was ". . . the humane work to which the Führer had devoted his life."[21]

If Ribbentrop proved a brick wall, Welles gleaned even less from Rudolph Hess, Hitler's deputy in the Nazi Party—a man whom Welles found exceedingly stupid. Hess never deviated from his script and gave the impression of an automaton. Four other meetings did, however, reveal at least a hint of Hitler's thinking and internal government dynamics. Ernst von Weizsacker, Welles's counterpart in the German Foreign Ministry and a traditional Weimar-era diplomat, revealed much when he explained that he had been strictly instructed not to discuss any subject relating to peace. That admission underscored the remoteness of establishing any last-ditch settlement. Then Weizsacker pulled his chair toward the center of the room and wordlessly indicated that Welles should do the same. The Nazi security service was listening, always, and every official had to operate under the weighty pall of surveillance. Welles asked if he thought that Mussolini might persuade the Führer to negotiate a settlement. Weizsacker felt that Ribbentrop would try to block any such attempt. As they parted, Weizsacker became teary-eyed, telling Welles that he hoped there might be a way that "an absolute holocaust could be avoided."[22]

At 11:00 on the following morning, officials arrived at Welles's hotel to escort him to the Chancellery. The Führer would grant him an audience. Inside the great marble hall, tapestries and sofas lined the corridors. Welles was ushered into a waiting room until Hitler was ready to see him. The Chancellor greeted Welles formally but pleasantly. Hitler looked fit, and taller than Welles had imagined. Throughout almost the whole of their meeting Hitler spoke eloquently in a calm and dignified demeanor. Though Welles could not have known it, that same day Hitler had issued orders to the Wehrmacht to prepare for an invasion of Denmark and Norway.[23]

Welles explained that he came as the representative of the President of the United States and that he would report only to the President and Secretary of State. He had no specific proposals, but he hoped to determine whether stability on the continent remained possible. "Was it not worth every effort to seek the way of peace," Welles asked Hitler, "before the war of devastation commenced and before the doors to peace were closed?" Such a peace, Welles explained, must include a contented and secure German people but also an international community that did not view Germany as a threat. Asked if the Chancellor could affirm that a possibility for peace still existed, Hitler quietly detailed his foreign policy over the previous seven years, exactly as Ribbentrop had done the day before. Welles had the distinct impression that every Nazi official he met with had been instructed to stick to the identical script.

Welles attempted to engage Hitler in a discussion of Germany's long-term economic interests, arguing that no country could benefit more than Germany from the resumption of liberal trade relations. Hitler said that the nations of central and southeastern Europe needed to purchase German industrial products (of the kind that those countries could not themselves produce), while Germany could import those nations' raw materials. Trade with the United States was not his priority. Welles countered that German luxury goods would not find markets in central and southeastern Europe, as those populations could not afford them. Only advanced economies such as the United States could provide sufficient consumers. War would disrupt Germany's best hopes of economic growth. Welles was trying to reason with the Führer by assuming that economic interests were one of his primary concerns. Either he did not grasp Hitler's underlying drivers, or he simply wanted to draw the Chancellor out in hope that he would reveal what he truly wanted. In part, Hitler did reveal himself.

Hitler replied that he had three aims: historical, political, and economic, in that order. Germany had once been an empire. It was the German people's right to demand that their historical position be returned to them. This much of Hitler's assertions was a true reflection of his aims, to restore a German Empire. The rest of what he told Welles was not simply false; it was also contrary to what he had written in *Mein Kampf*. Hitler assured Welles that Germany had no desire to dominate non-German peoples, only to ensure that they posed no security threat. Finally, he insisted on the return of German colonies taken by the Versailles agreement, as Germany needed them for their raw materials and as places for German emigration. In *Mein Kampf*, Hitler had argued that Germans required not colonies but contiguous land for food production and emigration. He now told Welles that, compared to the United States, Germany had to produce ten times the amount of food per square kilometer. Because of its population density, Germany, he insisted, needed Lebensraum in order to feed itself.[24] He did not remind Welles what he had written on this subject in *Mein Kampf*, that strong peoples take what they need by force, as this was the natural order of things. Equally telling in Hitler's comments was what he did not say. He avoided any reference to the Soviet Union—an omission that Welles noted in his report.

As the meeting drew to a close Hitler remarked, "The German people today are united as one man, and I have the support of every German." There could be no hope for peace, he declared, until the English and French will to destroy Germany was itself destroyed. He assured Welles that Germany was strong enough to prevail. If it were not, then "we would all go down together . . . whether that be for better or worse." Welles expressed the fleeting hope that if peace could be found, then no nation would need to go down. Hitler assured Welles that Germany's aim, whether through war or otherwise, was a just peace. On that note, their meeting ended.

If Welles and Roosevelt hoped to gauge Hitler's underlying drivers, the interview provided some useful information. It underscored Hitler's intention to create an empire in Europe. If they had compared his present claims with his statements in *Mein Kampf*, they could have spotted the inconsistencies, which in turn should have led them to expect Hitler to widen the war for control of eastern lands. In short, this meeting confirmed what they already expected. It did not provide any great revelations. Yet the way in which Hitler presented his aims did suggest that his key driver was messianic. Economic hegemony was not his prime concern. Instead, he coolly explained that he intended to restore Germany's historic greatness as an empire. He concluded the meeting with the notion that all countries would go down together, suggesting a fanatical devotion to his cause. For Roosevelt and Welles to know whether Hitler's words genuinely reflected his beliefs or were instead mere rhetoric, they would have had to consider Hitler's pattern breaks.

In the search for any last possible clues to Hitler's underlying motivations, Welles met with Field Marshall Hermann Göring. Rumors had spread of a possible rift between Hitler and Göring. Welles needed to see if such a division existed and could be exploited. Deep within a national game reserve, Göring had constructed a massive monument to his own bloated sense of self-importance. After a ninety-minute drive from Berlin through a heavy snowfall and biting winds, Welles was delivered in an open car to the Field Marshall's sanctuary at Karin Hall. From the entrance to the reserve, they rode another ten miles through pine and birch forest, past Göring's personal collection of rare aurochs, the stocky bull-like ancestor of the domestic cattle. Göring's dwellings were still in process of being expanded. When finished, they planned to rival the size of Washington's National Art Gallery. Inside the main log cabin, glass cases lined the walls, housing ornate cups, bowls, beakers, and various objects of solid gold.

Although Welles found his manner frank and unaffected, Göring's physical appearance suggested otherwise. Swathed in a white tunic emblazoned with brilliant insignias, Göring sported an iron cross around his neck and a monocle dangling on a black cord. His girth was monstrous, his arms and thighs tremendous. His hands resembled the "digging paws of a badger." Yet those thickish fingers bore dazzling gems. The ring on his right hand glittered with six enormous diamonds. The one on his left held an emerald a good square inch across.[25]

Göring made a sympathetic impression on Welles, but he left the Undersecretary with the clear idea that Hitler had hardened in his stance. The only verbal jousting in the course of their three-hour conversation came when Welles again brought up the touchy issue of Nazi treatment of the Jews. Göring maintained that he had always wished for positive relations with the United States but that German racial policies had proved a sticking point. Americans needed to understand, Göring explained, that if German policies seemed hard, it was because these methods were necessary for exerting counter-pressure. Then he pointed to America's own racial policies, observing that colored peoples were not even permitted to travel in the same railway cars as whites. Welles somewhat weakly countered that this was only in a small part of the United States, and he added that America even had a colored Congressman.[26] Welles failed to note this exchange in his own account of the interview. Later, Welles's brilliant career as a diplomat would meet a bitter end when his enemies within the State Department pressured President Roosevelt to sack him for having made homosexual advances to the Negro porters on a railway car in September 1940. Roosevelt had tried to protect his friend and trusted envoy, but he ultimately felt compelled to remove Welles from the government. At a time when homosexuality was widely considered immoral behavior, Welles's rivals held the upper hand.

Göring closed their conversation by insincerely wishing Welles success on his ostensible peace mission. If there were any way of averting the coming war, he declared, then the U.S. government "will have accomplished the greatest thing which human beings could desire." But Göring added fatalistically that he believed the war was unavoidable.[27]

What led President Roosevelt to hold talks with the enemy of America's closest ally, Great Britain, while a war was already underway? A cynical interpretation for FDR's actions is that, in an election year, the President wanted to garner votes from those who favored peace at all cost. A consummate politician, the domestic implications of foreign policy were never far from Roosevelt's considerations, but this explanation is not sufficient. Had political posturing been the sole reason for the Welles mission, FDR could have gained even more by sending a higher-level official in place of Welles. Secretary of State Cordell Hull, whom Roosevelt disliked, would have suited the purpose perfectly. Hull's higher rank would have played even better in the American press. But the President wanted someone whose judgment he could trust. FDR respected Welles's abilities more than Hull's. FDR and Welles had long family ties. Both he and Welles had attended Groton, the elite boarding school for upper-class boys. Welles had even served as an usher at FDR's wedding. Roosevelt used Welles to circumvent the State Department. He could be counted on to preserve any truly valuable information for Roosevelt's ears only. And it was information to enhance strategic empathy that Roosevelt hoped Welles might glean.

Months after the Welles Mission had faded from the news, the President explained his thinking to Assistant Secretary of State Breckinridge Long. On December 12, 1940, Long had entered the President's study to discuss another matter, but the President first turned the conversation to the Welles trip. FDR told Long that he had expected a German spring offensive and he had wished that Welles might be able to delay Hitler's plans by negotiating. Then the President confided that the only other reason for sending Welles to Europe was to learn what he could from Mussolini and Hitler. Sending Welles to Paris and London was just "window dressing." It was necessary to keep up the appearance of balance. He already understood what the British and French thought. What Welles had gone to Europe for really was to get the low-down on Hitler and get Mussolini's point of view.[28]

Only much later, at the close of 1942, did the Office of Strategic Services (OSS, the forerunner to the Central Intelligence Agency) produce a psychological assessment of Hitler. This study represented the first formal attempt by the American government to engage in this type of analysis of an enemy's underlying drivers. Completed on December 3, 1942, the report was not released to the public until the year 2000. From the vantage point of today, the study seems almost juvenile in some of its conclusions, particularly those focused on Hitler's sex life. The anonymous authors proposed that the whip that Hitler often toted substituted for his lack of sexual potency and reflected sado-masochistic tendencies. They viewed his wild gesticulations when orating as whip-like motions. They maintained, perhaps accurately, that Hitler believed an audience should be treated like a woman—with decisiveness and control.

The study veered into dubious scientific validity when it postulated that Hitler's sexuality was as dual-natured as his political views, suggesting that the authors grasped neither his sexuality nor his politics.

"He is both homosexual and heterosexual; both Socialist and fervent Nationalist; both man and woman." Asserting that the Führer's sexual situation was untenable and desperate, the authors claimed that Hitler sought a half-mother and half-sweetheart. Frustration over his failure to find such a partner had led him, the authors claimed, into "brooding isolation and artificially dramatized public life."[29]

No doubt recognizing the study's shortcomings, the OSS commissioned a separate psychological profile of Hitler, this time conducted by the psychoanalyst Walter Langer, brother of the renowned Harvard historian William L. Langer. Drawing on numerous interviews with those in the United States who had had personal contact with Hitler, Langer's assessments were more coherent than the prior study, though by today's standards the report still appears rudimentary. Psychobiographies remain a staple of intelligence communities' multifaceted efforts to understand the enemy. They can provide rich pictures of a foreign statesman's traits, habits, and predilections, but they suffer from the great mass of information problem. It is difficult to know which psychological traits are most meaningful at crucial junctures.

In 1940, Roosevelt did not need psychological assessments of the Führer of the kind the OSS would later produce. The President wanted a clearer sense of Hitler's more immediate intentions. Fortunately, Roosevelt did not engage in simulation theory. He did not project onto Hitler the same reasoning process that Roosevelt himself employed. Pattern breaks such as Kristallnacht underscored to FDR that Hitler possessed a fanaticism distinct from, and far beyond that of, the average Realpolitik-driven head of state.

Welles's reports only confirmed what Roosevelt already believed on this score. But what Welles may not have grasped from his visit was that Hitler harbored serious concerns about confronting the United States in war. Hitler used the Welles talks to demonstrate to Roosevelt his determination to prosecute and win the current conflict, or to see everyone "go down together." Although Hitler aimed to deter Roosevelt, his words only solidified the President's conviction that American entry into the war was inevitable.

Roughly eight months after Welles departed from Berlin, the Soviets would make their own attempt to probe the Führer's mind. A hint of Hitler's fear of facing the United States can be seen more directly in the conversations between Hitler and Stalin's special emissary to Berlin, though Stalin's purpose was more immediately to discern Hitler's intentions toward Russia.

Molotov's Mission

Grasping that secondhand accounts of Hitler, such as Herman Rauschning's book, could only reveal so much, Stalin instructed Molotov to meet with Hitler for the express purpose of divining the Chancellor's true intentions. It was a reasonable attempt at theory-theory, and a brief departure from Stalin's default mode of simulation, to which he would ultimately return. On November 11, 1940, Molotov arrived in Berlin for several days of discussions. Despite the pomp, those talks proved largely pointless. Hitler remained inscrutable, evading direct answers even when pressed. True to his reputation, the Führer held his cards too close to permit a peek.

Acting on Stalin's orders, Molotov struggled to make Hitler explain the presence of German troops in Finland and Romania, as this was one of the few aggressive German moves that genuinely concerned the Soviet leader. The Führer demurred, calling them a trifle. Seven months later, those troops would be part of the coming attack.

Hitler tried to explain away German military actions as merely the necessary measures during the life and death struggle with England in which Germany now found itself. If Russia were in a similar position, Germany would of course understand Russia's wartime actions. He assured Molotov that German troops in Romania would leave that country as soon as the war concluded.[30] When Romania, Finland, and other points of friction arose in conversation on the second day of talks, Hitler urged the Soviet Foreign Minister to recognize that any disagreements they presently faced were insignificant compared to the great advantages that both nations would reap in the future, provided they continued to collaborate, and provided that Soviet Russia did not interfere in German-occupied territories for the duration of the war.

There were a few brief, revealing moments in the course of these discussions. Hitler hoped to use these conversations as the mirror image of his talks with Welles, both serving as part of his larger deception campaign. With the Welles talks, Hitler hoped to deter Roosevelt from intervening by stressing Germany's intention to fight to the bitter end. In contrast, Hitler sought to use the talks with Molotov to lull Stalin into believing that peace between the two nations could continue. In both sessions between Hitler and Molotov on November 12 and 13, Hitler repeatedly stressed that no meaningful disputes existed between Germany and Soviet Russia. He asserted that political and economic interests could be oriented in ways that would guarantee that conflicts would be avoided for long periods.[31] This was what Stalin wanted to believe: that the war with Germany could be postponed until Soviet military strength could be enhanced.

At this point in the second day's discussions, Hitler made one of his boldest claims—one that should have caught Stalin's attention. The Chancellor invoked the immense power to result from joint German–Soviet cooperation: "The future successes would be the greater, the more Germany and Russia succeeded in fighting back to back against the outside world, and would become the smaller, the more the two countries faced each other breast to breast." If they fought together, and against the rest, Hitler insisted that there was no power on Earth that could oppose them.[32]

Neither Molotov nor Stalin could have taken Hitler's blandishments seriously. If Hitler were a realist, he would want to keep his Bolshevik enemy out of the war until victorious over Britain. But to insist that he desired to fight alongside his ideological foe against some unnamed opponent (presumably the United States) challenged credulity. Ludicrous comments such as these called into question the whole of Hitler's assurances that his actions in Finland and Romania were trifles and not directed against the Soviet Union. But Stalin's form of mentalizing stood in the way of drawing those conclusions.

That Stalin was duped by Hitler's promises of future collaboration is doubtful. That Stalin believed in Hitler's pragmatism is nearly certain. If indeed Stalin projected his own rationality onto the Führer, then he had to assume that Hitler would not attack while still at war with Britain. Stalin also learned from Molotov's mission that Hitler was concerned about the possible involvement of America. Hitler had pressed Molotov to state whether Russia would declare war on the United States if America entered the war. Molotov replied that this question was of little interest. Hitler retorted that if a new war did break out, it would then be too late for Russia to decide on its position. Molotov dodged any such commitments by saying that he saw little likelihood of an outbreak of war in the Baltic.[33] This time it was Hitler who could not pin down the Soviets. If Stalin paid attention to this exchange, it likely reinforced his view that Hitler was prudent in military matters—probing the balance of forces and assessing enemies and allies alike. Such a realist, Stalin assumed, would defer an attack on Russia until his rear was clear.

As if to underscore the dangers ahead for German–Soviet cooperation, the banquet Hitler held for the Soviet delegation was shattered by a Royal Air Force bombing raid. Attendees had to scurry for cover as the festivities dispersed. It mattered little. Molotov would return to Moscow empty-handed, no closer to grasping Hitler's underlying drivers or his more immediate intentions. Ten days after Molotov departed, Hitler issued the orders to his military to begin preparing Operation Barbarossa, the largest invasion in history.

Conclusion

Both Roosevelt and Stalin strove to gain strategic empathy for Hitler, for they fully recognized that their nation's fates depended on their ability to read him correctly. Both leaders sent their closest foreign policy advisors to meet with Hitler in 1940. Both leaders hoped to buy time before going to war with Germany, and both missions aimed at gleaning the Chancellor's will. One crucial difference between the two leaders' conclusions can be traced to the way that each man mentalized. Roosevelt tried to grasp how Hitler thought by constructing a theory of how the Führer would behave based on Hitler's own drivers and constraints. FDR recognized from episodes such as Kristallnacht that Hitler possessed a uniquely racist, extremist ideology that was more than mere rhetoric. Like Roosevelt, Stalin also recognized Hitler's ideology, but unlike FDR, Stalin simulated what he himself would do if he were in Hitler's place. Simulation theory best describes how Stalin typically mentalized. It explains his need to murder anyone who could threaten his power, from his colleagues to his officer corps. Stalin put himself in their shoes and decided that, if he were they, he would try to depose the leader. Therefore, he had to destroy his opponents before they could destroy him. Similarly, Stalin asked what he would do if he were in

Hitler's place. Because preserving his own power always took precedence to advancing an ideological agenda, Stalin projected that same view onto the Führer. Stalin's simulations proved the worst possible approach to Hitler: a man who was willing to risk his power, his life, and his nation rather than abandon or postpone his ideological mission.

Years later, after the war was over and some 20 million Russians lay dead, Stalin reflected on his mental debacle. He revealed to a small group of advisors a rare moment of self-reflection. "NEVER put yourself into the mind of another person," he warned them, "because if you do, you can make a terrible mistake."[34] The great simulator may at last have understood why his attempts at strategic empathy had gone so horribly wrong.

Following Stalin's death in 1953, communist leaders inside the Soviet Union and beyond continued to struggle with reading their opponents. For the ideologically minded Marxists in Vietnam, the challenge of reading the Americans was critical. As American involvement in Vietnam increased throughout the early 1960s, North Vitnamese leaders needed to gauge the likelihood of a full-scale U.S. escalation. And if the Americans did escalate, Hanoi needed a clear sense of its enemies' weaknesses in order to defeat them. Fortunately for Hanoi, a sober strategist and hardened fighter against the French had been steadily rising through the Party ranks. Despite never having visited the United States, this enigmatic Marxist managed to pinpoint his rivals' weakest links—and exploit them for all he could.

6

Hanoi's New Foe

Le Duan Prepares for America

The Underdog's Focus

It was summer in Paris, but the mood inside 11 Darthe Street on the outskirts of town was tense.[1] On July 19, 1972, American Secretary of State Henry Kissinger and his team were conducting six and a half hours of negotiations with Le Duan's right-hand man, the inveterate ideologue Le Duc Tho. In familiar fashion, Le Duc Tho offered up a historical lecture on Vietnam's great tradition of repelling foreign armies. Hoping to bring the conversation to meaningful discussions, Kissinger presented a five-point plan, which he referred to as America's last effort at peace, but the Vietnamese viewed it as simply more of the same old American proposals. Two days earlier, Hanoi had cabled its Paris delegation that the upcoming U.S. presidential election boded well for North Vietnam.[2] If George McGovern could win, American concessions would be even more favorable than what Nixon and Kissinger were offering. It was a remarkable assertion, given that President Nixon was far ahead in the national polls and widely expected to trounce McGovern, which he did in a landslide. Nonetheless, Hanoi believed it would be beneficial to hold out for a McGovern victory. For the time being, the talks were at an impasse. But then a curious incident occurred when the two teams broke for tea.

In a reflective moment, Kissinger allegedly remarked to his Vietnamese interlocutors that if the Vietnamese possessed merely courage, then the United States would already have crushed them on the battlefield. The problem, Kissinger opined, was that the Vietnamese were both courageous and intelligent. As a result, America was in danger of losing the war.

The room fell silent. Was this a Kissinger trap, one Vietnamese staff member recalled thinking. The staffers waited for their leader to respond. After some thought, Le Duc Tho asked Kissinger if this meant that he believed that the Vietnamese were more intelligent than the Americans. Le Duc Tho observed that the United States was far more advanced than Vietnam in science and technology, possessed high levels of education among its citizens, and contained more numbers of talented people than any other nation. Vietnam, he observed, was clearly the underdog. It was a small, economically backward, primitive agricultural state. Kissinger then asked, if America were so intelligent, why had it not defeated Vietnam? Le Duc Tho replied that twenty-four hours a day, every day, America must confront countless issues. As a result, its intelligence is dissipated. Vietnam, in contrast, had no choice but to concentrate its efforts on a single issue. ". . . We Vietnamese all just think about one thing 24 hours a day: How can we defeat the Americans?" Kissinger agreed that the issue was not which people were smarter but rather which was better able to apply its intelligence: " . . . I have to say that Vietnam uses its intelligence more skillfully than does the United States."[3]

This story was recounted by a member of Hanoi's negotiating team, and whether or not it is fully accurate, it highlights two important facts about the war. First, underdogs must concentrate their energies on a single aim—in this case, how to beat America. Overdogs, in contrast, with global commitments, have their energies dispersed. Second, underdogs must know their enemies better than their enemies know them. Without that knowledge, the underdog's chances of success are slim.

It has almost become a cliché to opine that America simply did not understand its enemy throughout the Vietnam War. If only the United States had possessed a deeper grasp of the Vietnamese people—their history, language, and culture—so the argument goes, the war might have gone much differently.[4] But such lamentations leave us wondering just how well the North Vietnamese leaders actually understood America. Does the Democratic Republic of Vietnam's (DRV) victory in 1975 stem from the fact that its leaders somehow knew their enemy better than the enemy knew them? How did they view

America's strengths and weaknesses, and how did they use this knowledge to best effect?

Hanoi's victory in the Second Indochina War has fostered a mystique of shrewdness on the part of its leadership—an image that has been preserved in part by the restricted access to key records about its decision-making. Scholars are still at an embryonic stage in determining how the North Vietnamese leadership functioned, thought, processed intelligence, and reached decisions. Because the most crucial archives—the Ministry of Foreign Affairs, the Ministry of Defense, and the Central Executive Committee Office—all remain largely closed, historians are limited in what they can assert. But thanks to the release of voluminous party records (*Van Kien Dang*[5]) and numerous Vietnamese official histories of the war,[6] along with burgeoning scholarship on internal Vietnamese Workers' Party (VWP) dynamics, we are gaining new insights into what the Party leaders actually thought about their principal foe.

This chapter and the next concentrate on the person who became the driving force within the Party and a key shaper of communist Vietnam's protracted war strategy. Much has been written on the person and policies of Ho Chi Minh, but Le Duan's powerful influence on strategy has been underinvestigated.[7] Though other Party leaders influenced wartime strategy, First Secretary Le Duan carried the greatest weight within the Politburo. He exerted the strongest influence over the southern communists, who were pivotal in fighting both U.S. and South Vietnam's forces. It was in this role as head of southern communists that Le Duan initially devised his strategies for defeating the Americans—concepts he developed and executed as his power grew. We therefore need to spotlight several recurrent themes in his thinking: the nature of a protracted war, the role of casualties, and America's global standing. Each of these subjects influenced how Hanoi intended to defeat the United States over the long term and offers insights into how Hanoi understood its enemy. In short, by excavating how Le Duan thought, we can better grasp how much strategic empathy the Party leader possessed for America.

When it came to recognizing the enemy's constraints, Le Duan's strategic empathy for America was strong. He saw that America was highly vulnerable in a protracted war, and he shaped Hanoi's behavior in ways that would exploit those weaknesses. With respect to America's key drivers, Le Duan never fully grasped the motivations of President

Johnson and his top advisors. In spite of this failing, he nonetheless recognized a break in the pattern of American behavior at a critical juncture in the conflict. He understood that the Tonkin Gulf episode represented a highly provocative act, one that presaged an American escalation.

Le Duan's strategic empathy for America stemmed from a careful consideration of enemy behavior and the context within which the Americans had to function. Although he was known for his strong ideological convictions, ideology did not cloud his conduct of strategy. As a new wave of scholarship on Vietnam has been evolving since the 1990s, researchers have been breaking with old preconceptions about the Indochina wars. One of the more prominent assertions has involved the ideological nature of Hanoi's thinking. Tuong Vu, for example, has elucidated the depth to which Marxist attitudes infused decision-making from the 1920s onward.[8] Others, such as Martin Grossheim,[9] have reinforced this notion. These authors have informed our understanding of the dogmatic (and often dangerous) world of domestic politics within the VWP.[10] There is evidence to suggest that many Party leaders were committed, true believers in communism. That faith helped galvanize their determination. It convinced them of the wisdom of collectivization, the merits of a centrally planned economy, and that their ultimate victory was historically inevitable. Yet in formulating particular strategies, Party leaders naturally could not be guided entirely by dogma. When assessing the Americans, rhetorical pronouncements of neo-imperialist plots were frequently balanced by sober calculations of America's key strengths and vulnerabilities. Ideology, therefore, could not always be paramount when it came to strategy. What Hanoi required for victory was not ideological fervor but strategic empathy, and it needed a leader who possessed it.

Le Duan's Ascension

The noted Vietnam historian Christopher Goscha has called Le Duan and Le Duc Tho the two most powerful Party leaders during the Vietnam War.[11] The historian Lien-Hang T. Nguyen placed both men at center stage in her recent study of DRV domestic politics and struggle for peace.[12] This belated attention is necessary, for while Le Duc Tho gained global prominence through his negotiations with Henry Kissinger and subsequent Nobel Peace Prize, Le Duan has long been thought of as a shadowy figure about whom little is known. Because it is now evident that his role atop the Party also enabled him to profoundly shape Hanoi's wartime course, we need to take a much closer look at Le Duan's sense of the American enemy. Scholars have yet to explore the roots and development of his strategic thinking, especially as it relates to the United States. In fact, Le Duan's notions of how to defeat the Americans are inseparable from the story of his rise.

Born in 1908 in Quang Tri Province, part of the central region of Vietnam, Le Duan traversed the country as a young man while working for the railways. Attracted to communism at an early age, he became a founding member of the Indochinese Communist Party in 1930. In 1931, he was arrested by the French for revolutionary activity and was later released in 1936 as part of a general amnesty offered by the new Popular Front government in France. Undeterred and more committed to the cause than ever, Le Duan established a Communist Party branch in central Vietnam and was once again imprisoned from 1940 to 1945. During this incarceration, Le Duan used his time to indoctrinate other inmates in Marxist ideology. Upon his second release, Ho Chi Minh appointed him to the Central Committee. Together with Le Duc Tho, he served as the Party's chief for South Vietnam. Le Duc Tho had initially been tasked in 1948 by the Central Committee to head the Party organization in the South, but for unknown reasons he decided to serve as Le Duan's deputy. Their collaboration continued into the 1980s. Le Duan's rise through Party ranks culminated in 1960, when he became the Party's General Secretary, serving in that post longer than any other party chair, relinquishing it only upon his death in 1986.

Part of the reason that he shunned the spotlight of world politics (in contrast to his better-known colleagues) may have been related to aspects of his personal life, which he strove to keep secret. Le Duan had two wives and children with each woman, though he managed to keep the existence of the second family quiet. He had married his first wife, a northerner, in the 1930s, prior to his imprisonment by the French. In 1948, while organizing the Party in South Vietnam, he married Nguyen Thuy Nga, a southerner. This second marriage was arranged by none other than Le Duan's close friend, deputy, and future Politburo colleague, Le Duc Tho. Although Politburo members were forbidden to have more than one wife, Le Duan flouted that requirement. In order to keep the second wife secret, he sent her to China to study and work in the late 1950s and early 1960s and subsequently dispatched her to South Vietnam to perform Party tasks. Despite their long separations and unorthodox arrangement, his private letters to Nga reveal a softer side to the dogmatic Marxist-Leninist who would erect and orchestrate a brutal police state.

In 2006, a Hanoi-based newspaper ran a five-part series on the late First Secretary's secret wife. Through these extended interviews with Nguyen Thuy Nga (now in her eighties), along with excerpts from her diaries and love letters she received from Le Duan, we see evidence of a devout revolutionary and passionate husband, as well as a man with something to hide.[13] On December 25, 1960, he professed his love and pleaded with her to trust him: "Do not let a few outward actions or a few unfortunate things that happened give rise to any misunderstandings that you might have about me." His letters reveal that his love for this woman was inextricably tied to the revolutionary cause:

> The deep love I have for you, the deep love that we have for our children, the deep love that we have for our revolutionary cause will let us live together and die together and leave behind us an inheritance for future generations—the inheritance that is our children and the inheritance that is our cause in which we were bound together, as if we were one person![14]

Around this same time, the late 1950s and early 1960s, Le Duan was also building relationships with cadres throughout the South. Part of Le Duan's rise within the Party was linked to his development of a wartime strategy against the Americans. Even prior to the French defeat in 1954, it had become clear to Party leaders that the United States would supplant France as a neocolonial adversary. As the United States was already paying roughly 80 percent of French war costs and had been supplying the French with war materiel since the Truman administration, VWP leaders understood that they were indirectly at war with America. At the Party's eighth plenum in 1955, this recognition took concrete form when the Party designated the United States as its principal adversary.[15]

Le Duan's most impactful early strategic assessment of America came in August 1956. Having risen to the post of Cochin China Party Secretary, essentially serving as the Party's chief representative in the South, he completed an analysis of America's intentions in South Vietnam. Working with Party members in each province of the Mekong Delta, Eastern Cochin China, and in Saigon-Cho Lon, Le Duan drafted a document that would serve as the political basis for future action. Noting that President Eisenhower's reelection campaign called for peace, Le Duan argued that even the war-mongering, imperialist nations have publics that desire peace.[16] Internal Party statements such as these belie its official proclamations in its newspaper, *The People* (*Nhan Dan*). That same year, the paper published a series of articles defending the DRV's democratic nature in the wake of the violent measures enacted during the land reform. Contained within these pieces, the Party denounced America as a false democracy whose news media were controlled by its capitalist elite.[17] Le Duan's comments reveal that Party leaders in fact believed that American politicians were beholden to the public, constrained at least in part by democratic processes. This recognition would serve Party leaders well in later years when they hoped that domestic opposition to the war would weaken American resolve.

Le Duan's thesis, "Tenets of the Policies of the Vietnamese Revolution in South Vietnam" (sometimes translated as "The Path to Revolution in the South"), advocated a period of peace, but it held out the possibility of war if conditions demanded it: "However, the fact that we firmly hold the banner of peace does not mean that the question of conducting armed insurrection as well as a war against foreign aggression will not be raised if the situation has completely changed."[18] This was the pacific note struck by his thesis. It tempered the more bellicose tones within the document: "The mission of the South Vietnamese revolution is to topple the dictatorial, fascist, American imperialist puppet Ngo Dinh Diem government and to liberate the South Vietnamese people from the yoke of imperialism and feudalism." And later, "Our people in South Vietnam have only one road to take, and that is to rise up against the Americans and Diem to save the nation and to save themselves. That is the path of the revolution. Other than that path, there is no other path that we can take."[19]

We cannot read these documents and the contradictions they embody without considering the context within which they were written. The mid-1950s marked an exceedingly turbulent period in the Party's history, for the North as well as the South. Almost immediately upon taking power, Hanoi experienced a mass exodus of Vietnamese from North to South Vietnam. We still do not know how many Vietnamese were executed during this period, though some estimates range in the tens of thousands.[20] The Party's disastrous land reform program resulted in the demotion of First Secretary Truong Chinh, paving the way for Le Duan's elevation. In addition, Khrushchev's policy of peaceful coexistence with the West greatly concerned the VWP leaders. At the 20th congress of the Communist Party of the Soviet Union, Khrushchev had boldly declared that nations could only choose between peaceful coexistence or the most destructive war in history. There was no middle ground. Consequently, in its thinking about waging a war against the South, Hanoi had to consider the Soviet Union's attitudes with care.[21] Meanwhile, in South Vietnam, the Diem regime was rounding up and executing Communist Party members, severely weakening its potential. Many of its leaders were forced underground, some having relocated to the Plain of Reeds. Under such circumstances, Le Duan, who had been ordered by Ho to direct the revolution in the South, was compelled to speak of peace while preparing for war.

A palpable tension existed between the southern communists' belief that armed struggle against the South was necessary on the one hand and the Central Committee's policy of peaceful political struggle under the framework of the Geneva accords on the other. As the official military command history of the Central Office of South Vietnam (COSVN) reveals, its armed squads were restricted from engaging in military operations in order to comply with Hanoi's instructions.[22] In December of 1956, the Cochin China Party Committee convened an enlarged session to discuss its strategy. Le Duan, as a Politburo member, presided, along with Nguyen Van Linh, the acting committee secretary. The group resolved that the time was not yet right to launch guerilla warfare. Instead, it would pursue armed propaganda. The purpose of propaganda units would be to encourage hatred of the enemy, suppress spies, win over the masses to their cause, and avoid combat that could reveal their forces to the enemy.[23] In other words, the Cochin China branch of the Party, under Le Duan's direction, determined to further the revolution by all means short of outright guerilla war.[24]

Militancy alone could not account for Le Duan's rapid rise within the Party. His elevation is a testament to his shrewd political skills and his manipulation of factional rivalries. By 1951 he was already a leading figure among the southern communists. In late 1956, Le Duan was reassigned to the North, signifying his rising status within the Party leadership. Following his journey with the delegation to the Moscow conference of communist parties in November 1957, he publicly emerged as the most important Party official after Ho Chi Minh. During these years, he continued to agitate for an armed struggle in the South, while his prominence within the Party grew.

In 1960, Le Duan ascended to the post of Party First Secretary, placing him in a powerful, though not unchallenged, position of influence over the Vietnamese Communist movement, both in the North and the South. As Le Duan's power base expanded, he applied increasingly harsh tactics to ensure that his own policies would be adopted and his opponents sidelined. On September 15, he succeeded in passing a Party statute that dramatically expanded the authority of the Secretariat, the government organ of which he was the head. Subsequently, Le Duan wielded enormous influence over government branches as varied as foreign affairs, finance, science, agriculture, propaganda, and beyond. More than this, Le Duan controlled the Ministry of Public Security, through which he could employ the harshest tactics of a modern state against his presumed opponents. It was a weapon he did not hesitate to use. DRV citizens, from Party intellectuals to political rivals, all felt the brunt of police state rule.[25]

Le Duan's opponents had good reason to fear his extensive reach, for in the wake of the Sino–Soviet split, the Party fractured along the lines of those partial to the Soviet Union (adhering to Khrushchev's policy of peaceful coexistence with the West) and those who favored closer ties to China (backing Chairman Mao's wish to support armed struggles against perceived neocolonialism). Le Duan and Le Duc Tho belonged to the pro-China faction. Those Vietnamese who had studied in the Soviet Union and now supported revisionism were especially vulnerable to Le Duan's and Le Duc Tho's attacks. A second, related rift emerged between those like Le Duan and Le Duc Tho, who advocated a south-first policy of war, and those who preferred a north-first approach focused on economic development of the DRV. Still a third important fissure developed within Party circles, with those who favored guerilla warfare in the South opposing those who advocated larger, conventional units being sent to fight alongside the southerners. Each of these swirling currents buffeted wartime strategy and policy, and Le Duan stood at the maelstrom's center.

In December of 1963, for example, subsequent to the Diem assassination, Le Duan pressed the Politburo to increase infiltration of the South and attempt to overthrow the southern regime, against the wishes of both Khrushchev and others within the DRV. Some of those opposed to his plans were arrested and removed from positions of influence.[26] In 1964, he moved to exert greater control over the southern communist forces by placing his own man, General Nguyen Chi Thanh, as head of the Central Office of the South Vietnamese Communist Party. By elevating General Thanh, Le Duan hoped to undercut the influence of the revered General Võ Nguyên Giáp, hero of the war against the French. Nguyen Chi Thanh was himself a Politburo member and seemed poised to rise even higher, but he died in 1967 under mysterious circumstances.[27] Some believe he was murdered by those loyal to General Giáp. Others claim he had a heart attack after a night of heavy drinking.[28] Whatever the case, Le Duan's appointment of Nguyen Chi Thanh to oversee COSVN reflects the First Secretary's intention to control the southern revolution. As for Le Duan's more heavy-handed efforts to influence events, Sophie Quinn-Judge has argued that during a Party purge in 1967 (the so-called anti-Party affair), Le Duan was again responsible for having opponents arrested and removed from power.[29]

Judging Le Duan's character is not as simple as it may seem. The evidence suggests a man driven to achieve his ends regardless of the costs to others. On the other hand, as a revolutionary leader, he clearly inspired many, whether as a teacher of Marxism-Leninism to other prison inmates or through his speeches and letters to the Party faithful.[30] Yet many of his contemporaries viewed him as deceptive and manipulative. According to Pierre Asselin, the General Secretary "found enemies almost everywhere." His paranoia and deceitfulness, Asselin observed, alienated many supporters of the revolution. More recently some of Le

Duan's colleagues have sought to defend his reputation through their reminiscences, though this has not shifted opinion in Western historiography.[31] His complex character aside, there is no doubt that as First Secretary of the VWP, Le Duan wielded enormous power over all organs of the state, including the military.[32] From such a formidable position, he was able to influence Hanoi's wartime strategy against America.

Le Duan and the Protracted War Strategy

Le Duan steadily advocated a dual approach: large conventional warfare when possible and protracted guerilla war when necessary. By bogging the Americans down in a war involving high numbers of casualties, Le Duan believed that domestic opposition within the United States would force Washington to withdraw from Vietnam if face-saving measures could be provided. Naturally, he would have been eager to achieve a quick victory if it had been possible, but even the general offensives of 1968 and 1972 did not produce a rapid triumph. Both methods—large-scale military offensives and long-term guerilla warfare—were employed to sap the Americans' will. While some scholars have highlighted Le Duan's interest in a rapid victory, this is only half of the story.[33] Le Duan frequently spoke and wrote, both in public pronouncements and private correspondence, of the need to wear the enemy down over a prolonged period. From his writings, we can see that he did not simply apply the same strategy against America that had been successful against the French. Instead, we find careful reasoning about the range of American strengths and weaknesses, from its nuclear capacity to its costly global commitments, particularly in Europe and the Middle East. In short, Le Duan thought in geostrategic terms, fully aware of the underdog's necessities and the overdog's constraints.

The First Secretary articulated the policy of protracted war to the southern communists in numerous letters. In April 1961, for example, he outlined Hanoi's guidance on southern strategy and tactics, along with a spirited urging to steep all Party members and the masses in the notion of a protracted war. Only by stressing the need for a long, arduous fight, he insisted, could they be certain of victory. President Kennedy, he claimed, had said that the United States would need ten years to snuff out the revolution in Vietnam. If the enemy was planning on a long war, then how could they fail to meet the challenge by doing the same, Le Duan asked rhetorically.[34]

Despite his reputation for militancy and advocacy of armed resistance, the Party First Secretary remained sensitive to strategic necessities. In a letter to COSVN in July 1962, Le Duan cautioned his comrades not to attack the cities at that time. Even though there were vulnerable areas, an attack would not be advantageous because it could incite the Americans to increase their intervention and expand the war.[35] Admonitions such as these demonstrated that Le Duan understood that provoking the Americans while COSVN forces were still weak was strategically unwise and potentially counterproductive. That recognition stemmed from an understanding of the balance of forces at the time. His critical assessment led to caution. This raises the question of why communist forces provoked America in 1964 at Tonkin and again in 1965 at Pleiku—a question to which we will soon return. Overall, the First Secretary observed that protracted wars must be fought in both the political and military arenas, and he pointed to the recent experiences of Laotians and Algerians in defeating their adversaries on the political front.

In this same letter, Le Duan clearly enunciated how he viewed America's greatest weakness and how Hanoi intended to exploit it. The movement, Le Duan explained, could not at that time destroy American forces. The enemy was too strong, both in military and financial resources. Instead, the aim was to attack portions of the Diem regime's forces, the "puppet army," and thereby cause the Americans to "sink deeper and deeper into the mire of a protracted war with no way out." This in turn would cause the Americans to become increasingly isolated domestically and globally, which would impel them to negotiate with Hanoi.[36] Hanoi would then call for the formation of a neutral South Vietnamese regime. Le Duan believed that the Americans would be willing to accept defeat provided that Hanoi advanced limited demands at a level that would not cause the enemy to lose too much face.[37] The overall plan was to weaken the Americans in phases, gradually pushing back the perceived expansion of neo-imperialist aims.

By 1963, the South Vietnamese regime was in deep turmoil. President Ngo Dinh Diem had pushed through turbulent land reform policies of his own, engendering resentment over forced resettlement programs. Diem's repressive policies fomented conflicts with communist units as well as with Buddhist and other religious minorities. Dissatisfaction with Diem's rule culminated in a coup on November 2, 1963, in which President Diem was assassinated.[38] Resentment at Diem's harsh rule had been brewing for several years, and although Hanoi recognized Saigon's instability as an opportunity, it was unable to capitalize on the situation. Following the coup, the key question facing Party leaders was whether the United States would increase its counterrevolutionary efforts in Vietnam. Would it expand the war? The month following the Diem coup, Hanoi analyzed the situation in a lengthy document.

In December of 1963, the VWP's Central Committee issued its Resolution from the Ninth Plenum. One section of this resolution covered issues surrounding America's intentions and capabilities. Hanoi's strategy seemed contradictory. It called for both a quick victory over the South and a protracted war. We know that Hanoi's leaders were flexible insofar as they were willing to adopt measures that worked. In this respect they were opportunistic, adapting their methods as circumstances dictated. But the apparent policy contradiction also likely reflected a compromise between competing factions within the Party. Internal Party disagreements were never aired openly, yet we know that various factions existed over time. One notable split existed between a more dovish branch favoring compromise and negotiation with the Americans and a more hawkish group, led by Le Duan, favoring all-out war.

The Resolution of December 1963 articulated some key elements in Hanoi's thinking about America. Given Le Duan's position atop the Party, it is certain that he influenced the resolution's final form and its treatment of the United States. The document was intended to spell out the likely prospects for the South Vietnamese revolutionary movement as well as outlining guidelines and responsibilities for victory. It asserted the standard and consistent line that the world revolutionary movement was in the ascendance and the global situation was increasingly unfavorable for the imperialists. It declared that Marxism-Leninism afforded the Party "a scientific foundation for our policy guidelines, formulas, and procedures for fighting the Americans" and that this could give the Party members great confidence in the Party leadership.[39]

Sandwiched between layers of Marxist historical analysis lay Hanoi's assessment of several specific challenges facing America. The first of these, a recurrent subtheme throughout the *Van Kien Dang*, involved the dispersal of U.S. forces. The Resolution observed that America's strength was spread around the world, making it difficult for the U.S. to concentrate sufficient force on any one region and allowing an opening for insurgencies to capitalize on this weakness. It argued that America had launched ten wars of aggression in the previous eighteen years but that it continued to be defeated, specifically in China, North Korea, Vietnam, Laos, and Cuba. Naturally, such comments might merely represent Hanoi's wishful thinking—attempts to spin its situation in a positive light. But since at other times Party leaders pointed to America's strengths and counseled caution, it is entirely possible that at least some Party leaders believed the above assessment of America. It suggests that they viewed the United States as weaker than its military and economic power would indicate.

Immediately thereafter, the Resolution broached the question of nuclear weapons. We do not have sufficient records to explain why Hanoi felt confident (if indeed it did) that America would not use its nuclear weapons against the North. We can surmise that Hanoi believed it fell under the Soviet Union's nuclear umbrella and that the United States would not want to risk widening the Vietnam War into a world war, its rhetoric to the contrary notwithstanding.

The Resolution's authors claimed that the United States had previously relied on its monopoly and superiority in nuclear weapons to influence world affairs. The Resolution called the Eisenhower administration's nuclear policy of "massive retaliation" one of brinksmanship. But the policy had failed, according to the authors, because of the Soviet Union's development of nuclear weapons as well as the rising strength of the socialist camp. As a result, the Americans were forced to adopt a new nuclear policy of "flexible response," in which they would launch special and limited wars while simultaneously preparing for a world war. The authors declared that although the imperialists, led by the United States, were still making feverish preparations for a world war, the odds of it occurring were diminishing. "If the imperialists are insane enough to start a new world war, the people of the world will bury them."[40]

Surprisingly, there is no mention in the Resolution of the Cuban Missile Crisis or other flashpoints such as Taiwan in 1958 or the Korean War, when the danger of an American nuclear strike was highest. Le Duan did, however, reference these episodes in May 1965, in a letter to

COSVN. There he argued that the United States had shown it would not dare to use nuclear weapons, even when that meant defeat. Le Duan cited America's failure to stop China's revolution, despite being allied with Chiang Kai-shek's 5 million troops. Le Duan interpreted this reluctance to use nuclear weapons as a sign of weakness. The same was true, he argued, in the Korean War as well as in the First Indochina War, when the United States backed the French. During the Cuban Missile Crisis, America showed some strength but failed "to intimidate a heroic nation with seven million inhabitants." America's willingness to accept a coalition government in Laos in 1962 only further demonstrated its impotence, he asserted.[41] Presumably, Le Duan, and probably all other Politburo members, had concluded that the United States would not introduce nuclear weapons into the Vietnam conflict based on its past unwillingness to deploy them.[42] In short, Hanoi was hoping that America's future behavior would resemble its past actions. Fortunately for Hanoi, its assumption turned out to be correct, though there were no guarantees that America would resist employing its nuclear option if conditions changed. VWP leaders did not know that President Nixon and Henry Kissinger would later consider using tactical nuclear strikes against them.

Turning to America's formation of the Southeast Asian Treaty Organization (SEATO), which Hanoi dubbed the Southeast Asian Aggression Bloc, the Resolution explained that the treaty was necessary because South Vietnam was the place of greatest revolutionary activity. Thus, U.S. military forces needed to be concentrated there in order to preserve American interests while propping up the supposedly crumbling capitalist system. The Resolution summarized America's three primary objectives as follows. First, it aimed to suppress the national revolutionary movement while implementing neocolonialism; second, it intended to construct military bases from which it would attack the socialist camp; and third, and most crucially, it sought to halt the spread of socialism throughout Southeast Asia. All of these points about SEATO suggest that VWP leaders accepted standard Marxist-Leninist dogma in this regard.

Trained to seek out internal contradictions within capitalist behavior, the authors observed that America was facing growing internal disagreements about its strong anticommunist policies in Vietnam, namely from the intellectual class. Hanoi followed the American media closely and frequently noted growing domestic opposition to the war.[43] Party leaders cited everything from public pronouncements against the war by U.S. Senator Wayne Morse,[44] to the 1960s' civil rights protests across the American South, to global opposition to American foreign policies. The *Van Kien Dang* reveal clearly that Hanoi fully intended to exploit those differences to its advantage. Ideological convictions may have led Party leaders to exaggerate the degree of internal dissention within America. Nonetheless, the Party's attention to those growing notes of discord would later, after 1968, prove useful.

The political scientist Carlyle Thayer has argued that Hanoi's decision-making must be understood as a complex interplay of individual leaders' aims, Party rivalries, and domestic constraints, along with the changing role of foreign powers, particularly China and the Soviet Union.[45] This is, however, precisely how VWP leaders tried to read Washington's decision-making. They considered the individual inclinations of Johnson and Nixon (as well as the plans advanced by figures such as General Maxwell Taylor and Defense Secretary Robert McNamara). They followed America's antiwar protests and other domestic issues to see how those movements might constrain Washington's actions. They examined the effects of the war on America's freedom of action globally. From this analysis, they sought to foresee how events would unfold.

The *Van Kien Dang* and other records demonstrate that Hanoi actively strove to understand its American adversary, partly by monitoring American news media and partly through espionage. Though more than thirty-five years have passed since the war's end, we still know remarkably little about the DRV's intelligence services. We know that Party leaders read summaries of foreign news and developments prepared by the Foreign Ministry. The military's intelligence branch also prepared reports on espionage activities and the interrogation of prisoners. It monitored foreign broadcasts and intercepted enemy communications.[46] The Ministry of Public Security also played a role, one similar to that of the Soviet KGB. In addition, the Party itself naturally operated its own External Affairs Department, which handled contact with other nations' communist and socialist parties. Hanoi's intelligence services cooperated with both their Soviet and Chinese counterparts, but the full extent of this collaboration is unknown.[47] Regardless of their sources,

Party leaders arrived in 1963 at seemingly incompatible conclusions about America's intentions.

Escalation Double-Speak

Did Hanoi believe that America would escalate the war, or did it instead think that the United States could be deterred? In order to predict the war's course, the Central Committee's December 1963 resolution differentiated between three types of wars that America could wage in Vietnam. Hanoi called the first type "special war," which Americans might have called a counterinsurgency war. In special war, which Hanoi considered to be the current type in 1963, the United States supplied puppet forces within Vietnam, providing them with military advisors and equipment. A transformation to the second type, or "limited war," would occur when U.S. forces became the primary combat forces within Vietnam. A "general war" would be one expanded to the North.[48] Hanoi anticipated that the current special war could transform into a limited war if the Americans held any of three beliefs:

1. American victory could only be guaranteed if it intervened in a massive way.

2. North Vietnam would not react strongly to greater U.S. intervention in South Vietnam.

3. Greater U.S. intervention would not spark strong opposition within the United States or around the world.

The resolution concluded that it was unlikely that America would expand to a limited war because of the risks: "They clearly realize that if they become bogged down in a protracted large-scale war, they will fall into an extremely defensive and reactive posture around the world."[49] Demonstrating that at least some in the Politburo feared a wider war despite these pronouncements, the authors quickly added that they should be prepared for the possibility of American escalation nonetheless. By bolstering the strength of southern units, Hanoi hoped it could cripple the southern regime and thereby dissuade America from expanding its commitment.

For several years Le Duan had been gradually increasing the flow of soldiers south to join the fighting. Throughout 1964, preparations intensified as nearly 9,000 soldiers and cadres, including two full-strength battalions, were sent south. Additionally, the DRV's Navy enhanced the frequency and tonnage of weapons shipments south via sea routes, employing steel-hulled vessels, which also served to transport mid- and high-level military as well as Party officials. During the 1963–1964 dry season, engineering units modernized the roads south, enabling the transportation of supplies to the battlefields to quadruple that of the previous year.[50] According to the official DRV history of the People's Navy, by late June the Navy had placed all of its forces on a war footing.[51] In the wake of these ongoing military preparations, Ho Chi Minh declared in a speech on March 27, 1964, that the DRV's aim was to see the Americans withdraw their forces as well as their weapons and support from South Vietnam.[52]

What then would have been the purpose of outlining the reasons America would not escalate if preparations for American escalation were considered necessary? One reason was to bolster morale among communist forces. Much of the resolution reads like a calculated effort by Hanoi to reassure its supporters that victory against the Americans was not only possible but in fact certain. Another explanation for this double-speak is that it reflects the internal contradictions within Party circles. Some may have believed that American expansion was unlikely, while others, Le Duan probably among them, insisted that a wider war was coming. If Le Duan believed any of the anti-American rhetoric he regularly expressed, namely that the United States was intent on expanding the war to impose neocolonial rule over Vietnam, then he would have seen an American escalation as inevitable and probably coming soon. Yet it did not require an ideological conviction to surmise that escalation was a strong possibility. By mid-summer of 1964, President Johnson had announced an increase of military advisors from 16,000 to nearly 22,000.[53] That wider war, it turned out, was close at hand. Though it would prove immensely costly to all concerned, it also offered some tangible advantages.

7

Counting Bodies

The Benefits of Escalation

ON AUGUST 2, 1964, the *USS Maddox* snaked its way through North Vietnamese waters. Its presence drew the enemy's attention. Three North Vietnamese torpedo boats fired on the vessel, most likely in response to U.S. shelling of two North Vietnamese islands a few nights before. What became known as the Gulf of Tonkin incident profoundly altered both American and Vietnamese history.[1] A suspected second torpedo attack on August 4 never actually occurred, but the episode enabled President Johnson to obtain Congressional approval for expanded military action. Although Hanoi had hoped to avoid a full-scale American intervention, communist forces continued to attack the Americans. On February 6, 1965, Viet Cong forces bombarded numerous military targets, including an American air base at Pleiku, killing nine servicemen and wounding 128. President Johnson responded with Operation Flaming Dart, a series of air strikes against enemy targets. It was the incident at Pleiku as much as Tonkin that triggered the deployment of U.S. ground troops. The first waves of Marines arrived on March 8, 1965. By the summer there would be roughly 85,000 of them. U.S. forces would ultimately total more than half a million. They would depart only after 58,000 of them had died and nearly 3 million Vietnamese had been killed, with millions more hideously wounded.

Why did Hanoi sanction attacks against Americans after the Tonkin Gulf incident? Hanoi did not desire an American escalation. Party leaders sought no wider war. Hanoi's policy had been to avoid an American escalation, to keep the special war from transitioning to a limited war in which American forces would be doing the bulk of the fighting. The last thing Hanoi should have wanted was to provoke a full-scale invasion by the United States, especially at such a precarious time. Nevertheless, communist forces in South Vietnam continued to strike American bases after Tonkin, when the risk of an American escalation was at its peak.

The reason for the attacks at Tonkin and Pleiku has never been fully clear. Lieutenant General Hoang Nghia Khanh was serving as Chief of Combat Operations Office A on the night of August 2, 1964, when the *Maddox* sailed into North Vietnamese territorial waters. His memoirs allege that the torpedo attacks were authorized by the high command, but he added that his superior, General Van Tien Dung, thought it a mistake to fire on the destroyer at a time when the North sought to limit the war from expanding in North Vietnam.[2] Hanoi's official history of combat operations states that it was an error for the General Staff command duty officer to have issued the order to attack the *Maddox*.[3] It is possible that the torpedo attacks were not directed from the highest Party officials but were rather a knee-jerk response from the high command to retaliate for both an incursion into territorial waters and the recent covert American shelling of the North's islands. If this were the case, it would indicate the inadequacy of Hanoi's command over its military, since the aim up to this time had been to avoid an American escalation. The fog of war could account for Hanoi's attack on the *Maddox*. But the situation becomes more curious when viewed in the context of subsequent attacks on Americans culminating at Pleiku.

On August 7, just days after the Tonkin episode, Ho Chi Minh presided over a ceremony to commend the Democratic Republic of Vietnam (DRV) forces on their fighting spirit in the Tonkin Gulf and subsequent air battle. The military had set about a "scientific analysis" of the strengths and weaknesses of the enemy's air force. As with any serious modern military, they scrutinized errors made during the battles in order to draw lessons and improve combat performance. At that time they mistakenly believed that they had shot down one American plane. Despite this erroneous belief, the DRV Navy had fought an American destroyer and fighter jets, yet all three of the DRV's torpedo boats survived. The tiny DRV Navy had acquitted itself well, but Ho cautioned his soldiers not to become complacent. He told the troops:

You have won a glorious victory, but don't become self-satisfied. Don't underestimate the enemy because of this victory. We must realize that, with regard to the American imperialists and their puppets, 'even in the face of death these leopards will not change their spots.' They still harbor many evil plots.[4]

That same day the Politburo issued a directive in which it assessed America's likely next steps. The Politburo concluded that America, despite having alternatives, would continue to escalate the war, particularly by increasing its attacks against the North.

Tonkin marked a break in the pattern of American involvement. Rather than advising and fighting alongside soldiers of South Vietnam, and rather than conducting intelligence or sabotage operations within the DRV, three American actions combined to heightenen Hanoi's fears of escalation. One was the shelling of islands on the night of July 30–31. The second was two bombing raids on August 1 and 2 over Laos and North Vietnam.[5] The third was the *Maddox* mission. Taken together, these suggested a sudden spike in American aggression. They appeared to Hanoi as serious, provocative acts. Following the attack, the *Maddox* was ordered back into the area. The ship's commander, John J. Herrick, suspected that he was being used in a game of cat and mouse, in which his ship was the mouse. Captain Herrick requested permission to withdraw, but Washington refused.[6] President Johnson's intentions aside, the question is whether Hanoi interpreted the *Maddox* and its attendant incidents as a provocation. Based on the Politburo's directive of August 7, it clearly did.

The post-Tonkin Politburo directive, titled "Increasing Combat Readiness to Counter All Enemy Schemes to Commit Provocations and to Attack North Vietnam," repeatedly spoke of the need to crush the enemy's expected provocations. The directive outlined America's three principal options for future action. First, it could intensify the war in the South and continue to provoke and sabotage the North in order to block the flow of supplies southward. Second, it could expand the war into the North. Third, it could seek a diplomatic solution. The directive concluded that the United States would choose the first option.[7]

According to the directive, the Politburo anticipated the Americans would engage in a variety of new and intensified provocations. These included the possibility of naval blockades, amphibious landings to destroy coastal areas and then withdraw, larger commando raids inside the DRV than those previously conducted, and inciting ethnic minorities and regime opponents to create disorder. The Politburo assumed that such actions could either be coordinated and launched simultaneously, or be taken in a gradual, step-by-step fashion for the purpose of testing the socialist camp's reactions.[8]

In light of the August 7 directive, it appears that Hanoi's leadership had by this point come to see a full-scale war with America as unavoidable, if it had not already reached this conclusion well before. In fact, by March 1964, Hanoi's military leadership already suspected that the covert American raids into North Vietnamese territory served as the precursor to a wider U.S. assault upon the North.[9] It is possible that Le Duan's adherence to Marxist-Leninist ideology convinced him that an American expansion was historically inevitable, deeply rooted in the nature of capitalist nations. More likely, his estimation was based on a careful observation of America's steadily growing involvement. By the time of Tonkin, there was little evidence to suggest that America planned to back down, regardless of prior Party insistence that it would surely be deterred.

Several months earlier, on May 20, 1964, President Johnson had tasked an executive committee to develop plans for graduated bombing against the North. Following the presentation of the committee's recommendations, Johnson cabled Ambassador Henry Cabot Lodge in Saigon with a synthesis of the group's conclusions: Southeast Asia could not be lost, time was on the communists' side, and Congress should authorize the administration to take all necessary measures before it was too late.[10]

Hanoi's assessment of U.S. options after Tonkin closely resembled the options being considered in Washington at the highest levels, suggesting that either its strategic empathy was especially strong at this time or Hanoi had penetrated the American Embassy in Saigon and was literally reading the enemy's thoughts. Unfortunately, DRV intelligence records from this period are still tightly guarded secrets. We therefore know little about how deeply Hanoi's espionage penetrated American sources. Nonetheless, the August 7 Politburo directive did accurately gauge the mood within Washington's innermost circle. President Johnson's executive committee, which included the various departmental principals, Secretary of State Dean Rusk, Secretary of Defense Robert McNamara, and National Security Advisor McGeorge Bundy, had all but excluded negotiation as an option, just as Hanoi recognized. Their idea of negotiation amounted to Hanoi's capitulation to America's main demands and therefore would not have been taken seriously by Hanoi. Instead, by the fall and early winter of 1964, the group was increasingly coming to press for attacks against the North, just as Hanoi anticipated, though no action would be taken before the Presidential election in November.[11]

If Hanoi believed that a U.S. escalation, which was already underway with respect to the number of military advisors, was soon to intensify, then what did it see as the purpose of continued attacks against American targets? If the attacks were intended to deter an American escalation, Hanoi would have had to have believed that the United States was in fact deterrable. Based on the *Van Kien Dang* records, it appears that opinion on this point was divided by the end of 1963. By August 7, 1964, following Tonkin, Politburo opinion clearly seems to have shifted to the view that the Americans intended to escalate. Deterrence, therefore, could hardly be effective if the decision to escalate had already been made. Nevertheless, Viet Cong attacks continued after Tonkin. On November 1, Viet Cong forces attacked the Bein Hoa airbase, killing four American airmen, wounding 72 others, and destroying five B-57 bombers. On December 24, Viet Cong units attacked the Brinks Hotel in Saigon where U.S. military personnel were housed. The assault resulted in the deaths of two Americans and 100 wounded. The February 6, 1965 attack on the Pleiku airbase at last produced a robust American response. All of these attacks occurred after Le Duan's carefully-selected General, Nguyen Chi Thanh, arrived in the south to take command of the Central Office of South Vietnam (COSVN).

If Hanoi had hoped to avoid provoking the Americans after Tonkin, it should have tried to restrict attacks on American bases. As head of the Party and having deep, intimate ties to the southern communist movement, and having installed his colleague General Nguyen Chi Thanh to oversee COSVN, Le Duan was exceedingly well-positioned to curb southern communist attacks. To do this, however, he would have needed to halt a common practice. Americans had long been considered legitimate targets by COSVN units. On July 20, 1956, a three-member commando team threw hand grenades into the U.S. Information Agency's office in Saigon. On July 7, 1959, as U.S. servicemen were enjoying an evening film, a six-member team brazenly fired their way into the U.S. Military Assistance and Advisory Group headquarters in Bien Hoa, killing two American soldiers and wounding one officer.[12] Viet Cong units employed terrorist methods as well. In March 1963, a covert Viet Cong operative working as an air controller at the Tan Son Nhat airfield met with his Vietnamese lover, chatting in the boarding area while roughly 100 U.S. military personnel waited for their flight. The woman, however, was not his lover but in fact another operative who had brought with her a bomb in a tourist bag. The "couple" switched their own bag with that of an American, who unsuspectingly carried it aboard. The bomb's timing mechanism malfunctioned, exploding only after the plane had safely landed in San Francisco, injuring two mail distribution clerks.[13] The most provocative act of all was the failed assassination attempt on Secretary of Defense Robert McNamara on May 2, 1964, when Nguyen Van Troi planted a mine below a bridge over which the Defense Secretary would travel. The mine was discovered in time, and Nguyen Van Troi was captured and executed by a firing squad at the hands of Army of the Republic of Vietnam (ARVN) forces. In commemoration of this assassination attempt, roads in Saigon and most major Vietnamese cities still bear Nguyen Van Troi's name. For COSVN forces to attack Americans or their bases was not unique. The question is what Hanoi hoped to gain by continuing those attacks after Tonkin, given that provoking the Americans risked expanding the war. The most provocative of those attacks culminated at Pleiku and provided President Johnson with the pretext he needed to begin the American escalation.

When, decades later, Robert McNamara convened a conference of former adversaries in June 1997 to reflect on the war, General Dang Vu Hiep claimed that the attacks at Pleiku had occurred solely at the local commanders' initiative. They were not, the elderly General asserted, directed by Hanoi, nor were they connected to Soviet Premier Alexei Kosygin's visit.[14] Subsequent to the McNamara meetings, General Hiep published his reaction to those discussions. He viewed Pleiku as an utterly ordinary attack, of lesser significance than others his side had struck against American targets. He could only understand the robust American reaction to Pleiku as intentionally blown out of proportion to serve as an excuse for expanding the war. He noted that the American air strikes, supposedly in response to Pleiku and which occurred on the following day, had to have been planned months in advance.[15]

But then the General added a curious note. The historian George Herring asked him who had planned the attacks. As mentioned above, the General affirmed that they had not been directed from Hanoi. Professor Herring asked if anyone had been criticized for launching the attacks. General Hiep replied that not only was no one criticized, his superiors commended them for the attack.[16] Commendations can help foster a fighting spirit, but if the goal had been to avoid American escalation, then such measures were ill-timed at best. Of course, the comments of Vietnamese officials must still be taken with great skepticism. We cannot conclude beyond doubt that Hanoi did not in fact direct the attacks at Pleiku or elsewhere. Nonetheless, the more important question is not whether Hanoi directed the attacks but rather why it did not seek to prevent them at such a crucial juncture.

The historian Frederick Logevall has advanced the standard interpretation that whether the attacks were directed by Hanoi or not, they were intended to destabilize the South Vietnamese government and not to engender an American retaliation.[17] In Logevall's view, Pleiku offered Washington the pretext for escalation it had been seeking. The Johnson administration immediately responded with air attacks against the North. Operation Flaming Dart deployed 132 U.S. and 22 South Vietnamese aircraft to strike four targets in the southern part of North Vietnam. America's direct combat against North Vietnam had begun.

Le Duan's writings to COSVN in February 1965 partly support Logevall's conclusion, but they do not tell the whole story. They show that the First Secretary hoped to weaken the Saigon regime before a full-scale American escalation could develop. In February 1965, Le Duan wrote to the southern communists to elaborate on points from the most recent Party resolution that year. It is unclear whether he wrote this letter before or after the Pleiku attacks. As he saw it, the aim was to fight in such a way that would "virtually eliminate" the possibility of an American escalation.[18] It had become a race against time to totally destroy the ARVN forces so that the United States could not rely on them any longer. "[The Americans] will only accept defeat when that source of support no longer exists."[19] And yet, based on the August 7

Politburo directive following Tonkin, it seems that Le Duan had already concluded that an American escalation could not be deterred. Why then would he have instructed southern communists that weakening ARVN forces could deter America?

Le Duan's next points bear close scrutiny. He argued that the United States would not be willing to expand because it understood that it could not afford to become bogged down in a protracted war, especially in light of its other global commitments. Destruction of the puppet army would lead the Americans into a quagmire in Vietnam, forced to deploy ever more troops. Since the United States was the world's leading imperialist power, it had interests and commitments around the globe, and becoming overcommitted and bogged down in Vietnam would limit its ability to act elsewhere.[20] This had been Le Duan's consistent line of reasoning for years. He possessed a firm grasp of geostrategic realities, always cognizant of his enemies' global advantages as well as their constraints. Yet we cannot rely solely on Le Duan's letters south as a Rosetta Stone for decrypting his beliefs. He was very likely convinced that America would be defeated in a protracted war, but, in contrast to what he told the southern communists, he probably did not think that the United States would soon back down.

Crippling ARVN forces was one thing; attacking Americans at so sensitive a time was quite another. If the standard interpretation for Pleiku and related attacks were correct—that the communists miscalculated—it would mean that Hanoi's strategic empathy for America (specifically for President Johnson and his top advisors) proved inadequate at one of the war's most critical turning points. This explanation, which we could call the "failed deterrence hypothesis," would mean that Le Duan, and presumably other Party leaders, believed that attacks on Americans after Tonkin would not be used by President Johnson as justification for escalation. It would mean that Hanoi believed that the relatively minor gains it could win by attacking American bases would not be offset by the tremendous costs of a large-scale U.S. military invasion. In other words, Hanoi badly misread its enemy's drivers.

This explanation assumes that Hanoi, and/or the southern communists, made a rational cost–benefit analysis of attacking Americans after Tonkin and calculated that Washington would back down. The political scientist James Fearon has argued that rationalist explanations for war must not only show how war could appear attractive to rational leaders; they must also show why states cannot find an alternative to the costly act of war.[21] On the eve of the Second Indochina War, Hanoi appears to have held what Fearon would call "private information" but that is in this case more precisely stated as a Marxist ideological conviction: that its victory was historically inevitable. Yet even this powerful belief did not go unquestioned. Le Duan himself had pointed to the Americans' success against revolutionary movements in Greece and the Philippines. The notion of ultimate victory, therefore, may have been a deep aspiration, an expectation, and a hope, but Party leaders understood that its realization depended on their ability to bring it to fruition.

The real problem with a rationalist interpretation is that the Politburo directive of August 7, 1964, shows that Le Duan expected America to intensify its commitment to the South—the opposite of backing down. It seems unlikely that the Party chief believed that America could be deterred by some relatively modest strikes. It is therefore worth considering some other possible explanations for the post-Tonkin attacks.

The second alternative is that the attacks on Americans from Tonkin through to Pleiku were simply ill-conceived, undirected, and divorced from any larger strategy. Poor communication between Hanoi and COSVN could have been at play. Hanoi might have been unable to restrain the southern attacks and subsequently felt it had to commend COSVN units on their heroic actions. But, as we have seen, in 1962 Le Duan was working to restrain COSVN by advocating caution. Since Le Duan had appointed his own man, General Nguyen Chi Thanh, to oversee COSVN, Le Duan should have had even greater influence over military actions in the South. To accept what we could call the "poor planning hypothesis," one must believe that on a subject of tremendous importance to Hanoi—the introduction of U.S. ground troops—Hanoi's oversight of COSVN actions was lacking.

There is another explanation for the attacks on Americans at this time, which we could call the "inevitable benefits hypothesis." There can be little doubt that most of Hanoi's leaders did not desire the massive deployment of American ground troops to South Vietnam. This was surely true of the Viet Cong fighters as well. One prominent Viet Cong leader recounted in his postwar memoir that he and his comrades viewed an American escalation as a "living nightmare," one that filled them with "sick anticipation of a prolonged and vastly more brutal war."[22] Yet if Le Duan had already concluded that the Americans intended to escalate, then there was little that Hanoi could do to prevent it. In that case, there would be certain benefits from attacking American bases. If successful, they could provide a substantial boost to morale and the southern communists' fighting spirit. Since the war to come was likely to be protracted, the southern communists would need to know that they had the ability to inflict real damage on the Americans, even against the invaders' own military bases.

One way of thinking about this preescalation period is as a time of undeclared war. Many overt wars are often preceded by a period of undeclared war. This was true of the United States and Germany prior to Hitler's declaration of war against America. Hitler's declaration merely acknowledged the reality that had existed between the two powers, as the United States had been providing financial support to the British, French, Soviets, and other allies via the Lend-Lease program. Even though no formal state of war existed between the two nations, German U-boats fired on American vessels in the Atlantic in an effort to disrupt the transfer of supplies. Similarly, the United States and Japan were in a state of undeclared war prior to Pearl Harbor, as the United States cut off oil supplies to Japan under President Roosevelt's quarantine policy.[23] During such times of undeclared war, there is often an incentive for each side to make the other launch the first strike. This enables the side being attacked to rally its people around the government as it portrays itself as the nation's defenders. This was true even of Hitler, who went to the trouble of casting Germany as a victim of Polish aggression on the eve of World War II. In the Gleiwitz incident, Hitler fabricated an attack on a German radio station by dressing up German soldiers in Polish uniforms. That drama enabled him to justify an invasion of Poland in September of 1939.

Given Hanoi's frequent wish to present itself as the victim of American aggression, and given that it expected an imminent American escalation, could Le Duan have encouraged the attacks on Americans (or at least failed to restrain them) in order to boost morale? Could he and others in Hanoi have reasoned that the time of undeclared war would soon be over and the time of a large-scale American invasion had come? This would not mean that Le Duan desired an invasion. It would instead mean that despite what he wrote to COSVN, he actually believed that deterrence had already failed, American escalation was inevitable, and it was best to strike the Americans hard in order to frame the Party as Vietnam's defenders. Viewed in this light, his written assurance to COSVN in February 1965 that they could still prevent an American escalation likely stemmed from a desire to embolden their forces. If instead he had informed them that the strongest, most technologically advanced military in the world was about to commit hundreds of thousands of combat forces to attack a relatively small South Vietnamese revolutionary army, the effect could have been highly dispiriting. Wiser, from Le Duan's perspective, would have been to urge the National Liberation Front (NLF) onward and persuade them that history was ultimately on their side. In the face of a large-scale war with America, morale would surely be at a premium.

The southern communist fighters were not all of one mind regarding strategy. Many favored guerilla warfare over Le Duan's preferred methods of large, conventional attacks.[24] Although General Thanh imposed Le Duan's policies on COSVN soldiers, Le Duan's letters also show the First Secretary's keen sense of his position. Unable to inflict the Ministry of Public Security apparatus upon southerners who rejected his plans, and recognizing that General Thanh's efforts would need help to overcome southern resistance, Le Duan tried to rally COSVN units behind large-scale attacks against ARVN forces. He tried to persuade them that his methods were the best way of defeating the Americans. Furthermore, permitting COSVN units to attack Americans directly, culminating in the brazen Pleiku assault, was a clever move by a leader sensitive to southern needs. These strikes helped to unify a diverse collection of divided forces.

Beyond the benefits to morale, Le Duan also recognized that escalation provided tangible advantages to the Party. Le Duan and other Party leaders expected a general uprising to occur in the South, which would overthrow the puppet government and pave the way for a socialist revolution. This uprising had been long awaited though thus far unrealized. An American escalation, invasion, and bombing of the North could prove fortuitous. It enabled the Vietnamese Workers' Party to frame itself even more clearly as the Vietnamese peoples' savior, heroically fighting against outside invaders. It furthered the conditions for attracting average Vietnamese, from the North and South, to the

Party's cause. Le Duan bluntly articulated this rather cold-hearted line of reasoning in December 1965:

> In fact, the more troops the Americans send into our country, the more bases they build in our country, and the more they employ the most vicious and barbaric methods to bomb, shoot, and kill our people, the most intense the contradictions between them and all classes of the population will become; the deeper the contradictions between them and the leaders of the puppet army and the puppet government will become; the more powerful will be the awakening of the spirit of nationalism among the majority of puppet army soldiers and puppet government officials will become; and the more difficult the lives of the residents of the cities and the areas under enemy control will become. This situation creates possibilities for us to further expand our political struggle movement and attract new forces to join the front. For that reason, our policy must be to strive to assemble a broad-based mass force from every class of the population and persuade members of the puppet army and the puppet government to join a truly broad-based resistance front to fight the Americans and save our nation.[25]

As Le Duan saw it, the American escalation offered two useful benefits to Hanoi's cause. First, as described above, it allowed the Party to frame itself as the nation's true defender against outside invaders—foreign forces who could be portrayed as cruel. This would attract more Vietnamese (from both North and South) to join the Party and support its aims. The propagandistic term "the resistance struggle against the Americans to save the nation" underscored this aim. The second benefit from escalation was that it provided greater opportunity to inflict casualties. The body count was seen as an essential component to Hanoi's overall strategy of protracted war. The higher the casualties, Le Duan reasoned, the more soldiers the United States would be forced to deploy, the more overstretched it would become, and American domestic support for the war would sink even lower.

In November 1965, with the American escalation well underway, Le Duan again wrote to the southern communists regarding the latest

Party resolution. Following the massive influx of U.S. ground troops and Hanoi's failure to prevent the Americans from expanding the war, the Party Secretary needed to reiterate the North's commitment to a protracted war strategy. He maintained that, despite America's escalation, the enemy's objectives remained consistent. He cited Secretary of Defense Robert McNamara's own words to a Congressional Armed Services Committee: "Even though our tactics have changed, our goals remain the same." Though he did not admit directly that the efforts to prevent escalation had failed, he did offer a new objective for Hanoi: to prevent the Americans from expanding the war to the North.

Hanoi had determined that in contrast to the preescalation phase, when ARVN forces constituted the primary targets, the postescalation phase meant that American soldiers as well as ARVN forces comprised the prime targets. "The dialectical relationship in this matter is that we attack U.S. troops in order to create conditions that will enable us to annihilate puppet troops, and, conversely, we annihilate puppet troops in order to create conditions that will enable us to attack and annihilate American troops."[26] Le Duan cautioned the southern communists to continue to avoid attacking the Americans where they were strong and to focus on attacking their weaknesses, but he added a new caveat: This instruction was not absolute; it was not cast in stone. The calculus had changed. Even striking Americans where they were strong could now be permitted.

Le Duan recognized that inflicting the greatest number of American casualties represented a crucial lynchpin in the protracted war strategy. Although the escalation posed new challenges and augured more exacting costs on Hanoi, it also provided more targets for communist forces. The Secretary envisioned a clear causal chain of events that would flow from killing Americans:

> . . . the more American troops that come to Vietnam, the more of them we will be able to kill. If large numbers of American troops are killed, the puppet army will disintegrate even faster, the U.S.'s hope of securing a victory through military means will collapse, and the American people's movement opposed to the U.S.'s dirty war in Vietnam will grow.

Later in that same missive, Le Duan set a specific kill quota. He advised the southern communists to kill at least 10,000 Americans in the coming spring–summer campaign. Within the next few years he suggested that they aim to kill between 40,000 and 50,000 American soldiers.[27] The bulk of this letter outlined the tactics that the southern communists should employ to accomplish their mission. One small part included training all classes of the population to profoundly hate the enemy.[28] In his 2013 study of American atrocities in Vietnam, *Kill Anything That Moves*, Nick Turse observed that U.S. military policy centered on maximizing the body count of enemy combatants.[29] It is striking that Le Duan adopted the same tactic toward the Americans.

The Party leader had read his own people well. By the spring of 1965, as American attacks against the North increased, the People's Army doubled its ranks.[30] For the time being, at least, Le Duan, the strategic empath, had bolstered support for his policies among northern and southern communists alike. Now the task ahead required even finer appreciation of America's constraints.

The Escalation Paradox

Le Duan argued repeatedly that America faced a dilemma. The more troops it deployed, the weaker it became. He articulated this and other assessments of American constraints at the close of 1965, as the escalation was fully underway. In December 1965, when Le Duan addressed the Twelfth Plenum of the Party's Central Committee, he explained more fully the policy of protracted war. His address began by observing that the war had developed precisely along the lines that the Party had laid out in the Ninth and Eleventh Plenums. (Those comments, however, were highly hedged, offering possibilities, not definitive futures.) He then noted that the situation had developed more rapidly than expected. In mid-1965, he alleged that the puppet army of the South had been on the verge of disintegration but that the Party did not have the necessary means at that time to force its collapse. Had the DRV been able to push the ARVN to the breaking point, he maintained, then the Americans might not have deployed massive ground troops. The lessons from this episode, he said, bore directly on the policy of protracted war.

The policy of protracted war, Le Duan explained, was to use weakness against strength. Even if the enemy deployed 400,000 troops to Vietnam (the United States ultimately sent more than a half million), the Vietnamese would defeat them by bogging them down in a stalemate. That policy, however, did not entail an orderly, step-by-step advance. Instead, it required massing forces against the enemy under specific conditions. The Americans are warmongers by their nature, Le Duan frequently declared. That was why they continued to escalate and expand the war. These appear to be Le Duan's true beliefs: that the Americans would continue to expand the war if the resistance was insufficient to deter them: and a protracted war would grind them down because it would increase American casualties, which in turn would bolster opposition to the war both within the United States and abroad.

The Politburo was not in complete agreement on these matters. In a rare admission of internal Party disagreement, Le Duan commented that differences of opinion on these matters still remained despite their lengthy, ongoing discussion. The First Secretary stressed that the Politburo was unanimous in its view that no matter how many troops the United States should send, the Vietnamese would defeat them. Further, they all agreed that the Politburo "must firmly maintain and study and digest even further our formula of fighting the enemy using both military and political means."[31] Le Duan insisted that unanimous agreement was essential, crucial to the success of the movement. And then the hint of dissent emerged:

> However, in a limited period of time we have not been able to carefully and thoroughly discuss every aspect of each individual issue, and therefore we may have some slight difference on one aspect or another, such as on our assessment of the American imperialists, on the nature and the form of the war, on the formula of a protracted war and striving to defeat the enemy within a relatively short period of time, about the effort to win the sympathy and help of our camp and of the international community, etc.[32]

Though couched in understated tones, the "slight disagreements" he described involved rather major issues. We can surmise that at this critical juncture in the war, the Politburo did not share a consensus view on either America's position or Hanoi's strategy. Le Duan, however, seems to have had strong opinions of his own, and he sought to push them through the Party bureaucracy to translate them into policy.

Following his admission of internal disputes, Le Duan launched into a new section titled, "Assessment of the American Imperialists." He asserted that, in devising Hanoi's war strategies, the most important question was to determine the balance of forces between the United States and Vietnam. It was a question, he stated, "of knowing the enemy and knowing ourselves." The lessons of Sun Tzu would not be lost on Le Duan.

A customary segment of many Party speeches included a historical analysis, which, heavily shaped by Marxism-Leninism, invariably illustrated both the enemy's waning fortunes and the Party's inevitable ascent. Le Duan thus laid out America's global position at the close of World War II, when its strength was unmatched by any rival. Under these conditions, the Americans, he claimed, "hatched their plot to take over and dominate the world."[33] Since its zenith of global power at the war's close, he continued, America's position had steadily eroded. Its loss of a monopoly on nuclear weapons; the recovery of the Soviet Union; China's rise; America's defeats in Korea, Cuba, Laos, and beyond; and its declining economy all combined to shift the balance of forces to the revolutionary camps around the world. He then cautioned that the American successes in "snuffing out" revolutionary movements in Greece and the Philippines could not be ignored. After recounting America's failures, from backing the French and paying 80 percent of their war costs only to be defeated at Dien Bien Phu, to now being bogged down in South Vietnam, Le Duan concluded that the Americans could not escape a crucial strategic contradiction. Although they possessed economic and military resources far greater than the DRV could muster, "the deeper they involve themselves in this war of aggression in the southern half of our country, the deeper they sink into a quagmire."[34] He observed that America's greatest problem was that it was waging an offensive modern war against guerillas. Using large units to fight guerrillas in South Vietnam, he said, was "just like punching water—when you pull your fist out, the water just flows right back in."[35]

The Secretary described America's military constraints as hinging on the asymmetric nature of the conflict, noting that this required the

Americans to disperse their forces. He devoted roughly equal attention to America's political weaknesses, as it faced growing internal and global opposition. He also added mention of American economic decline. So was this all pure propaganda aimed at rallying the Party to the cause? Not quite. Though his speeches and directives certainly contained heavy doses of propaganda, his assessments reflect some sober analysis of America's strategic situation. That knowledge no doubt contributed to Hanoi's willingness to prosecute its protracted war strategy despite the enormous toll it was taking on the Vietnamese people.

It was then time for the Party's First Secretary to speak about predictions. The underlying aim of developing strategic empathy, of knowing one's enemy, is of course to anticipate an opponent's actions. Le Duan proclaimed that the war would intensify, becoming more vicious in both the North and South. The scale of fighting would increase as the Americans stepped up their artillery and air strikes. The Americans would use chemical warfare and poison gas on liberated zones, even those adjacent to urban centers. The enemy would increase its bombing of North Vietnam, but it would focus on disrupting the transportation and supply lines from north to south. The Americans would attack key economic zones, the dike system, and residential areas. Finally, they would use psychological warfare and espionage to shake the will of the Vietnamese people.[36] Though none of this may have been difficult to predict (especially as much of it was already occurring), it was at least essentially accurate.

In order to counter the anticipated American intensification of the war, Le Duan spelled out the nature of Hanoi's protracted war strategy while also seeking a quick victory: two ostensibly contradictory positions. This policy, as suggested above, may have emerged as a compromise between divergent Party factions. Le Duan tried to square the circle this way:

> We have also clearly explained that these two things are not in contradiction to one another, because the basic condition for fighting a protracted war as well as for seeking victory within a relatively short period of time is to quickly develop our power and forces in all areas, and especially military forces, in order to change the balance of forces in our favor.[37]

The protracted war strategy was not, he explained, a policy of anni-
hilating all American forces down to the last man. Instead, as is well
known, it was a plan to sap the enemy's will to fight. It was also, he
added, to force the enemy to accept defeat with certain conditions.
This caveat indicates that Hanoi's "talking while fighting" tactic allowed
for the possibility that at least a faction within Hanoi's leadership was
willing to make certain concessions. Such a statement suggests that the
more compromising members of the Politburo who were open to negotiation with the Americans still held some sway over Party pronouncements. Le Duan would later silence this faction through intimidation
and arrest.

The tension between waging a protracted struggle and seeking a
rapid victory is perhaps best played out in this section of the speech. Le
Duan explained that Party leaders had a responsibility to understand
the psychological state of Southern Vietnamese. Although they had
been fighting the Americans officially since 1960, the revolution had
actually been fought for the past twenty years under savage conditions.
The Party leaders therefore had to make the greatest effort to shorten
the fighting as much as possible. And then he struck this compromising
note: "Naturally, our goal must be to win total, 100 percent victory, but
if in a certain situation we are able to achieve a 90 percent victory, we
can then bring the war to an end under conditions that are favorable
to us."[38]

Le Duan distinguished Vietnam's past struggles against the French
from the current war with the Americans. Though he had frequently
drawn comparisons between the two conflicts, he now identified the
significant differences. First, the strength of communist forces in both
the North and the South was far greater in 1965 than it had been in the
1940s and 1950s. Second, the communists in the North now possessed
a solid rear area backed by the socialist bloc. Third, the war against
the Americans and puppet government began with offensive, rather
than defensive, operations. He asserted that this time the Party held
the offensive initiative in its hands. Through the use of protracted war,
Le Duan believed that Hanoi would eventually win. The Party leader's
ability to recognize what was new in the current conflict enabled him
to adjust Hanoi's strategy to the enemy at hand, rather than applying a
one-sized approach to waging war. He was not fighting the last war with

yesterday's methods. Instead, he had the mental agility to see what was unique about his enemy and adapt accordingly.

Shortly after Le Duan's address, the Party convened a meeting of high-level cadres on January 16, 1966, for the purpose of studying the Twelfth Plenum's resolution. Although his folksy style stood in sharp contrast to Le Duan's more formal speeches, Ho Chi Minh showed himself in agreement with Le Duan's assessment of America. Addressing the assembled cadres, Ho confronted the challenges of fighting American soldiers. He observed that the Americans were well-fed and well-financed, receiving meat, cake, cigarettes, and chewing gum as typical rations. He claimed that supporting an American soldier cost fifteen times that of a South Vietnamese soldier. In addition, the Americans had just introduced a mobile division transported by helicopter. But then Ho outlined the enemy's weak points. First among these was their lack of mobility on the ground. Calling the Americans "big, heavy-set people," weighted down with all imaginable equipment, he observed that once they were on the ground, they could not move as quickly as the Vietnamese. Ho argued that although Vietnamese soldiers were smaller, they were faster, more agile, and therefore not at a disadvantage in hand-to-hand combat. Beyond these tactical appraisals, Ho underscored the view that body counts mattered for political reasons.

America's fundamental weaknesses, Ho asserted, centered on the growing domestic and global opposition to its intervention. He cited American youths setting themselves on fire in protest. He pointed to the violent uprisings by black Americans. Underscoring the same theme that Le Duan had stressed many times before, Ho assured the cadres that increased American casualties would only augment domestic opposition. He even cited U.S. Senator Morse as saying: "The more American troops we sent to South Vietnam, the more caskets that will be sent back home to the United States." Because victory hinged on what happened in South Vietnam, Ho concluded that "we must do whatever it takes in South Vietnam to destroy and shatter the puppet army and to kill large numbers of American troops. . . ."[39]

These same notions of America's vulnerability continued for years, even after the general offensive. Following the multiple attacks that together comprised the 1968 Tet Offensive, the Party's resolution of August revisited the current strategic balance, paying closest attention to the contradictions inherent in America's position. First, the resolution asserted that America's greatest contradiction was that it needed to confront the enemy directly, yet its current posture was defensive. It could not win without substantially increasing its troop strength, but deploying more troops would guarantee an even greater defeat. The next contradiction, as Hanoi saw it, involved de-Americanization, or what the Nixon administration would later dub "Vietnamization" of the war: transferring primary fighting responsibility to the ARVN. Hanoi maintained that ARVN's forces were becoming less effective as their morale deteriorated, but the Americans needed to place them in the principal fighting role. In addition, the Americans needed to mass their forces, though they were compelled to disperse them because they needed to defend the cities while simultaneously controlling the countryside.[40] In short, all of the weaknesses Hanoi had recognized years before were now exacerbated.

The same was true for the way Hanoi assessed America's international position. On August 29, 1968, a report to the Central Committee observed that Vietnam had hamstrung U.S. actions in other hot spots. Referring to the Soviet Union's invasion of Czechoslovakia, the report argued that America could not mount a serious response because it was tied down in Vietnam. It could not go deeper into the Middle East despite the recent Arab-Israeli War. It could not go deeper into Laos following its defeat at Nam Bak.[41] Despite Hanoi's military losses from the Tet Offensive, Party leaders still maintained that America's underlying constraints left its future prospects grim.

By the start of 1969, Le Duan recognized that American support for the war had reached a turning point after Tet. On January 1, the Politburo cabled Le Duc Tho and Xuan Thuy (two of the leading delegates to the Paris peace talks) to report on its discussions of American intentions. Party leaders believed that the key American policymakers wanted to end the war by withdrawing troops but maintaining a strong regime in the South. President Nixon, they presumed, was also compelled to follow this course, though he sought an honorable end to the war. In subsequent Politburo cables throughout January and February, Hanoi reiterated its belief that U.S. politicians wanted to deescalate and de-Americanize the war, though Nixon hoped to negotiate from a position of strength. Consequently, the Politburo concluded that the struggle must continue on all three fronts—military, political, and diplomatic. In order to maintain the protracted war strategy, the cable instructed that diplomacy must not give the impression that Hanoi desired a quick conclusion to the conflict.[42] On each of these three fronts, Le Duan continued to pursue an effective grand strategy of wearing the Americans down.

Conclusion

Le Duan's strategic empathy for America—his ability to identify America's underlying constraints—proved strong on the most crucial dimension. He grasped the enemy's sensitivity to casualties. He understood America's vulnerability to being bogged down, fighting for years without demonstrable progress. He comprehended that America's global commitments could be hamstrung if overextended in Vietnam. Ultimately, this was the most important assessment to get right, and on this point he succeeded in knowing his enemy well.

Le Duan also saw the shelling of North Vietnamese islands and the Tonkin Gulf episode as both a provocative act by America and a distinct break in the pattern of U.S. behavior. According to the Politburo directive of August 7, 1964, he expected America to intensify the war in the South and step up its measures against the North. Here, too, he correctly estimated his enemy's intentions.

Le Duan likely understood that President Johnson would retaliate against the post-Tonkin attacks culminating at Pleiku. Rather than halting COSVN assaults in order to avoid provoking an American escalation, Le Duan seems to have reasoned that since escalation at that point was both likely and imminent, attacking the Americans would boost morale, giving southern communists a resource that would be greatly in need throughout the protracted war to come. The fact that Le Duan permitted those attacks to continue after Tonkin strongly suggests that he recognized Tonkin as signaling an inevitable escalation. It is not clear that Le Duan ever comprehended why President Johnson and his advisors decided to expand the war, but his uncertainty is understandable, especially since even historians are divided on the matter. They have been debating the Johnson administration's motivations for decades and will no doubt continue to do so. Given Le Duan's in-depth, reasoned efforts to understand his American foes, we cannot attribute his predictions of American actions to his Marxist-Leninist convictions alone. The often conflicted nature of Hanoi's assessments of America show that ideology influenced, but did not determine, Hanoi's thinking. Instead, Le Duan's and Hanoi's strategic empathy derived from a complex interplay of pattern recognition, attention to pattern breaks, and an overlay of Marxist dogma.

Contingency and chance are always at play in every conflict. Rarely are any outcomes predetermined or ineluctable. Obviously there were many causes of Hanoi's ultimate victory, primary among them being the support it received from China and the Soviet Union, its ability to continue sending arms and materiel south via the Ho Chi Minh trail, and its willingness to allow its people to endure extraordinary suffering. We must add to that list Hanoi's strategic empathy for America. Despite its failings, that empathy proved an equally important factor in its final triumph.

Although Le Duan ultimately triumphed, he and other Party leaders still failed on numerous occasions to read their enemies correctly, most notably with their prediction that the South Vietnamese would rise up in revolution. Thus far we have examined cases in which the pattern-break heuristic played a helpful role (or could have, in the case of Stalin). I want now to turn to a different heuristic, one that sometimes undermines even the sharpest observers. I will call this the continuity heuristic: an assumption that the enemy's future behavior will mirror past behavior. To illustrate this mistaken mindset, we must look back at one of its earliest recorded cases, on the battlefields of ancient China. As the Han dynasty collapsed into warring factions, three kingdoms vied for supremacy over China's vast dominions. Amid countless generals, one strategic thinker stood apart. Though his fame was already secure, it turned legendary when he faced a massive onslaught with merely a hypnotic tune.

8

The Continuity Conundrum
When the Past Misleads

The Lute That Beat an Army

They called him Sleeping Dragon, though his mind was wide awake. Master Cun Ming's strategic insights were so renowned throughout China that his enemies shuddered at his name. When garbed in his white, silken Taoist robes embroidered with red cranes down the sides, it seemed hard to imagine that such a placid figure could be so dominant in battle. Yet through the careful, cautious application of superior force, Cun Ming had reached almost legendary status. But the Dragon's string of victories was about to end when he found himself left to defend a city with just 2,500 men. In the distance, Marshall Sima Yi advanced with the full might of his Wei army, nearly 150,000 troops. This time, even Sleeping Dragon could not hope to fight and win.

Cun Ming's officers were terrified. They knew a bloodbath was soon to come. Their foreboding only heightened as they received the Dragon's orders. After soberly assessing their impossible predicament, Cun Ming ordered the city gates flung open. Strangely, he did not issue the command to surrender. Instead, he instructed twenty of his soldiers to remove their uniforms and dress in the clothing of townsfolk. The disguised soldiers were to do nothing more than peacefully sweep the streets at the city gates. All other soldiers were to hide from sight. Any officer who so much as made a noise would be instantly put to death. Cun Ming then changed into his Taoist robes and ascended the roof of the highest building, armed only with his lute.

Had he gone mad? Was the strain of endless battle at last too much to bear? Or had he simply decided to meet his fate with the serenity of a peaceful spirit? As Sleeping Dragon played a haunting tune, Marshall Sima Yi's scouts surveyed the eerie scene. Uncertain as to its meaning, they hurried back and reported to their commander. Incredulous and slightly unnerved, Sima Yi ordered his army to halt while he advanced alone to observe the situation for himself. Sure enough, he saw precisely what his scouts had described. Townsfolk peered downward as they methodically swept the streets. Two ceremonial guards flanked Cun Ming atop the building: one bearing a sword; the other holding a yak tail, the symbol of authority. Cun Ming sat between them, absorbed in the playing of his lute, as if nothing at all were amiss.

Now Sima Yi's confidence was shaken. Cun Ming's lack of preparation had to mean a trap. But what exactly did he intend? By making the city appear undefended, Cun Ming must be planning an ambush, the Marshall had to conclude. Sima Yi's second son tried to offer counsel. "Why do you retire, father?" the boy asked. "I am certain there are no soldiers behind this foolery. Why do you halt?" But Sima Yi knew better. He had known Cun Ming for years and knew that the Master never took risks. If the city seemed defenseless, then he could be certain it was too strongly defended to attack. Sima Yi turned his entire army around at once. They headed for the hills in full retreat.

Upon seeing the massive ranks of soldiers fleeing from his lute, Sleeping Dragon laughed and clapped his hands with delight. "Sima Yi knows that I am a cautious man," Cun Ming explained to those around him. "But if I had been in his place I should not have turned away."

Because Cun Ming knew his enemy even better than the enemy knew him, Cun Ming was able to predict how his enemy would react to surprising information. Sima Yi did not possess the wit to accurately interpret the meaning of this pattern break, and Sleeping Dragon understood this. Instead, Sima Yi fled at the sound of a lonely lute. Later, when Sima Yi learned he had been tricked, he could only sigh resignedly. "Cun Ming is a cleverer man than I."[1]

Written in the fourteenth century, *Romance of the Three Kingdoms* is one of China's best-known and beloved novels. Based on the historical scholarship of Chen Shou in the third century, the novel imagines the thoughts and feelings of characters engaged in bitter conflict following the Han dynasty's collapse. The massive chronicle, all 800,000 words of it, embodies the principles outlined in an even older work: Sun Tzu's *The Art of War*. While it is tempting to focus on the cunning of Cun Ming, the story holds even greater value for what it suggests about Sima Yi. Though it does not make the point explicitly, the tale demonstrates an age-old problem in how too many leaders think.

Sima Yi fell victim to the continuity heuristic—the belief that the best guide to someone's future behavior is his past behavior. If an enemy has been aggressive previously, we can expect him to be aggressive again. In fact, many of us tend to use this same heuristic across a range of contexts, not just regarding leaders and their adversaries. We do this even when the cost of making the wrong decision would be dear.

The Pattern Problem

An example of the continuity heuristic can be seen in a surprising place. It is embedded in a story created by one of today's leading cognitive psychologists. Daniel Kahneman has studied heuristics and biases for decades. In his best-selling book, *Thinking Fast and Slow*, Kahneman constructs a hypothetical example of how we all tend to rely on what he calls the "availability heuristic." This is where we assume that the information available to us is, in fact, all the information we need to make the right decision. To illustrate his availability heuristic, he offers the following scenario.

An academic department is planning to hire a young professor and wants to choose the one whose prospects for scientific productivity are the best. The department narrows the choice down to two candidates, Kim and Jane. Kim is a Ph.D. student and the prototypical rising star. She arrives on campus with sterling recommendations from all of her instructors. She delivers a brilliant job talk and sails through her interviews with ease. She leaves a profound impression on the faculty that she is truly gifted. There is one problem, however. Kim has no track record of scholarly publications. She has yet to publish anything. Jane, in contrast, gives a less spectacular job talk and makes a less stellar impression in her interviews. But Jane has been working as a postdoc for the past three years and has an excellent publishing record. Which candidate should the department choose?[2]

Kahneman argues that to select Kim would be to fall victim to the availability heuristic. We simply do not possess enough information about her capacity to produce scholarship. Kahneman states that he would offer the job to Jane, even though Kim made the stronger impression. Jane is arguably the safer bet, whereas Kim is a gamble. Kim might produce path-breaking work, or she could just as plausibly fail to produce altogether.

Kahneman's availability heuristic is, of course, a very real and often disastrous mental shortcut. Yet Kahneman appears to be basing his decision to hire Jane in part on the continuity heuristic. This mental shortcut assumes that the future will resemble the past, even though conditions may well change.

I want to alter Kahneman's scenario slightly in order to illustrate the problem of the continuity heuristic. Instead of the academic department making a decision about a new hire, consider how it might make the decision to tenure Jane six years after she has been hired. (Six to seven years is the standard length of time after which young professors in America are tenured.) Receiving tenure virtually guarantees a scholar a job for life. Once the decision has been made, it is nearly impossible to fire that faculty member. One major purpose for granting tenure is to ensure that scholars will be free to publish any research findings that they deem true. Intellectual freedom ensures that scholars will not compromise their conclusions under political, financial, or other pressures. Naturally, tenure is a highly sought-after status within academia. If achieved, the scholar has tremendous job security. If denied, the scholar loses her job and typically must seek employment elsewhere. The stakes, therefore, are extremely high. From the standpoint of the senior faculty members, the stakes are almost as great. If they support a scholar's bid for tenure, they will have a colleague for life. But if they get it wrong by tenuring someone who ceases to work hard, someone who abuses the benefits of job security, then the department will be stuck with that person for decades.

One of the questions that the tenured faculty members must ask themselves when assessing a junior colleague is whether that scholar will be productive in the future. Will she continue to publish even after being tenured when the incentives have changed? To gauge this, they typically look back on that scholar's past productivity. The tenured faculty assume that past productivity is the best, or at least a very good indicator of future productivity—just as Kahneman believed in his scenario above. Often this turns out to be accurate. Yet frequently scholars receive tenure and cease publishing altogether, or they fail to publish anything of substance. They just dry up. Therefore, what the tenured faculty members needed to know was not the scholar's past record but rather why the scholar had been productive in the first place. Did she possess a genuine passion and capacity for her work, or was she simply publishing in order to get tenure? The pattern of past behavior does not reveal the scholar's underlying drivers. The continuity heuristic does not tell the hiring faculty members what they need to know. And knowing another's hidden drivers is essential to anticipating future actions, especially because future conditions are at some point certain to change.[3]

This is not a book about how to make tenure decisions, and in a moment I will return to how this applies to enemy assessments. Here I will just offer a few thoughts on a different and possibly better way to assess Jane. Rather than focusing primarily on her past productivity, I would try to examine two traits: her genuine passion for her work and her resilience in the presence of severe difficulty. If Jane speaks about her work with potent enthusiasm, or if she in some way conveys a deep love of what she does, then, unless she is an outstanding actress, I would believe that her underlying driver is to continue along a productive path. Of course, as we all know, in the real world, life has a way of interfering with our best intentions. The loss of a parent, a painful divorce, a child's illness, issues with our own physical or mental health—these things and countless more strike nearly all of us. Life has a habit of getting in the way of productivity. I would therefore try to discern Jane's level of resilience during prior periods of pattern breaks. In previous times of great difficulty when the unexpected occurred, how quickly and how well was she able to return to productivity? Although people can and often do improve their resilience over time, I would want to know at what level she is starting. Both these traits, her passion and her resilience, might best be revealed at pattern-break moments. I believe that this method of assessment would prove more predictive of Jane's future productivity than would her pattern of past productivity.

All of this bears directly on the central subject of this chapter because, unfortunately, statesmen and their advisors tend to rely on the same continuity heuristic when assessing enemy intentions. They look to an enemy's past behavior and assume that future behavior will be the same, without considering that a changed context might alter enemy actions.

Two of the twentieth century's most notable attempts to assess and predict an enemy's behavior—the Crowe Memorandum of 1907 and the Kennan telegram of 1946—were grounded in at least two unwise mental shortcuts. In the first shortcut, the authors of these reports attributed a fixed nature to their opponents, believing them to be aggressive by nature—what psychologists sometimes refer to as the fundamental attribution error.[4] When policy analysts convince themselves that an enemy has unchanging, aggressive traits, they typically also believe that the enemy only understands force and that he views compromise as a sign of weakness. These assumptions have at least three detrimental effects. First, they inhibit the assessor from recognizing that a change in context or conditions could change his enemy's behavior. Second, they lead the assessor to the only reasonable policy option—taking the toughest line possible. Third, they create a self-fulfilling prophecy. By adopting the hardest line possible against the enemy on the assumption that he is implacable, the enemy often becomes implacable, digging in his heels even on issues over which he might previously have been conciliatory.

The second major shortcut employed by these assessments involved the continuity heuristic. The assessors assumed that past behavior was the best predictor of future behavior. The idea that new contexts could substantially change the enemy's intentions formed only a secondary part of their analysis. While it is true that the future may often resemble the past, that does not tell us *why* it does. It is an assumption with no explanatory power. It tells us nothing about the underlying drivers of an individual or group. Consequently, when conditions change, as they inevitably do, the analysis cannot adequately explain or predict the enemy's behavior.

The Enemy Mind

On New Year's Day 1907, an ambitious and stridently self-confident member of the British Foreign Office laid out his views on what he perceived as the growing German threat. Germany's rising power, he insisted, made continued clashes with Britain inevitable. His analysis sparked much interest, even generating a reaction from the Foreign

Secretary himself. Unfortunately for the cause of peace, his sense of the German enemy was grounded in at least two fundamental flaws—flaws that have bedeviled international relations ever since.

Known today simply as the Crowe Memorandum, Eyre Crowe's assessment of Anglo–German relations laid out a conceptual framework for anticipating German behavior. The extent of the document's influence is still debated, yet it remains a compelling source in the history of international conflict in part because it so boldly ascribed a nature to the German people. That nature, Crowe claimed, was expansionist.

The child of a British father and German mother, Crowe was born in Leipzig and lived for a period in France. His trilingual fluency made him a natural fit for work in the British Foreign Office. Though he never held a diplomatic post overseas, Crowe steadily rose through the organization in Whitehall, was eventually knighted in 1911, and subsequently became Permanent Undersecretary for Foreign Affairs in 1920. Convinced of his own insights into the German nature, and vehement that Germany would continue to expand, Crowe offered his superiors an unsolicited assessment of the perceived German threat.

According to Crowe, German history led in a straight line toward ever more territorial aggrandizement. Crowe saw the modern German state as the inheritor of Frederick the Great's Prussia, which was forged by the sword. Bismarck then built upon Frederick's legacy, again by blood and iron. Crowe claimed that the idea of controlling a vast colonial empire had possessed "the German imagination." The German people, he insisted, believed that it was their natural right to spread their ideals and increase their control over territory. And this outward thrust would, inevitably, lead that nation into increasing conflict with Great Britain.

In his detailed review of Anglo–German relations over the previous twenty years, Crowe saw a consistent pattern of German aggressiveness and British acquiescence to German demands. Under Bismarck, Crowe alleged, the German Foreign Office browbeat Britain into friendship, but subsequent to the great Chancellor's departure, "the habit of bullying and offending England had almost become a tradition" in Berlin.[5] He likened German policy since 1890 to that of a professional blackmailer, forever extracting concessions by mere threat and bluster. Based on this reading of the relationship, Crowe advocated a far firmer stand in any future negotiations with the Germans, in the implicit expectation that Germany continued to seek expansion by any means. Like Marshall

Sima Yi, who assumed that his enemy Cun Ming would behave at present and in the future just as he had behaved in the past, Crowe assumed that German leaders as a whole would behave similarly in future as they had done in the past. The key difference was that Crowe applied the continuity heuristic to an entire group of leaders rather than to an individual opponent. Nonetheless, Crowe's and Sima Yi's style of thinking was essentially the same.

On one level, Crowe's analysis was based on a structural interpretation of international affairs. The growing strength of one state was seen as ineluctably clashing with that of the dominant world power. The only viable option, as he saw it, was to resist the pressure from the burgeoning threat. This is the standard interpretation of Crowe's text.[6] But Crowe's assessment was built on multiple assumptions. His structural interpretation ignored the possibility that individual German statesmen could shape Anglo–German relations in peaceful ways. He assumed that the distribution of global power necessitated that all German statesmen would relentlessly pursue their national interests in the same or similar manner, namely aggressively. He further assumed that each German statesman would perceive the national interests in the same way.

On a deeper level, the memorandum reflected a fundamental attribution error combined with the continuity heuristic. Crowe based his assessment in part on a particular interpretation of the German character. Despite the discussion of power and interests, there was something deeply personal embedded in his thinking. His language and his metaphors revealed prejudices about not just Germany as a government but about the German people as a whole. He proclaimed that it was not merely the Kaiser who demanded territorial expansion but also the entire spectrum of society, from statesmen to journalists to businessmen to the educated and uneducated masses alike. The German people cried out with one voice to demand colonies, "where German emigrants can settle and spread the national ideals of the Fatherland . . ."

Crowe believed that he could interpret and articulate the true German mindset. "The world belongs to the strong," he wrote, imagining that this is how most Germans thought and that these thoughts must dictate policy. "We have no designs on other people's possessions, but where States are too feeble to put their territory to the best possible use, it is the manifest destiny of those who can and will do so to take their places."

Crowe was so convinced that he grasped the German mentality that he implied that anyone who differed must not be able to enter the German mind: "No one who has a knowledge of German political thought, and who enjoys the confidence of German friends speaking their minds openly and freely, can deny that these are the ideas which are proclaimed on the housetops . . ." Those who could not sympathize with these sentiments, he maintained, were considered by Germans as prejudiced foreigners who could not recognize their real feelings.

To underscore his point that the problem lay with the German people, not simply its leaders, Crowe concluded his lengthy report with the final statement that a resolute, unbending British stance would be the best way to ensure the respect of not simply the German government but the German nation as well.

Even if Crowe had correctly articulated the general German public mood, his analysis overlooked the idea that public moods can shift, especially when leaders direct it. Crowe's weighty declarations garnered much attention inside Whitehall, reaching the man on top.

Sir Edward Grey, the British Foreign Secretary, praised the report's insights. Writing on January 28, he called it a "most valuable" memorandum that deserved to be studied and seriously considered. He described its overview of recent history as "most helpful as a guide to policy."[7]

There was, however, another view. Less often noted is a small but telling comment just below Sir Edward Grey's remarks, signed only with the capital letter "F." The words below were most likely penned by Edmond George Petty-Fitzmaurice, a Liberal politician who served as the Parliamentary Under-Secretary of State for Foreign Affairs from 1905 to 1908. Diplomatically couching his objections in caveats, Fitzmaurice noted the inescapable implications of Crowe's report.

The only other remark I make on this most able and interesting Memo[randum] is to suggest whether the restless and uncertain personal character of the Emperor William is sufficiently taken into account in the estimate of the present situation. There was at least method in Prince Bismarck's madness; but the Emperor is like, a cat in a cupboard. He may jump out anywhere. The whole situation would be changed in a moment if this personal factor were changed, and another Minister like General Caprivi [a former German Chancellor known for his pro-British foreign policy] also came into office in consequence.

Fitzmaurice's observation challenged the premise of Crowe's analysis. In Crowe's view, German behavior could be predicted based on its past behavior. Its past behavior was in turn based on a particular reading of events combined with an assumption that a German character not only existed but that this putative national character was also consistent, ubiquitous, and meaningful. Fitzmaurice was suggesting otherwise. If a change in personnel could cause a shift in policy, then there could not be a consistent German characteristic of aggressive expansionism. By the same token, although the structure of global power might make disputes more likely as interests collide, those disputes need not result in significant conflict if more moderate individuals were in charge.[8]

Do individuals matter in the formulation of policy, or are they instead bound by forces beyond their control? Clearly, such a sharp dichotomy oversimplifies the matter. Individuals have influence, and structural forces can shape their actions. Crowe was arguing in part that Germany's power had grown to a point where it would be uncontrolled if left unchecked. British interests would therefore continue to be threatened by German expansion because of the nature of German power.

Fitzmaurice tactfully presented the opposite view, or at least a modification of Crowe's view. He suggested that individuals do have agency and influence. Two different leaders can make different choices despite being bound by the same basic circumstances. This perspective not only challenges the notion of static national character traits but it also refutes the idea that individuals will invariably use whatever power they possess and that they will all use it in the same way. In contrast, those who believe that international relations are governed by immutable laws of power relations are more sympathetic to Crowe's views. Unfortunately, they are also often susceptible to Crowe's notions of national character. The two perspectives are often intertwined.

Crowe's memorandum had yet another, more pointed critic. Thomas Henry Sanderson had served in the Foreign Office for more than four and a half decades, rising to the post of Permanent Under-Secretary of State for Foreign Affairs. He therefore spoke with considerable authority. In Sanderson's view, Germany's past behavior had not, in fact, been unreasonable or unprovoked. In case after case, Sanderson argued that Germany had legitimate cause for its actions. If the acquisition of territory were a sin, Sanderson mused, then surely the British must be far guiltier than the Germans. He noted that even some British diplomats agreed that England had not always treated the Germans fairly. In one instance Britain had forcibly searched three German cargo ships full of passengers, yet found no evidence of wrongdoing. If the situation had been reversed and Germans had searched British ships, Sanderson opined, Britain would have denounced it as intolerable. In direct contrast to Crowe's depiction of the German people, Sanderson argued that popular opinion in Germany was "on the whole sound and prudent," and could be expected to "exercise an increasing amount of wholesome restraint." He concluded that a great and growing nation could not be repressed, but it was not necessary for Britain to block German expansion where the two nations' interests did not directly clash.[9]

Sanderson was countering Crowe in several ways. First, he disputed Crowe's entire depiction of Anglo–German relations, instead casting them as frequently cooperative and only sometimes caustic—and with Britain not blameless for the tensions. Second, Sanderson argued against the idea that the German people were relentlessly aggressive. Instead, he maintained that they were prudent and restrained. And third, he did not assume that conflicts would be inevitable because of clashing interests. On the contrary, he maintained that goodwill could be fostered through accommodation of German aims where Britain's vital interests were not at stake. His entire assessment of Germany stemmed from a rejection of the continuity heuristic and a repudiation of Crowe's blanket statements about the true German character. Unfortunately, it was Crowe's memorandum that garnered more attention.

The Oriental Mind

Crowe's way of thinking did not end in World War I. Instead, it is part of a long and potent tradition.[10] On February 22, 1946, the American Chargé d'Affaires in Moscow cabled the U.S. Secretary of State in

Washington with a secret report. The official aimed to analyze Soviet behavior and to forecast Soviet actions. The "long telegram," as it became known, was subsequently published in a somewhat different form in 1947, as an article in *Foreign Affairs* under the title "The Sources of Soviet Conduct." The telegram has since become what is arguably the most impactful and well-known diplomatic document of the twentieth century, while the published article remains one of *Foreign Affairs'* most memorable contributions. The ideas embodied in both the telegram and the article profoundly shaped the discourse on American Cold War strategy.

George F. Kennan's notions of containing Soviet aggression arrived in Washington to a receptive audience. Decision-makers needed a conceptual framework within which to fit the policies they were already crafting. President Truman tasked two top advisors to assess the Soviets' record of keeping their promises. The report was intended to remain close hold within the government, not for public scrutiny. The resulting Clifford-Elsey report drew upon Kennan's analysis and further concretized his assumptions of Soviet aggression into policy. Yet Kennan never intended for his reflections to be used to justify all manner of military interventions around the globe.[11]

One too often overlooked aspect of Kennan's analysis involves its assumptions about the Russian character. Like Crowe's memorandum some forty years before, Kennan looked to his adversary's history as having profoundly influenced its leadership: "From the Russian-Asiatic world out of which they had emerged they carried with them a skepticism as to the possibilities of permanent and peaceful co-existence of rival forces." Presumably, this "Russian world" from which they came precluded compromise and cooperation. Describing the Kremlin leaders, Kennan observed that they remained predominantly absorbed by the struggle to achieve and retain power, both within and beyond their nation's borders. Not only did Marxist-Leninist ideology convince them that the world was hostile, but history reinforced that view: "The powerful hands of the Russian history and tradition reached up to sustain them in this feeling." Just as Crowe saw the Prussian past, as far back as Fredrick the Great, reaching out to imprint itself upon German statesmen in 1907, so Kennan saw Russia's past—at least, one particular interpretation of that past—as shaping Soviet leaders in 1948.

There was a curious tension in Kennan's analysis. On the one hand, he was well aware of the obvious differences between Tsarist and Bolshevik rulers, with the latter embodying an ideology radically opposed to the former. On the other hand, Kennan perceived continuity between the two regimes, with each supposedly being influenced by the same historical forces. Kennan's article further revealed that he believed in a distinctly Russian deceitfulness, a legacy of the ancient past:

> Again, these precepts are fortified by the lessons of Russian history; of centuries of obscure battles between nomadic forces over stretches of vast unfortified plain. Here caution, circumspection, flexibility and deception are the valuable qualities; and their value finds natural appreciation in the Russian or the oriental mind.[12]

Passages like these suggest not simply that a Russian mind exists but that its nefarious qualities are permanent because of unchanging, deeply rooted historical conditions. In his original telegram, Kennan stressed that the Russian people are not hostile by nature but on the contrary are quite friendly to the outside world and eager to live in peace. It was to the Soviet leadership that he attributed the worst fundamental characteristics. He referred to the whole of Russia's leaders, past and present, as deeply insecure about their type of antiquated regime. He alleged that they were threatened by the West's greater competence. The rulers thus feared any contact between their own people and the West. He concluded with the chilling assertion that Russian leaders had learned to seek security only in a patient, deadly struggle for the total destruction of a rival power. They never, he proclaimed, sought accord with those rivals. If they did, it was only temporary and borne out of necessity.

Naturally, Kennan was insightful enough to accept the possibility that the Bolshevik system could change. He further recognized that, because of the Bolsheviks' deterministic ideology, they were unlikely to risk a cataclysmic war. But with such sweeping, categorical depictions, it was not at all surprising that his long telegram and subsequent article found many fans.[13] American Secretary of State Dean Acheson would later write: "His historical analysis might or might not have been sound, but his predictions and warnings could not have been better."[14] Strong statements about other peoples typically appeal to policymakers seeking simple guidelines. It was equally unsurprising that his prescriptions would be distorted from patient economic and diplomatic containment to an unrealistic, overzealous military doctrine of combating Soviet influence wherever it emerged. The remarkable aspect of Kennan's analysis was that it succeeded in predicting anything accurately about Kremlin behavior. When Kennan relied on reductive generalizations about Russian history and the character of Russian leaders, he omitted key facts and ignored evidence that would have forced him to qualify his claims. But when he generalized about the contemporary crop of Soviet leaders, his insights proved more trenchant. This is because while national character traits obviously exist, their consistency throughout a population is highly variable, and their salience in decision-making processes is only partial at most. Consequently, relying on national characteristics as a heuristic for prediction is of minimal utility. In contrast, when people willingly adopt an ideology and devote themselves to it as true believers, demonstrating that they are capable of killing or dying in the name of their beliefs, then it is perfectly possible to make certain predictions about their likely behavior. Kennan understood how Marxism-Leninism could affect its purest ideologues. His long telegram was premised on the belief that the current and future Kremlin occupants would doggedly adhere to their espoused convictions.

There was a problem, however, with the more persuasive part of Kennan's assessment. His heuristic of using Marxist-Leninist ideology as a predictor of Kremlin behavior rested on several assumptions. First, all Kremlin leaders would be devoted Marxist-Leninists, given to the same interpretation of that ideology. Second, those leaders could not change their views as circumstances and contexts changed. Third, power impelled all individuals and organizations to behave in similar fashion. In other words, if the enemy believed it had the ability to achieve a particular objective, it would act on that belief.

The results of these assumptions are predictable: tension and conflict. Not long after the Crowe and Kennan memoranda, World War I and the Cold War ensued. Obviously, a great many factors combined to produce these conflicts, but assumptions about the enemy's nature were an essential part of the mix.

Codes of Conduct

In the wake of Kennan's telegram, as the Cold War heated up, analysts devoted enormous energy to understanding and, with luck, predicting Soviet behavior. One of the hubs of Sovietology, where Kremlin-watchers scrutinized every aspect of Soviet society, was the RAND Corporation, a think tank headquartered in Santa Monica, California. In 1951, a RAND analyst named Nathan Leites authored a book titled *The Operational Code of the Politburo*.[15] He later developed those ideas in a subsequent book called *A Study of Bolshevism*.[16] Leites aimed to reconstruct how Soviet leaders thought—their operational code—based on key Marxist-Leninist texts and compared to Soviet behavior. Though his concept was slow to catch on, in 1969 the operational code was resurrected by the noted Stanford political scientist Alexander George. George applied the code to the study of political leaders' belief systems more generally.

One of the striking aspects of George's presentation of the code is that Soviet beliefs appear remarkably similar to those of American decision-makers. For example, the Bolsheviks' first strategy was said to be one that pursued graduated objectives, yet avoided adventures.[17] In other words, gain as much as you can, but don't be reckless. The code further stated, according to George, that Bolsheviks must "push to the limit" —engage in pursuit of an opponent who begins to retreat or make concessions—but "know when to stop." George cited Charles Bohlen, one of America's famed "wise men" in foreign policy and a Soviet specialist. Bohlen pointed to one of Lenin's adages that national expansion is like a bayonet drive: "If you strike steel, pull back; if you strike mush, keep going." Put another way, the Soviets would seek to maximize their gains in any encounter, but they would not push beyond what seemed reasonable in the face of strong resistance.

The difficulty, of course, was that these maxims were scarcely different from those employed by any statesmen in diplomacy and war. They were hardly unique to Bolsheviks in particular or communists more broadly. The operational code was an attempt to demystify the underlying drivers of Soviet behavior, but it had the opposite effect of cloaking the Soviets in the veil of a unique cognitive framework. Under closer scrutiny, the enemy's thinking did not sound all that different from that of American leaders.

Some of the code described Soviet aggression as based on a Marxist notion of historical inevitability, but this notion was so vague that it could hardly serve as much of a guide for action. According to the code, Marxists were instructed to bide their time indefinitely yet at the same time to seize any opportunity to advance their cause. This may well have been what Marxist dogma advised, but it did not help outsiders to predict which course the Party would pursue in any given context. Would it be patient or proactive? As George put it: "Action, therefore, tends to be either required or impermissible; there is nothing in between." Statements such as these offered outsiders (non-Bolsheviks) little concrete guidance and no predictive power.

More than this, however, the operational code overshadowed the fact that internal debates and Party factionalism were often crucial factors in Soviet policy outcomes, except during the period when Stalin's decisions went largely uncontested. In 1923, for example, it was Stalin who advised against pushing for revolution in Germany, while Trotsky and Zinoviev urged the revolution onward. At that time the latter two won out. The operational code would not have helped German statesmen to know what the Kremlin was likely to do because the decision depended more on the underlying drivers of those with the greatest influence at that moment. America's postwar Kremlin watchers obviously understood this, for they microscoped every shift in top personnel and dissected every statement from Moscow's leaders. Having a general idea of how Bolsheviks understood their own ideology sounded sensible, but the operational code lacked sufficient context to be of genuine value.

The most troubling aspect of the code was its notion that the Soviets perceived compromise as weakness. "When an opponent begins to talk of making some concessions or offers them, it should be recognized that this is a sign of weakness on his part. Additional and perhaps major gains can be made by continuing to press the opponent under these circumstances." George acknowledged that observations such as these lack "operational content," but while they cannot be readily applied in concrete situations, they probably represent "a valuable part of the cognitive and affective makeup of a good Bolshevik." These maxims beg the question: Do any statesmen fail to press an advantage? The larger issue, of course, is that enemies are frequently assumed to view attempts at compromise as signs of weakness. With this assumption as a starting point for understanding the enemy, compromise solutions are rapidly excluded.

Whenever an enemy is thought to view compromise as weakness, the prescription must always be at least steely resolve and at worst intransigence. Standing up to aggression is of course crucial. The problem is not with the prescription; the problem is with the analysis. The assumption is that the enemy always intends to be aggressive—to push until the other side yields. Therefore, all of the enemy's actions are interpreted as such, and a compromise solution is precluded.

Despite the problematic aspects of Leites's concept, many political psychology scholars have embraced his operational code as a useful means for understanding foreign policy decision-making. From studies in the 1970s by Margaret Hermann[18] and Ole Holsti,[19] to more recent works by Stephen G. Walker and Mark Schafer, scholars have sought to unravel the codes of statesmen from Bill Clinton and Tony Blair to Saddam Hussein and Kim Il Sung. At times, political psychologists have even sought to analyze the frequency and usage patterns of particular words that leaders employ in their public pronouncements.[20] These scholars acknowledge that speech writers and other government officials typically craft major policy addresses, not the leaders themselves. Nonetheless, those who dissect word usage believe that their methods can reveal hidden clues to a leader's worldview and future actions. Part of the impetus behind these projects is the desire to demonstrate that the beliefs of individual statesmen matter in policy formation—a fact that few historians would dispute but one that some international relations theorists cannot accept.

All statesmen have particular leadership styles, and these styles can and often do affect foreign policy decision-making. Leadership style is one factor among many that influences policy formation and outcomes. The same is true of worldviews. All statesmen have them, and their views impact policy. Beneath the superficial level of leadership style, and deeper down below the realm of worldviews, lies a single or small set of core drivers—the motivations most vital to a leader. These are the ambitions that propelled that person to seek and maintain a leadership role. They are the raison d'être of leadership, and they are specific to each statesman. At times of crisis, when the stakes are highest, a statesman's underlying drivers are revealed. Strategic empathy is the skill one needs to spot and comprehend them.

Crowe, Kennan, Leites, and many other policy analysts all committed the fundamental attribution error, convincing themselves and the statesmen they served that they truly grasped the enemy mind.[21] Scholarship on differing cultural norms can certainly provide insights into a group's behavior, but it cannot serve as a reliable guide to understanding the underlying drivers of individual foreign leaders.

These analysts simultaneously employed the continuity heuristic in formulating their policy recommendations. Crowe looked to prior German actions as the best guide to future behavior: "For there is one road which, if past experience is any guide to the future, will most certainly not lead to any permanent improvement of relations with any Power. . ." He concluded that because of an essentially aggressive German nature and Germany's rising power, British concessions could never be fruitful.[22] Similarly, in his long telegram, Kennan argued that the Soviets' pattern of past behavior clearly indicated the course of their future behavior. The type of analysis that both men used was strikingly akin.

The root problem with the continuity heuristic is that it identifies a behavior pattern, such as productivity or aggressiveness, without clarifying why that behavior exists. In contrast, the pattern-break heuristic focuses our attention on what underlies that behavior. It suggests why the enemy was aggressive in the first place by spotlighting what is most important to that individual or group.

The Empty Couch

The continuity heuristic is, of course, not simply applied to groups: Germans, Bolsheviks, or others. Statesmen and their advisors have often made similar assumptions about individuals. In 1965, the U.S. Central Intelligence Agency (CIA) established a division to assess the psychology of foreign leaders. It was a daring project, for it required psychoanalyzing individuals without the subject's presence.

At first, this group was housed within the CIA's division of medical services, but soon it migrated to the Directorate of Intelligence, the part of the agency that deals with analysis (as opposed to operations).

The Center for the Analysis of Personality and Political Behavior recruited highly-trained psychologists and other experts in the behavioral sciences to scrutinize foreign leaders' biographies. The teams of psychobiographers were tasked with inspecting a leader's early childhood and later life experiences, all in the hope of drafting a composite picture of that person's character. With good reason, presidents and principals (the heads of American national security departments) wanted to know what made foreign leaders tick.

For twenty-one years, Jerrold Post headed this division. In his book about psychobiography, he explains that his Center focused on the key life events that shaped each leader. Post makes the assumption behind the Center's work explicit:

> Moreover, one of the purposes of assessing the individual in the context of his or her past history is that the individual's past responses under similar circumstances are, other things being equal, the best basis for predictions of future behavior.[23]

As I argued above, scrutinizing past behavior does not tell you what you truly need to know. It cannot reveal someone's underlying drivers. At best it can provide reasonable predictions only if future conditions are sufficiently similar to prior conditions. Unfortunately, in international affairs, the most crucial decisions are typically made under dramatically new settings, when old patterns are being upended and standard procedures overthrown. At such times, what statesmen need is heuristics for discerning their opponent's underlying drivers—the things that the other side wants most. Psychobiographies can be helpful in many realms, such as determining an individual's negotiating style or understanding his personal quirks, but they are less valuable when statesmen need to anticipate an enemy's likely actions under fresh circumstances.

The history of twentieth-century conflicts has been marked by the inability to gain a clear sense of one's enemies. Grasping the other side's underlying drivers has been among the most challenging tasks that leaders have faced. The analysts discussed above were by no means fools. They were smart, sober-minded students of international affairs, but they sometimes lacked an essential component to policymaking: a deep appreciation for what drives one's enemies. Much of their difficulty stemmed from two flawed assumptions. First, the other side possessed a rigid, aggressive nature. Second, past behavior was the best predictor of future actions. Both assumptions not only proved to be untenable, they also helped to create a dynamic out of which conflict was more likely to flow.

If the twentieth century saw frequent cases of the continuity heuristic, the twenty-first has begun with its own form of mental shortcuts: an excessive faith in numbers. Modern advances in computing, combined with increasingly sophisticated algorithms, have produced an irrational exuberance over our ability to forecast enemy actions. While mathematical measures can offer much to simplify the complex realm of decision-making, an overweighting of their value without recognizing their limitations will result in predictions gone horribly awry. The crux of those constraints rests upon our tendency to focus on the wrong data. And although that mental error is not new to the modern era, it has been magnified by modernity's advances in technology. Our endless longing to use technology to glimpse the future might be traced back to the start of the 1600s, when a small boy wandered into an optics shop, fiddled with the lenses, and saw something that would change the world.

9

Number Worship
The Quant's Prediction Problem

NO ONE KNOWS PRECISELY how Hans Lippershey came upon the invention. One legend holds that some children wandered into his spectacle shop, began playing with the lenses on display, and suddenly started to laugh. Tiny objects far away appeared as though they were right in front of them. The miniscule had become gigantic. Though the truth of that tale is doubtful, the story of the telescope's invention remains a mystery. We know only that four centuries ago, on October 2, 1608, Hans Lippershey received a patent for a device that is still recognizable as a modern refractory telescope.[1]

Not long after Lippershey's patent, the device found its way to Pisa, where it was offered to the duchy for sale. Catching wind of this new invention, Galileo Galilei quickly obtained one of the instruments, dissected its construction, and redesigned it to his liking.[2] Galileo intended it, of course, for stargazing, but his loftier intentions were not shared by the Pisans. This new tool had immediate and obvious military applications. Any commander who could see enemy ships at great distance or opposing armies across a battlefield would instantly gain a distinct advantage. That commander would, in effect, be looking forward in time, and, with that literal foresight, he could predict aspects of the enemy's actions. The telescope offered its owner a previously unimaginable advantage in battle. It brought the invisible to light. It altered the perception of time. It presented a genuine glimpse into the future, beyond what the naked eye could see. We don't know whether

Lippershey, Galileo, or some other crafty inventor made the first sale of a telescope to a military, but when he did, that exchange represented one of the earliest mergers of Enlightenment science with the business of war. From that moment on, modern science has been searching for ways to extend its gaze into the future, and militaries have been eager to pay for it.

In the seventeenth century, merely gaining an early glimpse of the enemy's actions was enough to advantage one side over the other. By the twentieth century, strategists needed much more. They needed greater predictive power for anticipating enemy moves. Technology alone could not, and still cannot, fill that gap. Strategists have always needed to develop a sense of the enemy, but the craving for more concrete, reliable predictions has left militaries easily seduced by science. Lately, that longing has led them to focus on the wrong objective: predicting the unpredictable.

The Numbers That Count

The rush is on to quantify as much as possible and let the algorithms tell us what the future holds. While this method offers obvious advantages, it is not without serious pitfalls. In many realms of prediction, we often go astray when we focus on the facts and figures that scarcely matter, as Nate Silver has shown in his thoughtful, wide-ranging study, *The Signal and the Noise*. Silver is America's election guru. He has rocketed to prominence for his successful forecasts of U.S. primary and general election results. In his book, Silver concentrates on those predictions reliant on large, sometimes massive, data sets—so-called "big data." Silver himself dwells mainly in the realm of number crunchers. He quantifies every bit of data he can capture, from baseball players' batting averages to centuries of seismologic records, from poker hands to chessboard arrangements, and from cyclone cycles to election cycles. In short, if you can assign a number to it, Silver can surely crunch it.

After four years of intensive analysis, Silver concludes that big data predictions are not actually going very well. Whether the field is economics or finance, medical science or political science, most predictions are either entirely wrong or else sufficiently wrong as to be of minimal value. Worse still, the wrongness of so many predictions, Silver says, tends to proliferate throughout academic journals, blogs, and media reports, further misdirecting our attention and thwarting good science. Silver contends that these problems mainly result from our tendency to mistake noise for signals. The human brain is wired to detect patterns amidst an abundance of information. From an evolutionary perspective, the brain developed ways of quickly generalizing about both potential dangers and promising food sources. Yet our brain's wiring for survival, the argument goes, is less well-suited to the information age, when too much information is inundating us every day. We cannot see the signal in the noise, or, more accurately put, we often fail to connect the relevant dots in the right way.

Silver urges us to accept the fallibility of our judgment but also to enhance our judgment by thinking probabilistically. In short, he wants us to think like a "quant." A quant—someone who seeks to quantify most of the problems in life—adheres to an exceedingly enthusiastic belief in the value of mathematical analysis. I use the term *quant* with respect, not simply because mathematical agility has never been my own strength and I admire this ability in others but also because I recognize the tremendous value that mathematics brings to our daily lives.

Naturally, not everything is quantifiable, and assigning probabilities to nonquantifiable behaviors can easily cause disaster. Part of what makes Silver's book so sensible is that he freely admits the value in combining mathematical with human observations. In his chapter on weather forecasts, he observes that the meteorologists themselves can often eyeball a weather map and detect issues that their own algorithms would be likely to miss. And when discussing baseball players' future fortunes, Silver shows that the best predictions come when quants and scouts can both provide their insights. Software programs as well as human observations can easily go awry, and errors are most likely to occur when either the computer or the person is focused on the wrong data. If the software is designed to project a minor league pitcher's future strike-outs but fails to include information on the weakness of the batters that pitcher faced, then the pitcher will be in for a rough ride when he reaches the major leagues. By the same token, scouts who assess a player's promise by the athlete's imposing physique might overlook some underlying flaws. Though he does not state it directly, Silver finds that scouts do better when they focus on pattern breaks. "I like to see a hitter, when he flails at a pitch, when he takes a big swing and to the fans it looks ridiculous," one successful scout told Silver, "I like to look down and see a smile on his face. And then the next time—bam—four hundred feet!" There's no substitute for resilience, and it can best be seen at those times when things don't go as planned.[3]

While prudent, thoughtful quantification can serve us well in many areas, it cannot be applied in every area. As a case in point, toward the close of his book, Silver turns to intelligence assessments, drawing specifically on the failure to predict the attacks on Pearl Harbor and 9/11. On the one hand he advocates that intelligence analysts must remain open to all possibilities, particularly by assigning probabilities to all imaginable scenarios, no matter how remote they might seem. On the other hand, he assumes that analyzing individuals is a less profitable endeavor. Silver writes: "At a microscopic level, then, at the level of individual terrorists or individual terror schemes, there are unlikely to be any magic bullet solutions to predicting attacks. Instead, intelligence requires sorting through the spaghetti strands of signals . . ." Of course it is true that we have no magic bullets. Statesmen do, however, possess ways of improving their odds. Rather than mining the trove of big data for patterns in their enemies' behavior, or sorting through a sticky web of conflicting signals, statesmen can focus instead on the moments of pattern breaks. Again, it is obvious that this will not guarantee successful predictions, but it can help illuminate what the enemy truly seeks.

As a quant, Silver is understandably less comfortable analyzing how individuals behave. His forte is calculating how groups of individuals are likely to behave over the long run most of the time. Here then is a crucial difference between the type of predictions made by Silver and his fellow quants and those predictions made by statesmen at times of conflict. Quantitative assessments work best with iterative, not singular, events. The financial investor, for example, can come out ahead after years of profits and losses, as long as his overall portfolio of investments is profitable most of the time. Depending on the arena, a good strategy could even be one that makes money just 60 percent of the time, as is a common benchmark in personal finance. The same is true of the poker player, baseball batter, or chess master. When the game is iterative, played over and over, a winning strategy just has to be marginally, though consistently, better than that of a coin flip. But leaders, in painful contrast, have to get it right this one time, before lives are lost. In the dangerous realm of international conflict, statesmen must be 100 percent right when it matters most. They cannot afford to repeat again and again the Nazi invasion of Russia or the American escalation in Vietnam. Unlike in competitive poker, the stakes in this setting are simply too high.

The political scientist Bruce Bueno de Mesquita is arguably the king of quants when it comes to predicting foreign affairs. Frequently funded by the Defense Department, Bueno de Mesquita insists that foreign affairs can be predicted with 90 percent accuracy using his own secret formula. Of course, most of his 90 percent accuracy likely comes from predictions that present trends will continue—which typically they do.

The crux of Bueno de Mesquita's model rests largely on the inputs to his algorithm. He says that in order to predict what people are likely to do, we must first approximate what they believe about a situation and what outcomes they desire. He insists that most of the information we need to assess their motives is already available through open sources. Classified data, he contends, are rarely necessary. On at least this score, he is probably correct. Though skillful intelligence can garner some true gems of enemy intentions, most of the time neither the quantity nor the secrecy of information is what matters most to predicting individual behavior. What matters is the relevant information and the capacity to analyze it.

The crucial problem with Bueno de Mesquita's approach is its reliance on consistently accurate, quantifiable assessments of individuals. A model will be as weak as its inputs. If the inputs are off, the output must be off—and sometimes dramatically so, as Bueno de Mesquita is quick to note on his own website: "Garbage in, garbage out." Yet this awareness does not dissuade him from some remarkable assertions. Take for example the assessments of Adolf Hitler before he came to power. Bueno de Mesquita spends one section of his book, *The Predictioneer's Game*, explaining how, if politicians in 1930s Germany had had access to his mathematical model, the Socialists and Communists would have seen the necessity of cooperating with each other and with the Catholic Center Party as the only means of preventing Hitler's accession to Chancellor.[4] He assumes that Hitler's opponents could easily have recognized Hitler's intentions. He further assumes that the Catholic Center Party could have been persuaded to align against the Nazis, an assumption that looks much more plausible in a post–World War II world. In 1932, the various Party leaders were surely not envisioning the future as it actually unfolded. Their actions at the time no doubt seemed the best choice in a bad situation. No mathematical model of the future would likely have convinced them otherwise. Assessments are only as good as the assessors, and quantifying bad assessments will yield useless, if not disastrous, results.

None of this means that all efforts at prediction are pure folly. Bueno de Mesquita's larger aim is worthy: to devise more rigorous methods of foreseeing behavior. An alternative approach to his quantitative metrics is to develop our sense for how the enemy behaves. Though less scientific, it could be far more profitable, and it is clearly very much in need.

Quants are skilled at harnessing algorithms for spotting pattern recognition and also pattern breaks. But their methods work best when their algorithms can scan big data sets of iterative events, focusing on the numbers that truly count. Anyone who has ever received a call from a credit card company alerting her to unusual activity on her account knows that MasterCard and Visa employ sophisticated algorithms to identify purchasing patterns and sudden deviations. This is a realm in which computers provide enormous added value. But in the realms where human behavior is less amenable to quantification, we must supplement number crunching with an old-fashioned people sense. It is here that meaningful pattern breaks can contain some clues. Perhaps surprisingly, within the heart of America's defense establishment, one man and his modest staff have spent decades refining their strategic empathy. Their successes, as well as their failures, offer useful tips for those who would predict their enemies' behavior.

Yoda in the Pentagon

In October 1973, Arab states attacked Israel with overwhelming strength in numbers. The Egyptians deployed some 650,000 soldiers—a massive military force in its own right. Syria, Iraq, and other Arab states added another quarter of a million troops. Against these 900,000 enemies Israel could muster no more than 375,000 soldiers, and 240,000 of those were from the reserves. But the war was really a battle of tanks, and on this score the numbers looked even more daunting. Israel's 2,100 tanks confronted a combined Arab fleet of 4,500.[5] On the northern front when the war began, Syria massed 1,400 tanks against 177 Israeli—a crushing ratio of eight to one. Given the extraordinary disparity of force, after Israel recovered from initial losses and decisively won the war, most Western observers interpreted the conflict as proof of Israel's unbreakable will to survive. Yet when Andrew Marshall and his staff analyzed the numbers, they saw something else entirely.

Tucked into a nondescript section deep within the Pentagon's labyrinthine rings, the Office of Net Assessment had just been created the previous year. Studying the war's less glamorous details and drawing on the substantial research of others, Marshall and his team discovered an Egyptian army with a Soviet-style flaw. The entire military was astonishingly short on maintenance. When one of its tanks became damaged in battle, Egypt had no effective means for repairing it. Israel, in contrast, had well-trained technicians able to make rapid repairs. It turned out that on average Israeli tanks returned to battle three times, but Egyptian tanks were used only until damaged. In other words, the initial number of tanks was not the number that mattered.

Superior force, by standard measures, did not win. The number that truly counted was the one that revealed a tank's likely longevity. Counting tanks before the war was a necessary but insufficient exercise. It didn't tell observers what they needed to know in order to assess the net strength of each side in the conflict. "What impressed me about the '73 War," Marshall explains, "was how asymmetric it was. Israel was not only much better prepared to recover and repair its tanks, it also dominated the battlefield, making recovery possible."

When Marshall and his analysts next looked at the Soviet Union's capacity for repairs, they found that the United States had a distinct and meaningful advantage. The bulk of the Soviet forces were comprised of conscripts, young men compelled to serve for two years in the army or three in the navy. Most were poorly trained and lacking technical know-how. American soldiers, conversely, were given better, longer, and more specialized training. Each unit working on ships or aircraft contained men able to perform some repairs when necessary. The Soviet military didn't work that way. Most of the time, when an engine or other critical part of an aircraft, tank, or ship malfunctioned, the Soviets had to send that part back to a depot or factory for repair. The Soviet Air Force, for example, purchased six engines for each engine position on its aircraft. The United States bought only one and a quarter—a dramatic cost-saving measure when multiplied by thousands of planes. Those costs, of course, counted not just in rubles but in time. The Soviet delays in servicing aircraft parts meant that American planes would be available more of the time when needed most.

Likewise, American ships had on-board crews that could make repairs on the spot, but Soviet naval crews did not possess the same level of maintenance training. The longer their ships were at sea, the less effectively they would function. The numbers of ships in each side's fleet was not important. Marshall recognized that less obvious asymmetries mattered far more. The simple and seemingly insignificant difference in repair capabilities meant that Soviet forces would come under extreme pressure during a protracted conflict.

Ensuring that America could continue to strike and engage the Soviets in a prolonged military conflict meant that the United States would ultimately have the advantage. It was this type of thinking that contributed to America's Cold War strategy. In Marshall's case, the insight derived not from sophisticated algorithms but from unorthodox thinking about how best to compare competing military forces.

The Office of Net Assessment (ONA) director, Andrew Marshall, once a mathematical whiz kid, has one overriding mission: to assess the balance between competing militaries. At age ninety-two (that is not a typographical error), Marshall is not merely sharp but deeply engaged in running ONA's affairs. The office churns out countless reports analyzing military and strategic issues ranging across the globe, examining everything from advances in neuro-pharmacology to Swedish innovations in submarine design to the future of microrobot warriors, always with an eye to their impact on American national security. The fact that Marshall has remained ONA's sole director since its inception, serving eight Presidents and more than a dozen secretaries of defense over the past forty years, suggests that he either is exceedingly astute at political survival, provides a product of substantial value, or both.[6]

During the Cold War, Marshall and ONA paid careful attention to the numbers and patterns that mattered most—the ones that constrained enemy behavior. Many credit Marshall with contributing to the policy of spending the Soviet Union into bankruptcy. He allegedly encouraged keeping long-range bombers in service while developing a new generation, both of which forced the Soviets to invest in costly air defense systems, though Marshall would not confirm this. Perhaps it was this seeming inscrutability, maybe his political longevity, or simply his age that earned him the affectionate nickname "Yoda."

Trained as an econometrician (essentially, an economic quant), Marshall later switched fields to mathematical statistics because he objected to the then-dominant view in economics of rational decision-making. The notion that *Homo economicus* always sought and was informed enough to maximize benefits did not accord with Marshall's view of human behavior. It has taken economics decades to come around, grudgingly, to a more flexible view embodied in the emerging subfield of behavioral economics.

Early in his career, Marshall himself performed some number crunching to useful effect. After a brief teaching stint at the University of Chicago, Marshall married his facility with numbers to a study of national security. In 1949, he joined a project at RAND to study mental illness. Many at the time believed that modern societies were prone to higher rates of psychosis. During World War II, it appeared that a large number of soldiers were rejected from service for psychological reasons—a larger proportion than in World War I. If this reflected a general trend, then a still larger proportion would be rejected for service if the United States had to mobilize again. The implications were troubling. Analyzing a century's worth of data, Herbert Goldhamer with Marshall's assistance concluded that no significant rise in serious mental illness in the United States had occurred.[7]

The mental illness study was precisely the kind of nontraditional investigation at which RAND excelled. Its scholars moved beyond missile counting to explore the many other societal dimensions on which wars were fought and won. They asked the questions that others never dared. RAND in those days differed from the typical defense establishment think tanks. Although it focused predominantly on the Soviet Union and strategic issues surrounding nuclear war, it cultivated a free-flowing intellectual environment. The average age of its analysts was twenty-seven. These were energetic, inquisitive men, tackling the big questions of strategy in a nuclear age. And at that moment in history, the field was wide open. Too many military men and policy pundits were obsessed with missile counting—constantly weighing the balance of American and NATO forces against those of the Warsaw Pact states. RAND was different. It brought together many of the top young intellects working on strategy, and it offered them considerable latitude to explore fresh avenues of inquiry. It was within this intellectual incubator that Marshall developed some of the methods he would later apply to analyzing the Soviet military throughout the Cold War.

Part of ONA's mission is to recognize and gauge the impact of long-term trends. Marshall's background at RAND clearly contributed to this type of focus. In the 1950s, one of Marshall's RAND colleagues, Charlie Hitch, made a curious but seemingly innocuous observation. Hitch, a Harvard-trained Rhodes scholar who worked for the Office of Strategic Services during the Second World War, had been teaching at Oxford before RAND lured him away to its headquarters in Santa Monica. Studying 200 years of data, Hitch saw that America's economy had grown at a rate of roughly 1 percent more than Britain's annually. In any single year, or even within a span of a decade or more, the impact of this variation in growth rates would not be significant. But Hitch's point was that over a century or longer, the impact would be profound. Financial dominance would mean military dominance. It would result in the supplanting of Britain by America as a global superpower. It was not a foregone certainty that America would overtake Britain as it did. Many populous, resource-rich nations do not achieve great power status for countless reasons. Hitch believed that modest, sustained economic growth was one key cause of American ascendance. Though initially inconsequential, the net effect over time of a mere 1 percent difference would prove a monumental advantage.[8] That 1 percent was a number that counted. It was, at least for Hitch's purposes, the information that mattered most, for it graphically underscored the link between economic and military might. This type of analysis—the search for underlying drivers and constraints—shaped the training grounds on which Marshall flourished.

In 1972, Andrew Marshall was serving on the National Security Council under Henry Kissinger when President Nixon ordered the creation of a new group within the Council, one that Marshall would later lead. This group would be charged with an entirely different mission: it would look ahead to the strategic environment that the military would likely face in a decade's time. It would assess the trends affecting America's position vis-à-vis its peer competitor. It would scrutinize the relative strengths and weaknesses of the United States and the Soviet Union, as well as that of their allies. Understanding the net balance in these competitions enabled strategists to ask what opportunities were being missed, which strengths needed to be bolstered, and which weaknesses could be exploited. It also helped strategic planners to envision how adversaries might assess and attack America's vulnerabilities.

In November 1973, the group moved into the Pentagon to become the Office of Net Assessment. Marshall has remained its director ever since. ONA's reports, most of them highly classified, would be written for the highest-level decision-makers: the Secretary of Defense and his deputies.

From 1976 to 1978, ONA's attention turned to Soviet strategy in northern Europe. In contemplating the Soviets' likely moves in a European war, U.S. experts assumed that part of Soviet strategy would involve an attack down through Norway. The Barents Sea port at Murmansk represented Russia's western-most border of northern Europe in the divided Cold War world. If Soviet forces moved aggressively at any point along the borders between NATO and Warsaw Pact states, the United States was committed to a rapid deployment of ten American divisions to reinforce the central front of NATO—a massive and costly undertaking.

Most strategists assumed that the Soviets would send their attack submarines into the Atlantic in order to disrupt American deployments, but some military observers had noticed a surprising anomaly in Soviet naval operations. Although American attack submarines were positioned to intercept Soviet subs if they moved out from the Barents Sea, the Soviets were holding their subs back. They were not conducting operations as expected. Something didn't add up. This curious break in the pattern of Soviet behavior quickly drew the Pentagon's attention.

"One of the things that happens from time to time," Marshall told me in a windowless Pentagon meeting room, "is that you have to revise your entire notion of how your opponent sees things." After reviewing fresh analysis of Soviet doctrine and intentions, Marshall concluded that the Soviets actually saw this whole region in largely defensive terms.

"I remembered something that Norwegian military officials had said to me a decade earlier in 1964," he continued. "They realized that the Soviets must have viewed that sea region as essential to their air defense perimeter, and they would want to push their air defenses out." The Soviets, Marshall concluded, wanted to create and protect a bastion for their strategic missile submarines as well.

The surprising Soviet behavior could easily have been misinterpreted as aggressive. Any deviation from the norm in Soviet military operations raised grave concerns about what the Russians were up to. A spiral of action and reaction could then easily have led to heightened Cold War tensions, or worse. Focusing on pattern breaks can never guarantee that the correct analysis of that behavior will result. Instead, pattern-break moments provide an opportunity to reassess our beliefs about what the enemy really wants.

"Your view of what the enemy is up to and what he is thinking can shift very rapidly," Marshall says. "New data can surprise you and cause you to revise both your assessment of the enemy and the appropriateness of your strategy."

No high-tech computer algorithms were needed to change the U.S. perceptions of Soviet behavior. Years of studying Soviet strategy were necessary but not sufficient. The insight that Soviet strategy in the North Sea was defensive, not offensive, came instead by observing a meaningful pattern break in Soviet behavior. When the analysts encountered surprising new information, they took it seriously, rather than dismissing it because it did not conform to expectations. And after reassessing what they knew, they had to change what they believed.

Yet even the most ardent true believers in predictive prowess, quantitative or not, have had to admit that foreseeing massive changes, such as societal transformations, is still a distant dream. ONA's own foresights have not always been correct.

The Russian Riddle

In 1988, America's foremost strategic thinkers met at Harvard to cast their eyes just twenty years ahead. Marshall presided over the gathering, and many of his protégés contributed their expertise. In a studious final report summarizing their discussions, the experts soberly concluded that by 2008 the Soviet economy will have probably declined.[9]

They were right.

If in-depth analysis of a society's underlying trends truly aids prediction, many people have asked why those who were most invested in predicting international affairs—experts in government like Marshall or scholars of international relations theory—failed so stunningly to foresee the Soviet Union's demise. Marshall maintains that his office came closer than others in seeing the decline of the Soviet Union, though it did not predict the collapse.

According to Marshall, in 1988 the Central Intelligence Agency estimated that the Soviet economy stood at approximately 60 percent of the U.S. economy. ONA, in contrast, recognized it as not more than a third or a quarter the size of the U.S. economy. Experts at the time underestimated the percentage of the Soviet gross domestic product (GDP) devoted to military spending. Most thought it was only around 12 percent. ONA believed correctly, Marshall says, that it was actually about 30 to 35 percent. Nonetheless, he admits that he was surprised by the events just one year after the Harvard conference. He told *Wired* magazine: "I thought they were in trouble, but the rapidity and completeness of the withdrawal were really striking."[10]

Marshall and ONA have fared better when focused on the nearer-term future and specifically when assessing an enemy's underlying constraints. Foreseeing the Soviet Union's collapse was not possible, but neither was it necessary. Understanding Soviet behavior and influencing its decisions proved more useful. Whether it was in recognizing the implications of Soviet maintenance and repair capabilities, or its approach to its air defenses, ONA's ability to think like the enemy, to step out of the American mindset and into another's, represented true value. This is the skill set that America clearly needs more of in waging its current conflicts.

The Future of Futuring

One of President Barack Obama's rude awakenings came just two years into his first term, when the revolutions that spread from Tunisia and sparked the Arab Spring caught the American intelligence community mostly unawares. Despite an annual budget of roughly $80 billion—about the current GDP of Iraq—the analysts provided virtually no advanced warning of the upheavals. As administration insiders told *The New York Times*, the President let them know he was not happy about it. But this frustration was born of unreasonable expectations.[11] Just as ONA and all the experts failed to foresee the Soviet Union's demise, today's American intelligence community could no better anticipate the revolutions that shook the Arab world. Quantitative analysis is unlikely to assist because such dramatic episodes are not iterative, and no large data sets are likely to reveal a pattern for pinpointing the timing, scope, or nature of a revolution. Revolutions are launched by people, and people are notoriously diverse in the degree of oppression they are willing to endure. What we can do, instead, is to focus our attention on predicting the behavior of individuals and small groups, not with probability but with heuristics based on their underlying drivers and constraints.

The ability to get out of our own minds and into the heads of others is one of the oldest challenges we all face. It's tough enough to do with people we know well. Attempting it with those from foreign cultures is immeasurably harder. It should be obvious that even small-scale, individual actions can never be perfectly anticipated since so much of human behavior rests on contingencies and chance. That said, we can still enhance our strategic empathy by retraining ourselves to approach prediction differently. We may never find an algorithmic oracle that can reliably predict societal upheavals. But we can improve our strategic empathy for individuals and governments, beginning by focusing on meaningful pattern breaks. Even a modest refinement in our ability to think like others could have substantial payoffs both in winning wars and, more crucially, in sustaining peace.

Conclusion

Moon Over Miami

Kadeesha had a tip. It arrived by anonymous e-mail. "Watch the 9:20 race at Wolverhampton. The winner will be a horse called Boz."

Kadeesha was instructed not to place a bet; she was merely to watch. She had never put money on the races before. In fact, she had no history of gambling. Why would she, of all people, be receiving this tip? A single mom in Kew, England, working two jobs to support her son, Kadeesha barely had enough income to cover the monthly bills. "I never had a large sum of money," she explained, "'cause it always goes out 'cause of all the responsibilities I've got in life." But the sender insisted that he possessed a foolproof system for consistently predicting the winners at the race track. "I was gutted that I couldn't put a bet on, but I checked it out and it won."

Kadeesha was intrigued. The next e-mail came a few days later. Again it predicted the result of a race just twenty-four hours in advance, this one at Suffolk Downs in Boston. How could this "system" know anything about a race in America? Kadeesha figured, "I'm up for a laugh," and this time, as instructed, she put a small amount of money on Laced Up. Though not the favorite, her horse won again.

Now Kadeesha was hooked. When the third e-mail came, she zoomed out from her desk at work to the nearest betting shop. She put down 20 quid, which for her was not a small sum, on a horse named Naughton Brook, an eighteen to one outsider. Nervous and excited, she repeated to herself, "This had betta' win. Oh, God, this had betta' win." As the announcer declared the winner, Kadeesha shrieked, "Thank you, The System!" She had just won 360 pounds.

Race four took place back at Wolverhampton. The 2:45, a horse called Formation. The odds of correctly predicting four of these races in a row stood at nearly a thousand to one. But Formation did win, and Kadeesha had now made over 500 pounds. The System, it seemed, could not lose.

After race five, Kadeesha's confidence in The System had solidified. She was now ready to put down serious dough. She went to her father to ask for 1,000 pounds. "The most I ever put on a horse was 20 quid," her father told her, "and when I lost it, I said that's it. Never again." Nonetheless, the predictions had been right so far. Kadeesha then borrowed more money from a loan company. For race six she had assembled 4,000 pounds. She bet it all on Moon Over Miami, the horse in the green and white checks. "I'm really, really scared now," she admitted to the TV cameras filming her story. The worst part, she confessed, was gambling her father's money as well as her own.

What Kadeesha did not know but was about to discover was that The System was simply an exercise in probability. Derren Brown, a British entertainer, wanted to demonstrate how difficult it is for most of us to think rationally about prediction. No such system could exist for accurately predicting horse races, yet Kadeesha and thousands more like her are willing to believe in a bogus ploy. Soon after his first anonymous e-mail, Brown informed Kadeesha that he was the actual sender. She then agreed to let him film her as she bet her money. But what Brown did not reveal (not yet) was that the same e-mail Kadeesha initially received Brown had also sent to 7,775 other randomly selected people. The only difference in all those e-mail messages was that the recipients were divided into six groups and each group was given the name of one of the six horses in the race. Kadeesha just happened to be in the group that was told to watch for Boz. The five groups whose horses did not win were sent a follow-up e-mail, blaming the loss on a glitch in the system. They were never contacted again. Kadeesha's group, however, was then subdivided into another six groups, each given the name of one of the six horses in a new race, and instructed to bet. And thus the process was repeated, until by the fifth race, only six participants remained, each one betting on a different one of the six horses. Kadeesha just happened to be the lucky winner. By race six, however, she was the only one left. Moon Over Miami had as good a chance of winning as any other.

"Fuckin' hell!" was all Kadeesha could muster after Brown explained what he had done. "I'm gonna' be sick," she declared. And yet, even after the explanation, Kadeesha seemed in disbelief. "I was lucky all this time and now it's all gone wrong."

Moon Over Miami did not win. The lucky horse was Marodima.

Only moments after Kadeesha's horse had lost and her agony was plain, Derren Brown assured her that he had not actually bet her money on the unlucky steed. With dramatic flare, Brown handed her a ticket showing 4,000 on Marodima to win. (Most likely, he had put 4,000 down on each of the horses, just to be certain.) Kadeesha was about to receive 13,000 pounds in cash. She shrieked for joy. "I'm debt free for the first time in eight years!"

Brown's experiment tried to show how poorly most of us grasp basic concepts of probability. What he actually revealed was something he himself might not have realized. Kadeesha always had the upper hand, and she very likely sensed it. She had no way of knowing whether Brown's so-called system was legitimate or not. She probably lacked a firm grounding in the science of probability. What she really needed to know, however, was not whether Brown's system could find her the winning horse. Instead, she needed to know whether Derren Brown would permit her to lose her and her father's savings on national TV.

Kadeesha had two ways of thinking about what Brown would likely do. She could have tried to ascertain Brown's character, observing subtle cues to gauge his kindness and compassion—the underlying drivers that make him tick. The second method was for Kadeesha to contemplate the limits on what Brown could actually do, regardless of his inclinations. With this approach Kadeesha had to focus on Brown's constraints. The key question then would be not whether Brown, of his own volition, would let her lose, but whether his television network or the British TV-viewing public would permit a working-class single mom to be ruined by a clever TV host.

Kadeesha may not have had the skills to think deeply about the probability of predicting races, but rather than being a sucker for "The System," Kadeesha may have worked the system—the larger social system in which both Brown and Kadeesha have to function. Moon

Over Miami had little chance of winning, but placing her money as Brown instructed her to do proved the shrewdest guess she could have made.

We will never know what Kadeesha really thought, but we can use her predicament to illuminate the kinds of questions leaders face when thinking like the enemy. Exactly like Kadeesha, leaders must seek out their adversaries' underlying drivers and constraints. They must gather information, filter out the ocean of irrelevant data, and devise shortcuts for locating the points that matter most. I have called this exceedingly difficult endeavor strategic empathy.

Kadeesha's story also highlights a related problem in prediction. Quantitative methods often miss the mark because they calculate the wrong data, as I described in the previous chapter. Even if Kadeesha had possessed training in statistics, math, or the science of probability, seeing through Brown's system would have done her little good. Kadeesha walked away a winner: 13,000 pounds richer than before. Moon Over Miami's fate never mattered. The only odds that counted were the ones on what Brown would do to her in the public eye. And those odds were probably always in her favor. Knowing which data matter most is what strategic empaths do best.

I began this book by asking what produces strategic empathy—the crucial yet all-too-rare capacity for divining an enemy's underlying drivers and constraints. I have argued that when leaders focused on the right data—their enemy's behavior at pattern-break moments—they improved their chances of reading their enemies correctly. When they ignored the pattern breaks entirely, or else grossly misinterpreted them as in Stalin's case regarding Hitler, they thwarted their capacity for accurate assessments. I further argued that when leaders assumed that their opponents' future behavior would resemble their past behavior, they hindered their own ability to identify and correctly interpret surprising new information, which could have afforded them useful insight.

Mahatma Gandhi's recognition that the British leadership was not evil, as he frequently stated, but in fact remorseful over the Amritsar massacre emboldened him to pursue a strategy of aggressive nonviolence. He could do this in full faith that British authorities would not permit the repeated slaughter of unarmed, peaceful protestors.

He understood that British leaders were vulnerable to his brand of disobedience precisely because they could not stomach rule by tyrannical oppression. Against a Hitler, a Stalin, and possibly even a Le Duan, Gandhi's strategy could not have prevailed. But against the post–World War I set of British leaders, nonviolent resistance, or what Gandhi sometimes called "love force," had a genuine chance to succeed. The House of Commons debate on General Dyer's deeds made that plain.

In the turbulent 1920s, Stresemann's ability to read his opponents, particularly the Russians, greatly facilitated his task of maneuvering Germany back to equal status with the European powers. Gauging the Kremlin's drivers was especially challenging at this time in part because power was shifting in the wake of Lenin's illness and then death. As Stalin gradually consolidated his authority, Stresemann had to determine whether Stalin's pronouncements of socialism in one country were sincere. Would spreading communist revolution to Germany, as had been attempted in 1923, be subordinated to the interests of technological and military modernization in cooperation with Germany? By observing Soviet behavior after Scheidemann's embarrassing revelations, Stresemann recognized that he could continue the secret military collaboration without much fear of renewed revolutionary agitation against his government.

Yet Stresemann's acumen involved more than this. He mentalized in a thoughtful manner. He gradually constructed a picture of Soviet intentions during a time of change, as Trotsky was being out-maneuvered by Stalin for control of the regime. No doubt precisely because power was shifting inside the Kremlin, Stresemann wisely remained open to the possibility that Soviet objectives were in flux.

Stresemann faced the same type of conflicting information about his enemies that nearly all leaders confront. It was easy to build an argument that the Soviet regime was bent on spreading communist revolution to Germany and overthrowing the government. It was equally plausible, based on a separate pattern of behavior, that the Soviet regime wanted military cooperation with Germany. If Stresemann had assumed a fixed nature to the Soviets, as George F. Kennan and many of his contemporaries later would do, he might not have been receptive to the break in Soviet behavior that accompanied the Scheidemann affair. Instead, Stresemann saw that the Soviet leadership of 1926 was not the same as the leadership of 1923. Continuing the two countries' secret rearmament now mattered more than fomenting a German revolution. No one could say what the farther future would bring, but at least for the short and medium term, the Kremlin under Stalin favored military cooperation, and Stresemann had the strategic empathy to grasp this.

It is painfully evident that Stalin grossly misread Hitler's intentions in 1941, but he also misread Hitler's underlying drivers more generally. Stalin's strategic autism cost an estimated 20 million Russian lives and widespread devastation across eastern Europe. The Soviet leader's profound inability to understand Hitler was rooted in the specific way he mentalized. By employing simulation theory, Stalin projected his own form of rationality onto his opponent. Because Stalin would never have risked his power by waging a two-front war if he had been in Hitler's position, Stalin assumed that Hitler would be driven by the same calculations. But Hitler was primarily driven by his racist ideology. He was willing to risk his power, his life, and his nation's fate in order to achieve his twisted dogmatic ends. Stalin's further use of German history convinced him that Hitler would act in accordance with prior German leaders: avoiding a two-front war. In effect, Stalin employed the continuity heuristic, assuming that the behavior of past German leaders could predict the behavior of present and future German leaders. In short, he did exactly the opposite of what a good strategic empath should do—the opposite of what Stresemann had done. Stalin mentalized by simulation theory, and he relied on the continuity heuristic to interpret information. What he needed instead was to mentalize by employing the pattern-break heuristic. He should have focused on Hitler's behavior during two pattern-break moments: Night of the Long Knives and Kristallnacht.

If Stresemann and Stalin represent the two extreme ends on the strategic empathy spectrum, then the North Vietnamese leader Le Duan would fall closer to the middle. On the eve of American escalation in Vietnam, Le Duan accurately grasped America's most salient underlying constraints: its vulnerability to high numbers of casualties, its difficulty in maintaining support for a protracted war, and its distracting global commitments. This recognition shaped not only Hanoi's strategy but also the war's outcome. The Party leader further identified American actions surrounding the Tonkin Gulf incident as a provocative prelude to escalation. Yet while he was successful in spotting America's constraints, there is little evidence that he truly comprehended what drove President Johnson and his advisors. Because Le Duan is known as an austere Marxist ideologue, it is tempting to conclude that he could only view the Americans through that ideological lens. But given Le Duan's considerable efforts to understand his principal adversary, it is unlikely that he allowed his ideology to serve as his only means of thinking about America—his ample Marxist rhetoric notwithstanding.

Does He Sting, or Only Roar?

Entering another's mind is hard enough when we know that person well. It is vastly harder when that person comes from a foreign culture, speaks a foreign tongue, and thinks in ways distinctly different from ourselves. I have tried to show that the pattern-break heuristic enhanced leaders' ability to think like their enemies and that this ability affected key conflicts in the past century. Yet the pattern-break heuristic is not simply a tool of the past. It can be just as useful to present-day policy analysts seeking to predict their adversaries' likely actions. Although analysts should not overweigh the expected payoffs of this approach, they should weigh heavily the value of surprising information. When routine trends are broken and individuals behave in unexpected ways, that information can reveal more about an opponent's root ambitions than his actions under normal conditions. This is primarily true when an opponent's actions impose costs upon himself.

Just as the pattern-break heuristic can aid analysts contemplating the future, it can also assist historians examining the past. As I noted in the section on Gustav Stresemann, historians still debate the Foreign Minister's true objectives. Similar debates are common among most other historians struggling to comprehend why their particular subjects acted as they did. For the scholar and the policymaker alike, such disagreements are common because leaders frequently behave in complex, sometimes seemingly contradictory ways. Experts can then point to evidence to support competing interpretations of that leader's intentions. If we instead concentrate on behaviors at meaningful pattern breaks, we may come closer to exposing a historical figure's deeper aims.

All of this raises the question of whether individuals possess fixed or fluid motivations. This turns out to be a nontrivial problem, one that dates back at least to ancient Greece.

Most people know the fable of the scorpion and the frog. A scorpion asks a frog for a ride across the lake, but halfway across the water the scorpion strikes. As both are drowning, the frog asks the scorpion why he stung him, knowing it meant that both of them would die. The scorpion responds that he couldn't help himself. It was just his nature. The original tale probably traces back to Aesop, who related the same parable through a farmer and a viper, but the moral was the same. Some people just can't change their wicked ways.

The scorpion story would be a tremendously depressing commentary on human nature if it were not offset by another of Aesop's fables, one with a strikingly alternative lesson. In the story of Androcles and the lion, a slave in ancient Greece escapes his captors and flees into the woods. There he comes upon a roaring beast. Whereas others might have fled in terror, Androcles overcomes his initial fear and approaches the animal. He discovers that the lion has a painful thorn caught in its bleeding paw. Once he removes the thorn and binds the wound, the lion is not only grateful, he develops a genuine warmth for the human. Later, both the lion and the slave are captured. As punishment, Androcles is thrown into the arena, where the hungry lion is sent to devour him while the emperor and crowds look on in savage expectation. But when the lion rushes toward his prey, he recognizes Androcles. Rather than tearing him apart, the lion licks Androcles's hand in friendship. The moral Aesop had in mind had to do with gratitude. But the story conveys another equally important lesson. Sometimes our enemies are not enemies by nature but because of conditions external to themselves. They can be transformed into allies simply by a change in circumstance.

These two tales can easily serve as metaphors for a recurring debate within foreign policy circles. Leaders are frequently confronted by aggressive states. They must then devise strategies for dealing with them. It would be just as foolish to assume that all opponents are potential allies as it would be to think that all are implacable foes. One of the most crucial tasks of statecraft is to distinguish the scorpions who cannot change from the lions who can. It is here that pattern breaks can help.

Strategic empathy might seem useful only for getting the better of your opponent. Certainly that was its value to the leaders I described throughout this book. But strategic empathy can be used just as effectively to avoid or ameliorate conflicts. It can be a means not for outmaneuvering the enemy but instead for making amends. Obviously, some enemies cannot be accommodated. Some differences can never be bridged, but many can. Understanding what truly drives others to act as they do is a necessary ingredient for resolving most conflicts where force is not desired. It is, in truth, an essential first step toward constructing a lasting peace.

Afterword

Fitting In: Some Thoughts on Scholarship, Sources, and Methods

WARNING: THIS AFTERWORD IS intended for academics. I want to describe to them how this book fits in with the existing literature on decision-making and prediction as well as to explain how the findings from related fields have informed my own work. The title is slightly tongue-in-cheek, since fitting in is something I have never done well. Because this book does not resemble a traditional work of history, I need to explain my particular methodological approach and the sources I employ. If you are not an academic, you might want to avoid this afterword altogether. Alternatively, if you are not a scholar but you suffer from severe insomnia, then please read on. This chapter might just be the cure you've been searching for.

Skeptics and Signals

Though most of us long to know the future, especially in troubled times, lately behavioral scientists have been shattering our crystal balls. The noted psychologist Philip Tetlock has been widely cited for revealing that the more renowned the expert, the more likely his predictions will be false.[1] The Harvard psychologist Daniel Gilbert tells us that we cannot even predict what will bring us joy, since our expectations are almost always off.[2] And the gleefully irreverent market trader Nassim Taleb argues that the massive impact of black swans—improbable but surprisingly frequent anomalies—makes most efforts at prediction fruitless.[3] Most notable of all, the economist Dan Ariely has exposed the flawed models for predicting our behavior in everything from the products we buy to the daily choices we make.[4] Of course, they're all right. We are abysmal at prediction. But the skeptics have missed a crucial point: we have no other choice.

National leaders are always in need of thoughtful approaches to prediction, especially when lives are on the line in matters of war and peace. We therefore need to have some sense of what scholars from a range of disciplines have learned about predictions in general and enemy assessments in particular. One of the most recent observers to find fault with the prediction business is Nate Silver, the election guru whose work I described in chapter 9.[5] Silver is only the latest thinker to tackle the question of how we can enhance our predictive prowess. Much of this work has involved, in one form or another, the question of discerning signals amid noise. Writing in 1973, the economist Michael Spence asked how an employer can distinguish potential good employees from bad ones before hiring anyone.[6] Spence proposed that good and bad employees signal to employers by dint of their educational credentials. More recently, the sociologist Diego Gambetta has used signaling theory to understand criminal networks.[7] Gambetta observes, for example, that a mafia must be especially prudent before including members into its organization. If candidates are not carefully vetted, the mafia might enlist an undercover police officer. By asking new recruits to commit a murder, the mafia imposes a substantial cost upon the undercover agent, who, presumably, would be unwilling to pay that price. A genuine would-be mobster, in contrast, can signal his commitment with a single shot. In Colombia, youth gangs have even been known to require that prospective members first kill one of their closest relatives to prove their sincerity. Imposing high costs upon ourselves is one way of signaling what we value.

Another economist who focused on asymmetric information, George Akerlof, examined the market for used cars. In 1970, he suggested that because used-car buyers have no easy means of knowing the quality of a particular car, they will pay only what they believe to be the price of an average used car of a given model and year. As a result, owners of high-quality used cars (ones that were barely driven and well-maintained) will refuse to sell because they will not get the price they deserve, thereby reducing the overall average quality of used cars on the market. Although assessing enemy behavior and buying used cars are dramatically different realms, Akerlof's notions do suggest the dangers that result from assuming that the seller (or the enemy) is of low quality. In chapter 8 we saw what happens when statesmen and their advisers project negative qualities onto their opponents without an accurate understanding of the other side.

One obvious difference between these studies in economics and sociology on the one hand and the history of international relations on the other is that much of the time foreign leaders do not want to signal their true commitments. The strategic empath must therefore locate ways of identifying an adversary's drivers amidst conflicting signals. Nevertheless, the idea of costs is useful. At meaningful pattern breaks, statesmen make choices with significant costs to themselves and with likely long-term implications. These actions can be valuable signals to foreign statesmen, even though they are unintentionally transmitted.[8]

The natural sciences have also aided our understanding of prediction through the development of information theory. John Archibald Wheeler, the physicist who coined the term "black hole," is also famous for crafting the catchphrase "it from bit." Wheeler was a leading light in the development of nuclear fission, having studied under Niels Bohr and later having taught Richard Feynman. When Wheeler uttered his pithy slogan in 1989, he intended to imply that all matter as well as energy, the whole of our universe, emerged from information. The bit is a particle that cannot be split. Everything, in the end, reduces to information. But it was Claude Shannon, father of information theory in computer science, who truly brought about the information turn in scientific study.

Shannon recognized that not all information is created equal. To test this, he pulled a Raymond Chandler detective novel from his bookcase and read a random passage to his wife: "A small oblong reading lamp on the——." He asked Betty to guess which word came next. She failed to guess correctly at first, but once he told her that the first letter was *d*, the rest was easy. It was more than mere pattern recognition that mattered here. Shannon wanted to show that the information that counted most came before the missing letters, whereas the letters that followed the *d* in *desk* were of lesser value. For Shannon, information equaled surprise. The binary digits, or "bits," as they came to be known, that mattered in any message were the ones that gave us something new or unexpected.[9] It was a valuable insight, and one with applicability across fields. The historical cases in this book bore this out. Each case examined the particular bits of surprising information on which leaders focused and why that focus helped or hindered them.

Evolutionary biology, specifically regarding the literature on theory of mind, is equally important for historians of decision-making. The classic experiment on theory of mind involves researchers who placed a candy in front of two little girls. We'll call them Sally and Jane. The researchers then covered the candy with a box so it could not be seen. While Jane exited the room, the researchers removed the candy from under the box and hid it elsewhere, while leaving the box in place. When Jane returned, they asked Sally where Jane thinks the candy is located. Below the age of four most children think that Jane, the girl who did not see the candy being removed, will somehow know that the candy is no longer under the box. Most children believe that everyone else knows what they themselves know. It turns out that only after children reach the age of four do they discover that each of us has a distinct perspective on the world, shaped by access to different information. Before that age, children do not possess "theory of mind." They cannot imagine that someone else does not possess the same knowledge or perspective that they themselves do.

Compelling as they are, these theories have real limits when it comes to understanding the kinds of complex decisions that statesmen face. Although the theory of mind shows how we develop a kind of mental empathy—the ability to see things from another's point of view—this work was initially centered on primates and very small children. That said, there does exist work of relevance to statecraft. In a paper by Alison Gopnik and others, for example, researchers describe the differences between two common ways in which we predict the actions of others.[10] Most people, it seems, assume that past behavior is the best indicator of future behavior. If someone lied in the past, for example, that person can be expected to lie again. But others take a different view. Some people place greater weight on the current context. They do not discount past behavior, but they ask how the present context is likely to affect another's actions. In my own study of statecraft, I find that the leaders who succeeded most at anticipating enemy actions incorporated analysis of both prior patterns and current context, but they heavily weighted the information gleaned at certain moments.

One other scientific contribution bears indirectly, though significantly, on this book. Ray Kurzweil, the scientist who developed speech recognition software (and who is now the Director of Engineering at Google), has advanced a theory of how our brains function. In his 2012 book, *How to Create a Mind*, Kurzweil proposes the pattern recognition theory of mind to explain how the neocortex functions.[11] Kurzweil points out that the primary purpose of our brains is in fact to predict the future through pattern recognition. Whether we are trying to anticipate threats, locate food sources, catch a ball, or catch a train, our brains are constantly performing complex calculations of probability.

Kurzweil asserts that the neocortex—the large frontal region of the brain where most such calculations are conducted—is composed of layers upon layers of hierarchical pattern recognizers. These pattern recognizers, he maintains, are constantly at work making and adjusting predictions. He offers the simple sentence:

Consider that we see what we expect to—

Most people will automatically complete that sentence based on their brain's recognition of a familiar pattern of words. Yet the pattern recognizers extend far deeper than that. To recognize the word "apple," for example, Kurzweil notes that our brains not only anticipate the letter "e" after having read a-p-p-l, the brain must also recognize the letter "a" by identifying familiar curves and line strokes. Even when an image of an object is smudged or partially obscured, our brains are often able to complete the pattern and recognize the letter, or word, or familiar face. Kurzweil believes that the brain's most basic and indeed vital function is pattern recognition.

This ability is exceptionally advanced in mammals and especially in humans. It is an area where, for the moment, we still have a limited advantage over computers, though the technology for pattern recognition is rapidly improving, as evidenced by the Apple iPhone's use of Siri speech recognition software. For a quick example of your own brain's gifts in this arena, try to place an ad on the website Craigslist. At the time of this writing, in order to prove that you are a human and not a nefarious robot, Craigslist requires users to input a random string of letters or numbers presented on the screen. The image, however, is intentionally blurred. Most likely, you will have no difficulty identifying the symbols correctly. Robots, in contrast, will be baffled, unable to make sense of these distorted shapes. For fun, try the option for an audio clue. Instead of typing the image, listen to the spoken representation of those letters and numbers. You will hear them spoken in a highly distorted manner amidst background noise. The word "three," for example, might be elongated, stressed, or intoned in a very odd way. "Thaaaaaaaaa-reeeeeeee." It sounds like the speaker is either drunk, on drugs, or just being silly. The point is that a computer program attempting to access the site could not recognize the numbers and letters when they do not appear in their usual patterns. Our brains possess an amazing ability to detect patterns even under extremely confusing conditions. But before you start feeling too smug, Kurzweil predicts that we have until the year 2029, when computers will rival humans in this and other regards. So enjoy it while it lasts.

Let me sum up this section: Kurzweil's theory suggests that pattern recognition is the brain's most crucial function, and our sophisticated development of this ability is what gives human beings the edge over other animals and, for now, over computers as well. I suggest that the best strategic empaths are those who focus not only on enemy patterns but also on meaningful pattern breaks and correctly interpret what they mean. Next, Claude Shannon's information theory shows that it is the new and surprising information that is more valuable than other data. I observe that pattern breaks are, in fact, markers of new and surprising information, possessed of greater value to leaders than the enemy's routine actions. Finally, the theory of mind scholarship provides ways of thinking about how we mentalize, or enter another's mind, which I employed throughout this book, but especially when scrutinizing how Stalin tried to think like Hitler.

Before we grow too enamored of all these theories, we should remember that theories are not always right. Often their proponents, in their well-intentioned enthusiasm, exaggerate the scope and significance of their discoveries. This is particularly true of some recent works in social science—studies that bear directly on the nature of prediction.

How Silly Are We?

One of the striking features infusing much of the recent social science scholarship on prediction is its tendency to expose alleged human silliness. Across fields as diverse as behavioral economics, cognitive psychology, and even the science of happiness or intuition, studies consistently show how poor we are at rational decision-making, particularly when those choices involve our expectations of the future. Yet too often these studies draw sweeping conclusions about human nature from exceedingly limited data. In the process, they typically imply that their subjects in the lab will respond the same way in real life. Before we can apply the lessons of cognitive science to history, we must first be clear on the limits of those exciting new fields. We should temper our enthusiasm and must not be seduced by science.

Consider one daring experiment by the behavioral economist Dan Ariely. Ariely recruited male students at the University of California Berkeley to answer intimate questions about what they thought they might do under unusual sexual settings. After the subjects had completed the questionnaires, he then asked them to watch sexually arousing videos while masturbating—in the privacy of their dorm rooms, of course. The young men were then asked these intimate questions again, only this time their answers on average were strikingly different. Things that the subjects had previously thought they would not find appealing, such as having sex with a very fat person or slipping a date a drug to increase the chance of having sex with her, now seemed much more plausible in their excited state. Ariely concluded from these results that teenagers are not themselves when their emotions take control. "In every case, the participants in our experiment got it wrong," Ariely explains. "Even the most brilliant and rational person, in the heat of passion seems to be absolutely and completely divorced from the person he thought he was."[12]

Ariely is one of America's most intriguing and innovative investigators of behavioral psychology. His research has advanced our understanding of how poorly we all know ourselves. And yet there is a vast difference between what we imagine we would do in a situation as compared to what we would actually do if we found ourselves in that situation. In other words, just because a young man in an aroused state says that he would drug his date does not guarantee that he truly would do it. He might feel very differently if the context changed from masturbating alone in his dorm room to being present with a woman on the real date. Can we be so certain that he really would slip the drug from his pocket into her drink? Or would he truly have sex with a very overweight person if she were there before him? Would he have sex with a sixty-year-old woman or a twelve-year-old girl, or any of Ariely's other scenarios, if he were presented with the opportunity in real life? Life is not only different from the lab; real life has a funny way of being rather different from the fantasy.

A great many recent studies suffer from a similar shortcoming. They suggest profound real-world implications from remarkably limited laboratory findings. In his wide-ranging book on cognitive psychology, Nobel Laureate Daniel Kahneman describes the priming experiments conducted by Kathleen Vohs in which subjects were shown stacks of Monopoly money on a desk or computers with screen savers displaying dollar bills floating in water. With these symbols priming their subconscious minds, the subjects were given difficult tests. The true test, however, came when one of the experimenters "accidentally" dropped a bunch of pencils on the floor. Apparently, those who were primed to think about money helped the experimenter pick up fewer pencils than those who were not primed. Kahneman asserts that the implications of this and many similar studies are profound. They suggest that ". . . living in a culture that surrounds us with reminders of money may shape our behavior and our attitudes in ways that we do not know about and of which we may not be proud."[13]

If the implications of such studies mean that American society is more selfish than other societies, then we would have to explain why Americans typically donate more of their time and more of their income to charities than do those of nearly any other nation.[14] We would also need to explain why some of the wealthiest Americans, such as Bill Gates, Warren Buffett, Mark Zuckerberg, and a host of billionaires, have pledged to donate half of their wealth within their lifetimes.[15] Surely these people were thinking hard about their money before they chose to give it away. We simply cannot draw sweeping conclusions from snapshots of data.

I want to mention one other curious study from psychology. Its underlying assumption has much to do with how we behave during pattern breaks. Gerd Gigerenzer is the highly sensible Director of the Max Planck Institute for Human Development and an expert on both risk and intuition. Some of his work, which he related in a book titled *Gut Feelings*, was popularized in Malcolm Gladwell's *Blink*. Gigerenzer has never been shy to point out perceived weaknesses and shallow logic in his own field. He has written cogently on the flaws embedded in Daniel Kahnemann's and Amos Tversky's heuristics and biases project.[16] Yet even Gigerenzer has occasionally fallen into the "how silly are we?" camp, though the following topic he certainly did not take lightly. Unfortunately, this particular study suggests that Americans behaved irrationally after 9/11, though their reactions may have been perfectly sound.

Gigerenzer found that American fatalities from road accidents increased after 9/11.[17] Because many Americans were afraid to fly in the year following the attacks, they drove instead. Presumably, the increased number of drivers increased the number of collisions, leading to roughly 1,500 more deaths than usual. Gigerenzer's main aim is prudent and wise. Governments should anticipate likely shifts in behavior following terrorist attacks and should take steps to reduce indirect damage such as greater accidents from changed behavior. But the underlying assumption is that many Americans cannot think rationally about probability. Gigerenzer implies that the decision not to fly after 9/11 was based on irrational fears. Had they continued to fly instead of drive, fewer Americans would have died.

The problem with such reasoning, as you've likely already guessed, is that it ignores the pattern-break problem. A statistician might argue that, despite the 9/11 hijackings, the odds of dying in a plane crash were still extremely low. But those odds are based on a prior pattern—prior to a meaningful and dramatic pattern break. After 9/11, Americans had to wonder whether other terrorist plots using airplanes were still to come. If the terrorists could defeat our security checks once, could they do it again? Given that these were the acts of an organization and not of a single, crazed individual, and given that the leader of that organization vowed to strike America again, it was wise to adopt a wait-and-see approach. The past odds of flying safely no longer mattered in light of a potentially ongoing threat. Without any means of determining how great that threat would be, driving was a perfectly rational alternative, even knowing that one's odds of dying in a car crash might rise. Until a new pattern is established (or a prior one returns), the odds of dying in a hijacked plane might be even higher.

In his article, Gigerenzer did observe that following the Madrid train bombings in 2004, Spaniards reduced their ridership on trains, but those rates returned to normal within a few months. Gigerenzer speculates that one reason might have been that the Spanish are more accustomed than Americans to dealing with terrorist attacks. In other words, the Madrid train bombings represented less of a pattern break than did 9/11.

Another way of thinking about this problem is to compare it with the horrific movie theater shootings in Aurora, Colorado, on July 20, 2012, in which a lone gunman shot twelve people to death and wounded fifty-eight others. As frightening as this incident was, it would not have made sense for Americans across the country, or even in Aurora, to have stopped attending films in theaters. The incident marked no new breach in security and no innovation in killing techniques. The same risk has long been present. The assailant operated alone, not as part of an international terrorist network. While there is always the chance of copy-cat attacks, it remained valid to consider the odds of being murdered in a movie theater based on the pattern of past killings in theaters or in public spaces in general. The Aurora attacks did not represent a meaningful break in the pattern of American gun violence. Like Spaniards and the Madrid train bombings, Americans have sadly become accustomed to episodes like these.

Judging probability is an excellent way of assessing risk only when we focus on the right data and recognize when the old odds no longer matter. The famed English economist John Maynard Keynes is often quoted for his snappy remark, "When the facts change, I change my mind. And what do you do, sir?" I would offer a variation of Keynes's quip.

When the pattern breaks, I change my behavior.

How about you?

My goal in this discussion is not to disparage the work of behavioral scientists. On the contrary, their work can help us challenge the assumptions we have too long taken for granted. My aim instead is to caution us against carrying the implications of such studies too far. The experiments of behavioral scientists can help guide our thinking about how we think, as long as we remain cognizant of the gulf between labs and real life.[18] And here is where I believe historians can add true value.

The Standard Works

Although history holds great potential for understanding how we think, historians typically focus their studies on how one or two particular individuals in a narrow time period thought. For example, the historian might derive deep insight into the thinking of key historical figures, such as Abraham Lincoln or John Brown. Alternatively, historians might trace a particular historical event across time, such as the slave trade or the abolition movement, scrutinizing its many causes and consequences. As a result, they might comprehend how large groups of people thought about a particular subject over time. Rarely, however, do historians attempt to investigate types of thinking across both time and space—meaning at various historic moments in various regions of the world. That is what this study of historical decision-making aimed to do.

In contrast, the subfield of political science known as international relations often examines disparate cases of conflict across time and space, but it does so with definite theories it seeks to prove. Beginning with the assumption that nations relate to each other according to fixed laws of behavior, international relations scholars aim to advance, refine, or refute existing theories. When such theories are actually grounded in richly corroborated historical sources, awareness of these theories can be highly useful to the historian because they can alert us to common patterns in international conflict as well as cooperation.

This book does not advance a theory of how states behave—at least not in the traditional sense. My argument is both generalizable and parsimonious, but it is not predictive. It does not suggest that if x and y occur, then z will result. Instead, this book makes observations about how particular cases of twentieth-century conflict unfolded. It draws modest conclusions about how certain leaders have thought about their enemies, and it does this by probing a handful of key clashes.

Fostering a sense of the enemy typically involves gathering information specifically on intentions and capabilities. By examining these two elements of power, the experts believe they can comprehend or even anticipate that adversary's behavior. This categorization is, however, far too narrow. A more inclusive categorization focuses instead on drivers and constraints.

The first step in strategic empathy involves a cold assessment of constraints. We look first not at what the other side might want to do but at what it is able to do based on context. Capabilities are not constraints. Capabilities are what enable us to achieve our wants, but constraints are what render those capabilities useless. The worst strategic empaths think about capabilities in mainly military terms. They count missiles and tanks, factor in firepower, and dissect strategic doctrine for clues to enemy intentions. If China today builds an aircraft carrier, it must be planning to challenge America on the high seas . . . or so the thinking goes. But military capabilities, just like intentions, are often constrained by nonmilitary factors, such as financial, political, organizational, environmental, or cultural impediments to action. Even something as ineffable as the *Zeitgeist* can be a powerful constraint, as Egyptian President Hosni Mubarak and Libyan leader Muammar Gaddafi recently discovered, much to their regret. The best strategic empaths seek out the less obvious, underlying constraints on their enemy's behavior as well as their own.

Once the underlying constraints are grasped and it is clear that the enemy actually has room to maneuver, strategic empaths then turn to exploring the enemy's key drivers. (In reality, of course, most leaders cannot set the order in which they assess these factors. Typically that analysis occurs in tandem or in whichever order circumstances allow.) If intentions are the things we want to do, drivers are what shape those wants. We can be driven by an ideological worldview, such as communist, capitalist, or racialist dogma. We can be driven by psychological makeups, with all the myriad complexes and schema they entail. Or we could be driven by religious and cultural imperatives: to conquer the infidels, to convert the heathens, or to Russify, Francofy, or democratize the Other. Political scientists have produced a vast literature on enemy intentions. Each scholar offers an ever more nuanced explication of how states signal their intentions and how other states perceive them. Yet intentions are best anticipated, and strategic empathy is best achieved, when the underlying drivers are clearly understood.

International relations has a long tradition of scholarship on recognizing enemy intentions. As this discipline is frequently concerned with how states manage threats in foreign affairs, it has developed numerous studies dealing specifically with the failure to predict correctly. More often than not, states are caught off-guard when prior trends are broken. Blame then falls first upon the spies. A body of literature on intelligence failures has recently cropped up. These studies deal in part with assessing enemy intentions, but they are largely America-centric, spurred by the failures to predict the 9/11 attacks and to correctly estimate the presence of Iraq's alleged weapons of mass destruction. These works include Richard Betts's *Enemies of Intelligence*,[19] Robert Jervis's *Why Intelligence Fails*,[20] and Joshua Rovner's *Fixing the Facts*.[21] One work focused primarily on assessing military threats is Daryl Press's *Calculating Credibility*, in which the author argues, unconvincingly in my view, that leaders do not concern themselves with an enemy's past behavior when determining the extent of that enemy's likely threat.[22] A more recent study of assessing enemy intentions that expands its scope to cover statecraft as well as intelligence agencies is the doctoral dissertation and now book by Keren Yarhi-Milo, *Knowing the Adversary*.[23] That author concludes: "Decision-makers' own explicit or implicit theories or beliefs about how the world operates and their expectations significantly affect both the selection and interpretation of signals."[24] In other words, our beliefs affect how we think.

A Sense of the Enemy is not part of this political science canon. Rather than focusing only on failure, it also studies success. Instead of positing theories, it seeks explanations for why events unfolded as they did. It moves beyond the America-centric or Anglocentric story by concentrating on German, Russian, Indian, and Vietnamese leaders as well as American statesmen. And it aims not primarily to improve intelligence work but instead to understand how one aspect of statecraft contributes to shaping historical outcomes.

In addition to the many political scientists who have tackled the problem of enemy assessment, most notable among them being Alexander George,[25] historians have also specifically sought explanations for how opponents understand each other. In *Knowing One's Enemies: Intelligence Assessments Before the Two World Wars*,[26] a cast of distinguished historians investigates the faulty intelligence estimates within all combatants prior to war. Again, this work centers on the intelligence assessments rather than the statesmen. It focuses on failures, not successes, and it does not ask the question: What enabled statesmen to think like their enemies?

In 1986, the editor of *Knowing One's Enemies* teamed up with another Harvard scholar, Richard Neustadt, to assist policymakers with a book called *Thinking in Time*. The authors drew upon recent American history at the highest levels of decision-making, mainly over four decades from Roosevelt to Reagan. By examining a series of case studies and analyzing what went right and wrong—but mostly what went wrong—they hoped to provide sensible guidelines that would help dedicated public servants to perform better. Their conclusions could hardly be faulted: challenge your assumptions, be wary of historical analogies, distinguish what is certain from what is presumed, and read as much history as you can. Within their narratives, they also revisited the question of how we can know our enemies. They urged policymakers to engage in "placement": the act of placing individuals in their historical context in order to determine which major events, both public and personal, shaped their worldviews. Placement, they argue, can offer clues to another person's views, including that person's opinions of others. Sensibly, the authors conceded that placing others in historical context cannot guarantee correct predictions about their actions. I could not agree more, but the question remains how to know which information matters.

At one point the authors give examples of the key bits of information that would have helped predict particular decision-makers' actions during the lead-up to American escalation in Vietnam. They argue, for example, that to understand Defense Secretary Robert McNamara, ". . . It appears worth knowing that he made his way at Ford and built his reputation there from a base in statistical control." Regarding the Secretary of State, Dean Rusk, the authors observe that it helps to know that Rusk had served in the Army in World War II and that General George C. Marshall was his hero and role model. "Each piece of information from the rest of personal history," they maintain, "enriches or enlivens guesses drawn from conjunctions of age and job."[27]

The crucial phrase here is "it appears worth knowing." It only appears worth knowing these facts in retrospect. It is far harder to know at the time which of the countless bits of data about a person's life will be most salient in shaping his actions in a given moment. Placing others in their historical context is essential to learning about them, but it cannot reveal that person's underlying drivers. The basic problem with Neustadt's and May's notion of placement is not that it suffers from "hindsight bias," the tendency to view outcomes as inevitable and predictable. While it is unreasonable for historians to look back at events and assume that their outcomes were foreseeable, it is perfectly legitimate for scholars to analyze what occurred and identify which information would have been useful at the time, regardless of the ultimate outcome. The real problem with "placement" is that as a guide for policymakers it is too diffuse. It leaves one with too much information and no guide to identifying the right chunk.

Methods and Sources

I did not begin this study with a hypothesis about pattern breaks. I started only with a question: What produces strategic empathy? When leaders do get it right, is their success random—a product of pure luck—or could there be a signal amidst the noise? After analyzing in depth the cases described in this book, I found one such signal: an enemy's underlying drivers and constraints became apparent at times of pattern breaks.

All decision-makers need heuristics for cutting through the excessive amount of data about their opponents to distinguish what moves them to act. This book focuses on pattern breaks as a heuristic for exposing hidden drivers. It is not intended primarily as a guidebook to policymakers, though if it could be of use to them, that can only be to the good. It is instead a study of history, yet it differs from standard histories in two main ways.

The first unorthodox aspect of this book is that, unlike traditional diplomatic histories, this study strives to incorporate the useful, recent findings in decision-making gleaned by other fields, especially those from cognitive neuroscience, information theory, and psychology. Like many historians, I am skeptical of sweeping generalizations drawn from limited data. Yet we cannot allow skepticism to produce obscurantism. We simply know much more today about how the mind works than we did in the 1980s when Neustadt and May were writing. If one goal of historians is to understand how their subjects were thinking—and that is certainly a major goal of this book—then we have a responsibility to be informed by advances in knowledge of the decision-making process. Naturally, we can only be informed by this knowledge; we cannot apply it indiscriminately to the figures we want to understand. Since we cannot place Hitler or Stalin inside an fMRI machine any more than we could place them on the psychologist's proverbial couch, we dare not draw definitive conclusions about how those figures thought. But what we can do is to use the historian's craft of combing the extant records, diaries, memoirs, and private and official papers and combine those concrete insights with an understanding of how most people process information. Again, we can never reach total certainty about how historical actors thought, but we can sometimes get pretty close. The rest is left to our own judgment about what is reasonable and likely.

This is, in fact, the approach taken by Christopher R. Browning in his thoughtful historical study of Holocaust murderers, *Ordinary Men*. In attempting to understand how these seemingly average individuals came to act as cold-blooded killers of innocent Jewish men, women, and children, Browning cautiously applies insights drawn from psychology. Most notably, he considers the lessons from two separate and equally shocking experiments conducted by Stanley Milgram and Philip Zimbardo, both of which explored questions of conformity and deference to authority. Yet Browning remains judicious in his application of these findings and modest in his conclusions. Here is how Browning explains both the limits and benefits of psychology to history:

> Was the massacre at Józefów a kind of radical Milgram experiment that took place in a Polish forest with real killers and victims rather than in a social psychology laboratory with naïve subjects and actor/victims? Are the actions of Reserve Police Battalion 101 explained by Milgram's observations and conclusions? There are some difficulties in explaining Józefów as a case of deference to authority, for none of Milgram's experimental variations exactly paralleled the historical situation at Józefów, and the relevant differences constitute too many variables to draw firm conclusions in any scientific sense. Nonetheless, many of Milgram's insights find graphic confirmation in the behavior and testimony of the men of Reserve Police Battalion 101.[28]

I believe that precisely this type of cautious yet open-minded approach is not only sensible but invaluable for studies of decision-making. Today, the historian has the benefit of more than just psychology for understanding how people think. In the twenty years since Browning wrote *Ordinary Men*, we have made astonishing advances in cognitive neuroscience and other related fields, all of which have expanded our knowledge of how the human brain functions.

The second curious aspect of this book is that it combines two forms of scholarship: original, primary-source historical research and interpretive essays reflecting how historical actors thought about their enemies. To accomplish this, the book draws on a wide range of English, German, Russian, and Vietnamese primary sources, many of which are published archival records, as well as the substantial secondary literature on relevant topics. Like all historians, I plumb the extant record, watch for corroborating evidence, try to ascertain causes and verify claims. But I also apply a conceptual framework to my analysis by focusing on the effects of pattern breaks on the way that leaders thought.

For the chapter on Gandhi's assessments of the British I draw heavily on the *Collected Works of Mahatma Gandhi*. I also use memoirs of one close to the Mahatma during the events in question, as well as British newspaper accounts and the *Hansard* transcripts of debates in the House of Commons.

For the section concerning Germany in the 1920s, I use materials as diverse as Reichstag session transcriptions, records of Cabinet meetings, newspaper accounts, and the diaries and memoirs of leading decision-makers. I harness all of the standard resources available to diplomatic historians, such as the *Foreign Relations of the United States* series, *Documents on German Foreign Policy*, and *British Documents on Foreign Affairs*, including the more selective *Confidential Print* series.

For the section on Roosevelt's and Stalin's attempts to think like Hitler, I rely on similar sources as noted above, as well as the reports of Under Secretary of State Sumner Welles in private communication with President Roosevelt on the Welles mission in 1940 to see Hitler and Mussolini. I tapped the Franklin D. Roosevelt President's Secretary's Files, particularly Parts I and II, with their records of correspondence between the President and the American Ambassador to Germany, William E. Dodd. I also consult the published Soviet archival documents concerning Stalin's intelligence on the eve of Operation Barbarossa, including materials from the Stalin Digital Archive.

In the section on North Vietnamese statesmen I employ a variety of newly available sources. The Vietnamese state has recently released a massive collection of Politburo and Central Committee directives, cables, and speeches (called the *Van Kien Dang*), providing the first official glimpse into Hanoi's decision-making over several decades. This section also makes use of official Vietnamese histories of its military and diplomatic corps. These include histories of the Foreign Ministry, the People's Army, the People's Navy, the Sapper Forces, the Central Office of South Vietnam, histories of combat operations, histories of the Tonkin Gulf incident, memoirs of prominent military and diplomatic officials, records of the secret negotiations with the Johnson administration, and some Vietnamese newspapers.

I have engaged all of these sources in an effort to gain purchase on how strategic empathy shaped matters of war and peace. I selected these cases both for their significance to twentieth-century international history and their capacity to illuminate strategic empathy's impact.

One of my goals in this book, as in my previous work, is to use history to help us understand how people think. Whereas the cognitive sciences can suggest much about our decision-making process in the lab, the study of historical decision-making can provide us with real-life subjects under genuine pressures. Historians must examine how people behaved not in the confines of controlled procedures but in the real world, where so much is beyond anyone's control. If we want to understand how people think, it makes sense to probe historical cases for clues. In this way, studies of historical decision-making can greatly complement the cognitive sciences.

Ultimately, history must never be a mere recounting of facts, strewn together into a story about the past. Instead, it must be used to advance our understanding of why events occurred and why individuals acted as they did. Viewed in this way, historical scholarship holds enormous practical value for anyone who seeks to comprehend the world around us. As the international historian Marc Trachtenberg put it, the aim of historical analysis is to bring forth the logic underlying the course of events. "In working out that logic," he writes, "you have to draw on your whole understanding of why states behave the way they do and why they sometimes go to war with each other."[29] Part of our understanding—our whole understanding—must come not only from assessing the structure of state relations at the systemic level, or by analyzing the domestic-level and organizational politics affecting state behavior, but also from a study of how individual leaders thought about the other side.

ACKNOWLEDGMENTS

MY FIRST AND DEEPEST thanks must go to the staff and fellows of Stanford University's Center for Advanced Study in the Behavioral Sciences. The Center is a magnificent environment for any scholar, and I greatly benefitted from my interactions with academics across a wide range of disciplines. The Andrew W. Mellon Foundation provided generous financial support during my stay there, enabling me to develop this project.

Many other colleagues and friends assisted me in this work, either by reading early drafts or by sharing their expertise. They include Nil Demirçubuk, Alison Gopnik, Christopher Goscha, Michael Hechter, Peter Hobson, Alec Holcombe, Dominic Hughes, Frances Hwang, Stephen Kosslyn, Robert Kurzban, Thomas R. Metcalf, Merle Pribbenow, Kristin Rebien, Sangeetha Santhanam, Arlene Saxonhouse, Stephen Schuker, James Sheehan, Marla Stone, Hanh Tran, Tuong Vu, Barbie Zellizer, and Peter Zinoman. I am also indebted to two reviewers for Oxford University Press who kindly waived their anonymity in order that we could discuss this manuscript. Both Robert Jervis and Aviel Roshwald provided incisive comments that have made this a much stronger book.

The staffs at Doe Library of the University of California at Berkeley and Knox Library of the Naval Postgraduate School were always exceedingly patient in helping me to locate occasionally obscure materials. At various stages in this project I received thoughtful and diligent research assistance from Anthony Le and Alfred Woodson. Toward the project's close Diana Wueger tenaciously tracked down key records, exhibiting a "never give up" spirit that I greatly admire. Leslie Chang deserves special mention. She assisted me in this project for nearly two years, straining her eyes on barely legible microfilm, poring over dusty, out-of-print volumes, and working with me for hours at a stretch. I was especially lucky to have found her.

Naturally, I am thankful to my editor at Oxford University Press, David McBride, and my agent, Will Lippincott. To all these individuals, I am truly grateful.

Zachary Shore
Berkeley, California
November 2013

NOTES

Introduction

1. See Dexter Filkins and Carlotta Gall, "Taliban Leader in Secret Talks Was an Impostor," *The New York Times*, November 2010. See also Joshua Partlow, "British Faulted for Taliban Impostor," *Washington Post*, November 26, 2010.

2. Malcolm Gladwell graphically illustrated the dangers of choosing the wrong slice. See Malcolm Gladwell, *Blink: The Power of Thinking Without Thinking* (New York: Back Bay Books, 2007).

3. Isaiah Berlin, "On Political Judgment," *New York Review of Books*, October 3, 1996.

4. Christopher Chabris and Daniel Simons, *The Invisible Gorilla: And Other Ways Our Intuitions Deceive Us* (New York: Crown, 2010), p. 38.

5. Jonathan Steinberg, *Bismarck: A Life* (New York: Oxford University Press, 2011), p. 11.

6. Christopher Chabris and Daniel Simons, *The Invisible Gorilla: And Other Ways Our Intuitions Deceive Us* (New York: Crown, 2010), p. 157.

7. See for example the classic work on the pitfalls of analogical reasoning: Yuen Foong Khong, *Analogies at War: Korea, Munich, Dien Bien Phu, and the Vietnam Decisions of 1965* (Princeton, NJ: Princeton University Press, 1992).

8. Henry Kissinger, *Ending the Vietnam War: A History of America's Involvement in and Extrication from the Vietnam War* (New York: Simon & Schuster, 2003), p. 71.

9. For a short overview of the Chernobyl accident see W. Scott Ingram, *The Chernobyl Nuclear Disaster* (New York: Facts on File, 2005).

10. Writing about U.S. strategy in the nuclear age, the historian Marc Trachtenberg makes a similar observation, namely that few people ever extend their reasoning processes to third- and fourth-order calculations. Marc Trachtenberg, *History and Strategy* (Princeton, NJ: Princeton University Press, 1991).

Chapter 1

1. For a thorough account of the massacre, see Nigel Collett, *The Butcher of Amritsar: General Reginald Dyer* (London: Palgrave, 2005).

2. "Congress Report on the Punjab Disturbances," *The Collected Works of Mahatma Gandhi* (New Delhi: Publications Division, Ministry of Information and Broadcasting) (hereafter *Collected Works*), vol. 17, pp. 114–292.

3. For a thoughtful essay on Gandhi's interactions with the British see George Orwell, "Reflections on Gandhi," in *A Collection of Essays* (New York: Harcourt, 1946).

4. *Collected Works*, vol. 18, pp. 89–90. From *Young India*, July 28, 1920.

5. Guha Chāruchandra (Khrishnadas), *Seven Months With Mahatma Gandhi: Being an Inside View of the Non-Co-Operation Movement* (Madras, India: Ganesan, 1928).

6. Mahatma Gandhi, *An Autobiography or the Story of My Experiments with Truth* (Ahmedabad, India: Navajivan Publishing House, 1927), p. 439.

7. William L. Shirer, *Gandhi: A Memoir* (New York: Simon & Schuster, 1979), p. 31.

8. Judith Brown argues that Gandhi used the massacre as a political issue to advance the cause of Indian self-rule. See Judith M. Brown, *Gandhi's Rise to Power: Indian Politics, 1915–1922* (London: Cambridge University Press, 1972), pp. 244–47.

9. *Collected Works*, vol. 18, pp. 89–90. From *Young India*, July 28, 1920.

10. *Collected Works*, vol. 17, p. 23–26. Before February 11, 1920.

11. *Collected Works*, vol. 17, p. 38. From *Young India*, February 18, 1920.

12. For other useful syntheses of Gandhi's actions and thinking at this time see Stanley Wolpert, *Gandhi's Passion: The Life and Legacy of Mahatma Gandhi* (New York: Oxford University Press, 2001); Barbara D. Metcalf and Thomas R. Metcalf, *A Concise History of India* (Cambridge, UK: Cambridge University Press, 2002); Louis Fischer, ed., *The Essential Gandhi: An Anthology of His Writings on His Life, Work, and Ideas* (New York: Vintage Books, 2002); Judith M. Brown, ed., *Mahatma Gandhi: The Essential Writings* (New York: Oxford University Press, 2008); Gene Sharp, *Gandhi as a Political Strategist: With Essays on Ethics and Politics* (Boston: Porter Sargent, 1979); Norman G. Finkelstein, *What Gandhi Says About Violence, Resistance, and Courage* (New York: OR Books, 2012). Finkelstein argues, as do many others, that Gandhi in part sought to strike at the conscience of the British people in order to make them see the wrong they had done to India.

13. *Collected Works*, vol. 16, p. 330. December 7, 1919.

14. *Collected Works*, vol. 16, p. 361. From *Young India*, December 31, 1919.

15. Collett, *Butcher*, p. 283.

16. Collett, *Butcher*, pp. 405–6.

17. "Amritsar Debate," *Times of London*, July 9, 1920. See also "Commons Scenes in Amritsar Debate," *Manchester Guardian*, July 9, 1920.

18. Arthur Herman, *Gandhi and Churchill: The Rivalry That Destroyed an Empire and Forged Our Age* (New York: Bantam Books, 2008), p. 254.

19. "Army Council and General Dyer," *Hansard*, July 8, 1920, pp. 1719–34. Available at http://hansard.millbanksystems.com/commons/1920/jul/08/army-council-and-general-dyer.

20. "Army Council and General Dyer," pp. 1719–34.

21. "Army Council and General Dyer," pp. 1719–34.

22. Herman, *Gandhi and Churchill*, pp. 393–98.

23. "Army Council and General Dyer," pp. 1719–34.

24. "Army Council and General Dyer," pp. 1719–34.

25. Collett, *Butcher*, p. 386.

26. Even in his later years, Gandhi remained attuned to the evolution of British attitudes. After the Second World War, he noted that a new type of Briton had come into being, "burning to make reparation for what his forefathers did." *Collected Works*, vol. 82, p. 155, on or after December 1, 1945.

27. Judith M. Brown, *The Cambridge Companion to Gandhi* (Cambridge, UK: Cambridge University Press, 2011), ch. 12, "Gandhi's Global Impact."

Chapter 2

1. Gustav Stresemann, *The Stresemann Diaries* (New York: MacMillan, 1935), preface.

2. The Nobel Foundation did not award a Peace Prize in 1925. In 1926 it retroactively awarded the Peace Prize of 1925 to Charles Dawes and Austen Chamberlain while simultaneously awarding the Peace Prize of 1926 to Stresemann and Briand.

3. Antonina Vallentin, *Stresemann* (London: Constable & Co., 1931), Foreword by Albert Einstein, pp. v–vi.

4. For an early important work on Locarno see Jon Jacobson, *Locarno Diplomacy: Germany and the West* (Princeton, NJ: Princeton University Press, 1971).

5. Vallentin, *Stresemann*, p. 26.

6. For a thorough overview of Chicherin's background, see Timothy E. O'Connor, *Diplomacy and Revolution: G. V. Chicherin and Soviet Foreign Affairs, 1918–1930* (Ames: Iowa State University Press, 1988).

7. Stephen White, *The Origins of Détente: The Genoa Conference and Soviet Western Relations, 1921–1922* (Cambridge, UK: Cambridge University Press, 1985).

8. White, *Origins of Détente*, p. 181.

9. Philipp Scheidemann, *The Making of New Germany: The Memoirs of Philipp Scheidemann*, vol. 2, trans. J. E. Mitchell (New York: D. Appleton, 1929), p. 355. According to Scheidemann, the Kassel police repeatedly warned him of threats to his life.

10. For a more recent account of Stresemann's anti-inflation policies, see Liaquat Ahamed, *Lords of Finance: The Bankers Who Broke the World* (New York: Penguin, 2009).

11. See Patrick Cohrs, *The Unfinished Peace After World War I: America, Britain, and the Stabilisation of Europe, 1919–1932* (Cambridge, UK: Cambridge University Press, 2006), pp. 112–13.

12. For more on the Buchrucker affair, see John Wheeler-Bennett, *The Nemesis of Power: The German Army in Politics, 1918–1945* (New York: Palgrave MacMillan, 2005).

13. Jon Jacobson, *When the Soviet Union Entered World Politics* (Berkeley: University of California Press, 1994).

14. Werner Angress, *Stillborn Revolution: The Communist Bid for Power in Germany, 1921–1923* (Port Washington, NY: Kennikat Press, 1972).

15. *Akten zur Deutschen Auswaertigen Politik, 1918–1945* (hereafter *ADAP*), Series A, vol. 8, doc. 161, pp. 410–11.

16. *ADAP*, Series A, vol. 8, doc. 165, pp. 419–21.

17. *ADAP*, Series A, vol. 9, doc. 32, pp. 74–76. See also Stresemann, *The Stresemann Diaries*, Stresemann to Brockdorf-Rantzau, December 1, 1923.

18. *ADAP*, Series A, vol. 9, doc. 76, pp. 193–94. December 29, 1923, Schubert to Brockdorff-Rantzau.

19. *ADAP*, Series A, vol. 8, doc. 137, pp. 354–57.

20. *ADAP*, Series A, vol. 9, doc. 170, pp. 451–58.

21. *ADAP*, Series A, vol. 10, doc. 50, pp. 129–30.

22. *ADAP*, Series a, vol. 10, doc. 59, pp. 144–45. See also *ADAP*, Series A, vol. 10, doc. 65, pp. 162–63.

23. *ADAP*, Series A, vol. 10, doc. 112, pp. 274–75.

24. *ADAP*, Series A, vol. 10, doc. 131, pp. 319–22.

25. In fact, as historians now know, Trotsky's fortunes were already in decline and Stalin was in ascendance, having managed to suppress Lenin's scathing written criticism of the coarse Georgian. Nonetheless, Stresemann and other outsiders, of course, could not have known for certain the actual state of power politics inside the Kremlin at this time.

26. *ADAP*, Series A, vol. 10, doc. 213, pp. 534–38.

27. *ADAP*, Series A, vol. 11, doc. 93, pp. 219–20.

28. Nachlass Stresemann, Reel 3120, Serial 7178, Band 17, doc. 157411–19.

29. Nachlass Stresemann, *Politische Akten*, October 29, 1924, reel 3111, pp. 147173–76.

30. *ADAP*, Series A, vol. 11, doc. 265, pp. 661–62.

31. Nachlass Stresemann, Stresemann to Houghton, June 4, 1925, reel 3114, pp. 148780–93.

32. Nachlass Stresemann, June 11, 1925, Reel 3113, Serial 7129, Band 272, doc. 147850.

33. Gaines Post, *The Civil-Military Fabric of Weimar Foreign Policy* (Princeton, NJ: Princeton University Press, 1973), p. 114, fn. 60.

34. Gustav Stresemann, *Gustav Stresemann: His Diaries, Letters, and Papers*, vol. 1, trans. Eric Sutton (New York: MacMillan, 1935), p. 489.

35. Nachlass Stresemann, undated entry by Stresemann, Reel 3112, p. 147736.

36. Although Locarno was a Western-oriented policy, the foreign ministry's overall approach throughout the 1920s was one of *Schaukelpolitik*, a balancing between East and West while steadily regaining strength through revision of Versailles.

37. The Serbian official represented the country then known as the Kingdom of Serbs, Croats, and Slovenes. The country's name was later changed to Yugoslavia in 1929.

38. Military Intelligence Division, "German Soviet Relations," *U.S. Military Intelligence Reports, Germany, 1919–1941*, NA RG 165, microfilm, University Publications of America, August 9, 1925, 2: 207.

39. Wright, *Stresemann*, p. 324.

40. *ADAP*, Series A, vol. 14, doc. 109, pp. 284–91.

41. *ADAP*, Series A, vol. 14, doc. 109.

42. *ADAP*, Series A, vol. 14, doc. 110.

43. Peter Krüger, *Die Aussenpolitik der Republik von Weimar* (Darmstadt, Germany: Wissenschaftliche Buchgesellschaft, 1985), p. 209. Krüger writes: "Der deutschen Aussenpolitik kamen Stresemanns Realismus, seine rasche Auffassungsgabe und Intelligenz ebenso zugute wie die so dringend benoetigte Klarheit und Konsequenz seiner Poltik und vor alllem seine Besonnenheit, die . . . stets das uebergeordnete, wesentliche Kennzeichen seiner Aussenpolitik blieb." [Author's translation: "German foreign policy benefited from Stresemann's realism, quick-wittedness and intelligence and from the urgently needed clarity and forthrightness of his politics, and especially from his caution which always remained the overriding, essential hallmark of his foreign policy."]

44. *ADAP*, Series B, vol. II/1, doc. 112, pp. 280–83. "Wir haetten aber die Erfahrung gemacht, wir den in Deutschland immernoch sehr gefaehrlichen Kommunismus, der von Russland genaehrt wuerde, dann besser bekaepfen koennten, wenn wir mit Russland gut staenden."

45. Mary Habeck, *Storm of Steel: The Development of Armor Doctrine in Germany and the Soviet Union, 1919–1939* (Ithaca, NY: Cornell University Press, 2003), p. 81. For a much earlier work on Russo–German cooperation in this period see Gerald Freund, *Unholy Alliance: Russian–German Relations from the Treaty of Brest-Litovsk to the Treaty of Berlin* (London: Harcourt, Brace, 1957).

46. Nachlass Stresemann, December 22, 1925, Reel 3113, Serial 7129, Band 272, doc. 148109–18.

47. For more on internal Bolshevik power politics, see Robert W. Service, *A History of Twentieth-Century Russia* (Cambridge, MA: Harvard University Press, 1997).

48. *ADAP*, Series B, vol. II/2, doc. 37, pp. 90–93.

49. *ADAP*, Series B, vol. II/2, doc. 44, pp. 105–6.
50. *ADAP*, Series B, vol. II/2, doc. 64, p. 143.
51. *ADAP*, Series B, vol. II/2, doc. 80, p. 182.
52. Germany was permitted to maintain armament levels for self-defense, including an army of 100,000 men.

Chapter 3

1. "German Royalists Accused of Raising Huge Secret Army," *Washington Post*, December 17, 1926.
2. *Truppenamt* was the Army's euphemism for the General Staff.
3. *Verhandlungen des Reichstages*, vol. 391, doc. 1924, pp. 8577–86.
4. *Verhandlungen des Reichstages*, vol. 391, doc. 1924, pp. 8577–86.
5. *Verhandlungen des Reichstages*, vol. 391, doc. 1924, pp. 8577–86.
6. *Verhandlungen des Reichstages*, vol. 391, doc. 1924, pp. 8577–86.
7. Perhaps part of Scheidemann's anger can be traced to his personal grief. Only four months prior to this passionate address, Scheidemann's wife had died of a stroke.
8. *Verhandlungen des Reichstages*, vol. 391, doc. 1924, pp. 8577–86.
9. "German Royalists Accused of Raising Huge Secret Army," *Washington Post*, December 17, 1926.
10. "Germany's Cabinet, Defeated, Resigns in Face of Charges," *Washington Post*, December 18, 1926.
11. "Wild Scenes Mark Reichstag Session," *The New York Times*, December 17, 1926. See also "Christmas Crisis," *Time*, December 27, 1926.
12. "The Distrust of Herr Gessler," *Manchester Guardian*, December 17, 1926, p. 11.
13. "German Gun-Running," *Manchester Guardian*, December 18, 1926, p. 11.
14. "The Exposure of German Militarists," *Manchester Guardian*, December 21, 1926, p. 7.
15. "German–Soviet Alliance?" *Times* (London), May 1, 1922, p. 11; "German Ascendancy in Russia," *Times* (London), May 8, 1922, p. 9.
16. "Attack on Marx Cabinet," *Times* (London), December 17, 1926.
17. Post, *Civil-Military Fabric*, p. 118. See Dirksen notes of meeting with Schubert, Wetzell, and Major Fischer, January 24, 1927. AA 4564/E163483.
18. "Summary of the Final Report of the Inter-Allied Military Commission of Control into the General Inspection of German Armaments, February 15, 1925," *Documents on British Foreign Affairs: Reports and Papers From the Foreign Office, Confidential Print*, Part II, Series F, Vol. 36, pp. 61–65. The final sentence states: "All these infractions taken together are, in the opinion of the Commission, sufficiently important to require putting right, and the Commission will not, on its own initiative, be able to declare the military clauses fulfilled until these points are sufficiently advanced as to have attained the degree of disarmament required by the Treaty, which is now far from the case" (p. 63).

19. "World Statesmen Get Nobel Prizes," *The New York Times*, December 11, 1926, p. 5.

20. "World Statesmen," p. 5.

21. "A German Statesman," *The New York Times*, July 4, 1927, p. 14.

22. For a useful biography see David Dutton, *Austen Chamberlain: Gentleman in Politics* (Bolton, UK: Ross Anderson Publications, 1985).

23. Minutes of the British Cabinet, CAB 23/53, Cabinet Office Papers, National Archive, London, December 1, 1926.

24. The total number of IMCC inspections stood at 33,381, at an average of 28 inspections per day. The total cost reached $38,713,976. Michael Salewski, *Entwaffnung und Militaerkontrolle in Deutschland, 1919–1927* (Muenchen: R. Oldenbourg Verlag, 1966), p. 375.

25. Minutes of the British Cabinet, CAB 23/53, Cabinet Office Papers, National Archive, London, December 15, 1926

26. Minutes, December 15, 1926.

27. Minutes, December 15, 1926.

28. Richard Shuster has referred to Locarno as the "swan song of Allied efforts toward the enforcement of disarmament," arguing that henceforth Chamberlain accepted German promises over proof of disarmament. See Richard Shuster, *German Disarmament after World War I: The Diplomacy of International Arms Inspection, 1920–1931* (New York: Routledge, 2006), p. 194. Another thorough work on disarmament is Thomas E. Boyle's unpublished dissertation, "France, Great Britain, and German Disarmament," State University of New York at Stony Brook, 1972. Available through University Microfilms of America Inc.

29. Gustav Hilger and Alfred Meyer, *The Incompatible Allies: A Memoir-History of German-Soviet Relations, 1918–1941* (New York: MacMillan, 1953), p. 207.

30. Sir Ronald Lindsay to Sir Austen Chamberlain, December 18, 1926, *British Documents on Foreign Affairs: Reports and Papers from the Foreign Office Confidential Print*, Part II, Series F, vol. 37, Germany, 1926, Doc. 317, "Nationalist Associations," pp. 313–17.

31. Hans Gatzke, *Stresemann and the Rearmament of Germany* (Baltimore: Johns Hopkins University Press, 1954), ch. 2, "The End of Military Control."

32. *ADAP*, Series B, vol. II/2, doc. 173, pp. 439–40.

33. Nachlass Stresemann. Aufzeichnung, January 5, 1927. Reel 3167, Series 7337, Band 48, doc. 163495–6.

34. *ADAP*, Series B, vol. IV, doc. 169, pp. 365–66.

35. *ADAP*, Series B, vol. IV, doc. 174, pp. 378–79.

36. *ADAP*, Series B, vol. VI, doc. 108, pp. 229–30.

37. See for example Hans Gatzke, *Stresemann and the Rearmament of Germany* (Baltimore: Johns Hopkins Press, 1954).

38. See for example Jonathan Wright, *Gustav Stresemann: Weimar's Greatest Statesman* (New York: Oxford University Press, 2002), and Patrick Cohrs, *The Unfinished Peace after World War I: America, Britain, and the Stabilisation of Europe, 1919–1932* (Cambridge, UK: Cambridge University Press, 2006).

39. Henry Kissinger, *Diplomacy* (New York: Touchstone, 1995), p. 284.

40. Hans Gatzke's bibliographical note summarizes the early literature on the Foreign Minister. Among others, he cites the following as especially sympathetic to their subject: Walter Görlitz, *Gustav Stresemann* (Heidelberg: Ähren-Verlag, 1947); Prinz zu Löwenstein, *Stresemann: das deutsche Schicksal im Spiegel seines Lebens* (Frankfurt am Main: H. Scheffler, 1952).

41. Hans Gatzke, *Stresemann and the Rearmament of Germany* (Baltimore: Johns Hopkins University Press, 1954). See also Henry L. Bretton, *Stresemann and the Revision of Versailles* (Stanford, CA: Stanford University Press, 1953), p. 38. Bretton cited Edgar Stern-Rubarth, one of Stresemann's aides, as follows: "Stresemann's ultimate hope, as he once confessed to me, was: To free the Rhineland, to recover Eupen-Malmedy, and the Saar, to perfect Austria's Anschluss, and to have, under mandate or otherwise an African colony where essential tropical raw materials could be secured and an outlet created for the surplus energy of the younger generation." Peter Krüger addressed the Stresemann problem by arguing that the Foreign Minister's aims were less important than his style of seizing opportunities as they arose. See Peter Krüger, *Die Aussenpolitik der Republik von Weimar* (Darmstadt, Germany: Wissenschaftliche Buchgesellschaft, 1985). Other useful works on Weimar era foreign and military policy include John Wheeler-Bennett, *The Nemesis of Power: The German Army in Politics, 1918–1945* (New York: St. Martin's Press, 1954); F. L. Carsten, *The Reichswehr and Politics, 1918–1933* (New York: Clarendon Press, 1966); Gaines Post, *The Civil-Military Fabric of Weimar Foreign Policy* (Princeton, NJ: Princeton University Press, 1973).

42. Jonathan Wright, *Gustav Stresemann: Weimar's Greatest Statesman* (New York: Oxford University Press, 2002).

43. Cohrs, *Unfinished Peace*.

44. Stephen A. Schuker, "Review of Patrick Cohrs, *The Unfinished Peace after World War I: America, Britain, and the Stabilisation of Europe, 1919–1932*," *Journal of American History*, vol. 94 (2007), p. 319.

45. In a much earlier work, Schuker observed that Stresemann had no intention of going to war while Germany was still weak. Stephen Schuker, *The End of French Predominance in Europe: The Financial Crisis of 1924 and the Adoption of the Dawes Plan* (Chapel Hill, NC: University of North Carolina Press, 1976), p. 267.

46. Cohrs, *Unfinished Peace*, p. 229.

47. Wright, *Stresemann*, p. 508. Wright does note that because Stresemann also believed firmly in restoring Germany's equal rights among the states of Europe, the revision of Versailles would ultimately leave Germany as the strongest power on the continent, save for Russia. These two aims had an inherent contradiction, but Wright concludes that Stresemann remained increasingly wedded to achieving strength through peace.

48. Wright, *Stresemann*, p. 386.

49. One could argue that Stresemann's refusal to agree to fixed borders in the east represented a break in the pattern of cooperation commensurate with the Spirit of Locarno. However, this would only indicate his intention to revise those borders; it would not have been evidence of an intention to redraw those borders by military means.

50. MID, "Stresemann's Speech Before the Reichstag," *U.S. Military Intelligence Reports, Germany, 1919–1941*, NA RG 165, microfilm, University Publications of America, February 24, 1928, 2.418. The full sentence read: "We are disarmed, we have concluded the Locarno treaties, we have subjected ourselves to the jurisdiction of the Hague World Court by signing the optional clause for all international conflicts of a legal nature and we have created an almost complete system of arbitration and adjustment treaties."

51. Schuker, *End of French Predominance*, p. 267.

52. Robert Kurzban, *Why Everyone (Else) Is a Hypocrite: Evolution and the Modular Mind* (Princeton, NJ: Princeton University Press, 2010), p. 170. For a separate discussion of cognitive psychology and the modular view, see Timothy Wilson, *Strangers to Ourselves: Discovering the Adaptive Unconscious* (Cambridge, MA: Harvard University Press, 2002.)

53. In this book I observe two common heuristics among foreign policy analysts: one helpful to the decision-maker—the pattern-break heuristic—and one harmful to the decision-maker—the continuity heuristic. Unlike a psychologist, I make no claims regarding how most people think. Instead, I assess how particular historical figures thought and how their thinking influenced historical events. I do, however, relate some of the findings from fields beyond history in order to provide alternative ways of conceptualizing historical problems. Whenever I relate such findings, I do so with considerable caution. For example, some psychologists dispute the validity of much of the scholarship on heuristics and biases. They correctly observe that scholars have identified countless biases and their opposites, making it impossible to conclude how people typically think. Other critics, Gerd Gigerenzer primary among them, note that heuristics need not always be seen as flaws in rational decision-making. Instead, they suggest that heuristics can also make us smart by simplifying our decision-making processes with helpful rules of thumb. In the Afterword I say more about the risks of being seduced by science. For one thoughtful challenge to mainstream notions in social psychology see Joachim I. Krueger and David C. Funder, "Towards a balanced social psychology: Causes, consequences, and cures for the problem-seeking approach to social behavior and cognition," *Behavioral and Brain Sciences*, vol. 27, no. 3 (2004), pp. 313–27.

54. Hitler's own strategic empathy proved far less sound than Stresemann's. It was long believed that Hitler possessed an innate knack for divining the weakness of his enemies, but this view has not withstood closer scrutiny. See Zachary Shore, *What Hitler Knew: The Battle for Information in Nazi Foreign Policy* (New York: Oxford University Press, 2003), particularly ch. 3, "Risk in the Rhineland."

Chapter 4

1. David Murphy, *What Stalin Knew: The Enigma of Barbarossa* (New Haven, CT: Yale University Press, 2005), p. 87.

2. Gabriel Gorodetsky, *Grand Delusion: Stalin and the German Invasion of Russia* (New Haven, CT: Yale University Press, 1999).

3. Murphy, *What Stalin Knew*.

4. Dmitri Volkogonov, *Stalin: Triumph and Tragedy* (New York: Grove Weidenfeld, 1991).

5. Geoffrey Roberts, *Stalin's Wars: From World War to Cold War, 1939–1953* (New Haven, CT: Yale University Press, 2008).

6. David Holloway, "Stalin and Intelligence: Two Cases," forthcoming. Stanford Professor David Holloway kindly shared his unpublished article with me.

7. John Lewis Gaddis, *The Landscape of History: How Historians Map the Past* (New York: Oxford University Press, 2002), p. 126.

8. Norman Naimark, *Stalin's Genocides* (Princeton, NJ: Princeton University Press, 2010), p. 82. Naimark writes: "The vulnerability of the Soviet borders is a matter of historical dispute. But one might suggest that in an environment in which railway accidents, shortfalls in mining production, and grain spoilage were routinely attributed to Trotskyite subversion and Japanese-German spies, resulting in tens of thousands of arrests, torture and forced confessions and thousands of executions, the war scares and spy mania in the borderlands were part of the same process of inventing enemies and destroying people ultimately for no other reason except to maintain the suspicious and vengeful dictator in power."

9. One can debate whether "genocide" is the proper term for Stalin's crimes. At the very least we can consider them as mass murder.

10. Roberts, *Stalin's Wars*, p. 48.

11. For details on the origins of this pact see Zachary Shore, *What Hitler Knew: The Battle for Information in Nazi Foreign Policy* (New York: Oxford University Press, 2003), ch. 1, "Hitler's Opening Gambit: Intelligence, Fear, and the German–Polish Agreement."

12. Robert O'Neill, *The German Army and the Nazi Party, 1933–1939* (London: Cassell, 1966), p. 38.

13. Anastas Mikoyan, *Tak bylo* (Moscow: AST, 2000), p. 534.

14. For more on both theory-theory and simulation theory see Jason P. Mitchell, "The False Dichotomy Between Simulation and Theory-Theory," *Trends in Cognitive Sciences*, vol. 9 (August 8, 2005). See also Rebecca Saxe, "Against Simulation: The Argument from Error," *Trends in Cognitive Sciences*, vol. 9 (April 4, 2005).

15. Mikoyan, *Tak bylo*, p. 534. See also Simon Sebag Montefiore, *Stalin: The Court of the Red Tsar* (New York: Knopf, 2004), p. 376.

16. Mikoyan, *Tak bylo*, p. 376.

17. Adolf Hitler, *Mein Kampf*, trans. Ralph Manheim (Boston: Houghton Mifflin, 1943; Boston: Mariner Books, 1999), p. 654. Citations refer to the Mariner edition.
18. Hitler, *Mein Kampf*, p. 655.
19. Hitler, *Mein Kampf*, pp. 660–661.
20. Hitler, *Mein Kampf*, p. 661.
21. Montefiore, *Stalin*, p. 272.
22. Montefiore, *Stalin*, p. 298.
23. Montefiore, *Stalin*, pp. 309–310.
24. Some scholars still maintain that the Welles Mission of 1940 represented a genuine effort for peace. See Christopher O'Sullivan, *Sumner Welles, Postwar Planning, and the Quest for a New World Order, 1937–1943* (New York: Columbia University Press, 2008), ch. 3.

Chapter 5

1. Franklin D. Roosevelt Library and Museum, Collection: Grace Tully Archive, Series: Marguerite ("Missy"), LeHand Papers, Box 10; Folder = Correspondence: Roosevelt, Franklin D.: Transcripts of Longhand, 1934. Sunday July 1, 1934.
2. *Foreign Relations of the United States, 1934, Vol. II: Europe, Near East and Africa* (Washington, DC: U.S. Government Printing Office, 1934), pp. 241–43. Letter 1072 from William E. Dodd, the Ambassador in Germany, to Cordell Hull, the Secretary of State, July 24, 1934.
3. *FRUS, Volume II: Europe, Near East and Africa*. Memorandum from Cordell Hull, the Secretary of State, July 13, 1934, p. 238–39.
4. Edgar B. Nixon, *Franklin D.Roosevelt and Foreign Affairs* (Cambridge, MA: Belknap Press, 1969), vol. II, pp. 180–81.
5. Nixon, *Franklin D. Roosevelt and Foreign Affairs*, vol. II, pp. 186–87.
6. Nixon, *Franklin D. Roosevelt and Foreign Affairs*, September 7, 1934, pp. 207–8.
7. Dodd was far from the only foreign observer to be distressed by the heightened militarism suffusing German daily life at this time. One young American who was studying at Oxford travelled to Germany in 1934. While there he attended a Hitler Youth camp outing and was startled to see how much it resembled military exercises, complete with drills, calisthenics, and instruction in the dismantling and reassembling of weapons. Later, Dean Rusk would write, "This was no Explorer Scout outing or weekend in the fresh air of the countryside." Rusk could not then recognize the direction in which Germany was headed. In a speech to the World Affairs Council of Riverside, California, he adopted a wait-and-see attitude about Hitler's regime. He would look back on his myopia with regret. We can only speculate that this experience was a meaningful episode that shaped his worldview and influenced his decision-making while Secretary of State during the Vietnam

War. Dean Rusk, *As I Saw It*, as told to Richard Rusk, edited by Daniel S. Papp (New York: Penguin Books, 1991), p. 79.

8.   Nixon, *Franklin D. Roosevelt and Foreign Affairs*, November 5, 1934, Dodd to Moore, pp. 274–77.

9.   Nixon, *Franklin D. Roosevelt and Foreign Affairs*, May 9, 1935, Dodd to FDR, pp. 499–503.

10. Memorandum by Mr. S. R. Fuller, Jr., of a Conversation With Dr. Hjalmar Schacht, Minister of Economics and President of the Reichsbank of Germany, Berlin, September 23, 1935, *Foreign Relations of the United States, 1935. Volume II: The British Commonwealth, Europe* (Washington, DC: U.S. Government Printing Office, 1935), pp. 282–86.

11. Memorandum, *FRUS 1935*, pp. 282–86.

12. President's Secretary's File (Dodd), Part 2, Reel 11. FDR to Dodd, December 2, 1935. Roosevelt reiterated his concern over media control in Germany in a letter to Dodd on August 5, 1936, going so far as to liken the Nazi's media control to the Republicans' control over American media. "The election this year has, in a sense, a German parallel. If the Republicans should win or make enormous gains, it would prove that an 85% control of the Press and a very definite campaign of misinformation can be effective here just as it was in the early days of the Hitler rise to power. Democracy is verily on trial. I am inclined to say something a little later on about the great need for freedom of the press in this country, i.e., freedom to confine itself to actual facts in its news columns and freedom to express editorially any old opinion it wants to." PSF Dodd, Part 2, Reel 11, August 5, 1936.

13. Ian Kershaw, *Hitler: 1936–1945, Nemesis* (London: Penguin, 2000), p. 141.

14. Draft Statement on Kristallnacht, November 15, 1938, President's Secretary's Files: Diplomatic Correspondence, Germany 1933–1938 (Box 31).

15. Thomas E. Ricks, *The Generals: American Military Command from World War II to Today* (New York: Penguin, 2012), p. 27.

16. The political scientist Barbara Farnham has argued that the Munich Crisis of September 1938 convinced Roosevelt that Hitler represented a genuine threat to the Western democracies, America included. Barbara Farnham, *Roosevelt and the Munich Crisis: A Study of Political Decision-Making* (Princeton, NJ: Princeton University Press, 1997). In contrast, I have suggested that FDR grasped the nature of Hitler's regime and its dangers long before Munich. I have not focused on the Munich crisis here because it did not represent a pattern break but was instead the continuation of a pattern in Hitler's diplomatic style.

17. Kershaw, *Hitler: 1936–1945*, p. 153.

18. The historian David Irving has argued that Hitler was unaware of the plans for Kristallnacht, and once he learned of it, he sought quickly to end it. This claim is exceedingly hard to support, given, among other issues, Hitler's close collaboration and personal friendship with Josef Goebbels, who orchestrated the pogrom. Irving subsequently went to prison in Austria for denying the Holocaust.

19. *Documents on German Foreign Policy, 1918–1945* (hereafter *DGFP*), Series D, Memorandum by the Führer, "Directive for the Conversations with Mr. Sumner Welles," February 29, 1940, doc. 637, pp. 817–19.

20. Montefiore, *Stalin*, p. 312.

21. *DGFP*, Series D, Supplement to Memorandum of the Conversation between the Foreign Minister and Sumner Welles on March 1, 1940, doc. 641, p. 829.

22. *Foreign Relations of the United States, vol. 1, 1940*. Memorandum by Under-Secretary of State Welles, March 1, 1940.

23. *DGFP*, Series D, "Directive by the Führer and Supreme Commander of the Wehrmacht," March 1, 1940, doc. 644, pp. 831–33.

24. *DGFP*, Series D, "Conversation Between the Führer and Chancellor and American Under-Secretary of State Sumner Welles, in the Presence of the Foreign Minister, State Secretary Meissner, and American Charge d'Affaires Kirk," March 2, 1940, doc. 649, pp. 838–45.

25. *Foreign Relations of the United States, vol. 1*, March 2, 1940. See also Welles's subsequent account in Sumner Welles, *Time for Decision* (New York: Harper and Brothers, 1944), ch. 3, "My Mission to Europe: 1940."

26. *DGFP*, Series D, vol. VIII, "Conversation Between Field Marshal Göring and Under-Secretary of State Sumner Welles," March 3, 1940, doc. 653, pp. 853–62.

27. *FRUS*, Welles Report on conversations with Göring, March 2, 1940.

28. Fred L. Israel, *The War Diary of Breckinridge Long: Selections From the Years 1939–1944* (Lincoln: University of Nebraska Press, 1966), p. 64. One scholar of the Welles mission concludes that FDR had multiple aims in mind beyond seeking a peace initiative, including gleaning information on Hitler's and Mussolini's views, prolonging the Phoney War, and continuing Italy's neutrality. See C. J. Simon Rofe, *Franklin Roosevelt's Foreign Policy and the Welles Mission* (London: Palgrave MacMillan, 2007).

29. OSS Study of Hitler, 1943, Hitler 201 File, RID/AR, WASH X-2 PERSONALITIES #43

30. *DGFP*, Series D, vol. XI, doc. 326, Berlin, November 16, 1940, p. 547.

31. *DGFP*, Series D, vol. XI, doc. 326, Berlin, November 16, 1940, p. 542. Record of the conversation on November 12, 1940. People present: Hitler, Molotov, von Ribbentrop, Dekanozov, Hilger, and M. Pavlov.

32. *DGFP*, Series D, vol. XI, doc. 328, Berlin, November 15, 1940. Record of the conversation on November 13, 1940. People present: Hitler, Molotov, von Ribbentrop, Dekanozov, Hilger, and M. Pavlov, p. 554.

33. *DGFP*, Series D, vol. XI, doc. 328, Berlin, November 15, 1940. Record of the conversation on November 13, 1940. People present: Hitler, Molotov, von Ribbentrop, Dekanozov, Hilger, and M. Pavlov, p. 557.

34. Montefiore, *Stalin*, p. 350. Montefiore has offered this quote from an unpublished collection of notes by Reginald Dekanozov, son of the Soviet Ambassador to Berlin and Deputy Foreign Minister Vladimir Dekanozov. I have therefore not corroborated the quote from Montefiore's book with the original that he claims is found in the son's notes.

Chapter 6

1. This chapter and the subsequent one previously appeared as an article in the *Journal of Cold War Studies*. I am grateful to the journal for its permission to reprint the work here.

2. Lien-Hang T. Nguyen, *Hanoi's War: An International History of the War for Peace in Vietnam* (The New Cold War History) (Chapel Hill: University of North Carolina Press, 2012).

3. "The Historic Talks: 35th Anniversary of the Paris Agreement, 1973–2008," Diplomatic History Research Committee of the Foreign Ministry, ed. Vu Duong Huan [Vũ Dương Huân] (Hanoi, Vietnam: National Political Publishing House, 2009), p. 101.

4. This lament is made most famously by Robert McNamara, *In Retrospect: The Tragedy and Lessons of Vietnam* (New York: Random House, 1996), p. 32. McNamara wrote that neither he nor the Presidents he served nor their top advisors possessed any appreciation for or understanding of Indochina, "its history, language, culture, or values."

5. The *Van Kien Dang* is a collection of Politburo and Central Committee directives, speeches, and cables, emanating from Hanoi and covering most of the post–World War II era. The collection is assessed in the *Journal of Vietnamese Studies*, vol. 5, no. 2 (2010).

6. From among the many official DRV histories, this article has been informed in part by the histories of the Foreign Ministry, the People's Army, the People's Navy, the Sapper Forces, the Central Office of South Vietnam, histories of combat operations, histories of the Tonkin Gulf incident, the memoirs of prominent military officers, records of the secret negotiations with the Johnson administration, and some Vietnamese newspapers.

7. Pierre Asselin has highlighted the Party Secretary's importance in state building. See his article, "Le Duan, the American War, and the Creation of an Independent Vietnamese State," *The Journal of American—East Asian Relations*, vol. 10, nos. 1–2 (2001). A 2007 biography of Le Duan, which is essentially a hagiography by the official state-run publishing house, covers his general background and impact on Vietnamese history. See Tong Bi Thu, *Le Duan: Party General Secretary Le Duan* (Hanoi, Vietnam: VNA Hanoi Publishing House, 2007).

   Liên-Hang T. Nguyen's *Hanoi's War* spotlights intra-Party factionalism, emphasizing the roles of Le Duan and Le Duc Tho. Still largely absent from the literature is a focus on the Party General Secretary's ability to know his American enemy and its effect on the war.

8. Tuong Vu, "From Cheering to Volunteering: Vietnamese Communists and the Coming of the Cold War, 1940–1951," in *Connecting Histories: The Cold War and Decolonization in Asia (1945–1962)*, eds. Christopher Goscha and Christian Ostermann (Stanford, CA: Stanford University Press, 2009), pp. 172–204; and also "Dreams of Paradise: The Making of Soviet Outpost

in Vietnam," *Ab Imperio: Studies of New Imperial History and Nationalism in the Post-Soviet Space*, no. 2 (2008), pp. 255–85.

9. Martin Grossheim, "'Revisionism' in the Democratic Republic of Vietnam: New Evidence from the East German Archives," *Cold War History*, vol. 5, no. 4 (2005), pp. 451–77.

10. For an excellent analysis of just how dangerous Party rivalries could be, consider Le Duan's maneuvers to sideline General Võ Nguyên Giáp and force the Tết Offensive. See Merle L. Pribbenow, "General Võ Nguyên Giáp and the Mysterious Evolution of the Plan for the 1968 Tết Offensive," *Journal of Vietnamese Studies*, vol. 3, no. 2 (2008), pp. 1–33.

11. Christopher E. Goscha, *Historical Dictionary of the Indochina War (1945–1954): An International and Interdisciplinary Approach* (Nordic Institute of Asian Studies) (Copenhagen, Denmark: NIAS Press, 2011), p. 261.

12. Nguyen, *Hanoi's War*.

13. Hanoi's official commemorative biography of the Party First Secretary states that Le Duan was granted an exemption from the rule limiting Politburo members to one wife. In the arduous resistance war, Le Duan had close relationships with southern compatriots and comrades. In 1950 he was allowed by the Party organization to obtain a second marriage to Ms. Nguyen Thuy Nga. Tong Bi Thu, *Le Duan: Party General Secretary Le Duan* (VNA Hanoi Publishing House, 2007), p. 5.

14. "The Southern Wife of the Late Party General Secretary Le Duan," Installment 3, *Tien Phong*, July 9, 2006., Accessed July 10, 2006, at http://www.tienphongonline.com.vn/Tianyon/Index.aspx?ArticleID=52871&ChannelID=13.

15. Carlyle Thayer, *War by Other Means: National Liberation and Revolution in Vietnam, 1954–1960* (Sydney: Allen & Unwin, 1989). See chapter titled "The 8th Plenum, August 1955."

16. As translated by Robert Brigham and Le Phuong Anh, the relevant text reads: "Recently, in the U.S Presidential election, the present Republican administration, in order to buy the people's esteem, put forward the slogan 'Peace and Prosperity,' which showed that even the people of an imperialist warlike country like the U.S. want peace." Le Duan, "The Path of Revolution in the South," 1956. Available at http://vi.uh.edu/pages/buzzmat/southrevo.htm.

17. See *Nhan Dan*, no. 975 (November 5, 1956); "Some Observations Regarding the Recent General Election in the U.S." no. 981 (November 11, 1956); "Is That Actually Democratic?" no. 993 (November 25, 1956); "Democracy and Dictatorship," no. 1000 (November 30, 1956).

18. *Historical Chronicle of the Cochin China Party Committee and the Central Office for South Vietnam, 1954–1975* (Hanoi, Vietnam: National Political Publishing House, 2002), pp. 119–20. This history discusses the significance of Le Duan's thesis, placing it in the context of COSVN activities at the time.

19. *History of the COSVN Military Command, 1961–1976*, ed. Colonel Ho Son Dai (Hanoi, Vietnam: National Political Publishing House, 2004), p. 44.

20. Alec Holcombe, "The Complete Collection of Party Documents: Listening to the Party's Official Internal Voice," *Journal of Vietnamese Studies* vol. 5, no. 2 (2010), pp. 225–42.

21. Thayer, *War by Other Means*. See chapter titled "The Fatherland Front and Renewed Political Struggle, September 1955–April 1956." For more on Moscow's influence over Hanoi, see Ilya Gaiduk, *The Soviet Union and the Vietnam War* (Chicago: University of Chicago Press, 1996).

22. *History of the COSVN Military Command*, p. 42. "Faced with the duplicity and the brutal terrorist actions of the U.S. and their puppets, starting with 200 officers and men we had left behind to support the political struggle movement, the self–defense and armed propaganda forces of the B2 Front had expanded to form 37 armed propaganda platoons. However, these units only conducted limited operations because of the fear that they might be violating the Party's policy at that time, which was to conduct political struggle only."

23. *Victory in Vietnam: The Official History of the People's Army of Vietnam, 1954–1975*, trans. Merle L. Pribbenow (Lawrence: University Press of Kansas, 2002), p. 43.

24. For more on armed propaganda, see Greg Lockhart, *Nation in Arms: The Origins of the People's Army of Vietnam* (Sydney: Allen and Unwin, 1989).

25. For more on the construction of Le Duan's police state, see Nguyen, *Hanoi's War*, ch. 2.

26. See William J. Duiker in the Foreword to *Victory in Vietnam*, p. xiii.

27. The U.S. Central Intelligence Agency had closely followed General Thanh's rise and analyzed his influence. It was well-aware of his closeness to Le Duan within the Politburo. Following the General's death, the Agency assumed that his replacement would indicate whether Pham Van Dong and the moderates or Le Duan and the militants had greater power within the Party. See CIA Directorate of Intelligence, *Intelligence Memorandum* (July 11, 1967), No. 1365/67, "Problems Posed for North Vietnam by Death of Politburo Member Nguyen Chi Thanh."

28. See Asselin, "Le Duan."

29. Sophie Quinn-Judge, "The Ideological Debate in the DRV and the Significance of the Anti–Party Affair, 1967–1968," *Cold War History*, vol. 5, no. 4 (2005), pp. 479–500.

30. Asselin, "Le Duan." One of Le Duan's close supporters has published a memoir, attempting to defend his former boss's reputation. Tran Quynh served as Deputy Prime Minister of the Socialist Republic of Vietnam from 1981 to 1987. See Tran Quynh, "Reminiscences of Le Duan." Self-published recollections were available at http://d.violet.vn//uploads/resources/492/369514/preview.swf at the time of this manuscript's submission.

31. See Tran Quynh, "Reminiscences of Le Duan." The author served as Deputy Prime Minister of the Socialist Republic of Vietnam from 1981 to February 16, 1987, and worked closely with Le Duan. Self-published recollections were

available at http://d.violet.vn//uploads/resources/492/369514/preview.swf at the time of this manuscript's submission.

32. For a helpful summary of communist states and the primacy of the Party, see Archie Brown, *The Rise and Fall of Communism* (New York: Ecco, 2009).

33. Liên-Hang T. Nguyen argues that in 1963 Le Duan abandoned a protracted war strategy in favor of "big war" involving conventional forces aimed at a rapid victory. My own view is slightly different. I note that Le Duan preferred "big war" but recognized the need for protracted war against America for a variety of both military and political reasons. Nguyen's view is detailed in both *Hanoi's War*, ch. 2, and "The War Politburo: North Vietnam's Diplomatic and Political Road to the Tết Offensive," *Journal of Vietnamese Studies*, vol. 1, nos. 1–2 (2006), pp. 4–58.

34. *Letters to the South* [Tho Vao Nam] (Hanoi, Vietnam : Su That Publishing House, 1985). Letter to Muoi Cuc (Nguyen Van Linh) and the Cochin China Party Committee [Xu Uy Nam Bo], April 20, 1961, p. 48. Because the English translation of *Letters to the South* does not contain all of the letters in the Vietnamese version, I have drawn on both editions. The letter referenced here, for example, is not found in the English edition.

35. *Letters to the South*. Letter to Muoi Cuc (Nguyen Van Linh) and the Cochin China Party Committee [Xu Uy Nam Bo], July 1962, p. 50. "Currently, even though there are some cities where the enemy is vulnerable, it is not yet the time to attack and occupy them. From an over-all strategic standpoint, such a victory would not yield positive results at this time, because it could incite the American imperialists to increase their intervention and to expand the war."

36. *Letters to the South*, July 18, 1962, p. 65. A slightly different version of this letter is reprinted in *Van Kien Dang*.

37. *Letters to the South*, July 18, 1962. Le Duan wrote: "If we present limited demands that allow the enemy to see that, even though they must lose, they can lose at a level which they can accept, a level that the enemy can see does not present a major threat to them, then they will be forced to accept defeat. We have put forward goals and requirements for the National Liberation Front for South Vietnam that we have calculated are at the level necessary for us to be able to win and for the enemy to be able to lose."

38. For a thoughtful revision of Diem's reputation, see Philip E. Catton, *Diem's Final Failure: Prelude to America's War in Vietnam* (Lawrence: University of Kansas Press, 2002).

39. *Van Kien Dang*, 1963, p. 818.

40. *Van Kien Dang*, 1963, p. 815.

41. Le Duan, *Letters to the South*, May 1965. English edition.

42. For an interesting assessment of the hollowness of America's "flexible response" approach see Marc Trachtenberg, *The Cold War and After: History, Theory, and the Logic of International Politics* (Princeton, NJ: Princeton University Press, 2012), ch. 6, "The Structure of Great Power Politics."

43. *Van Kien Dang*, 1963, p. 813.

44. Wayne Morse, a Republican turned Independent turned Democrat, represented Oregon in the Senate from 1945 to 1969. He was one of only two Senators to vote against the Tonkin Gulf Resolution. The other was Ernest Gruening, a Democrat from Alaska.

45. Carlyle Thayer, *War By Other Means: National Liberation and Revolution in Vietnam, 1954–1960* (Sydney: Allen & Unwin, 1989).

46. Bui Anh Tuan ed., *Ministry of Public Security* (Hanoi, Vietnam: People's Public Security Publishing House, 2004), pp. 156–71. This official history describes some of the radio communications counterespionage against the Americans and acknowledges the Soviet Union's assistance in establishing those operations in the 1950s.

47. Two sources offering a glimpse into Hanoi's intelligence apparati are Larry Berman, *Perfect Spy: The Incredible Double Life of Pham Xuan An, Time Magazine Reporter and Vietnamese Communist Agent* (New York: Smithsonian Books, 2007), and a declassified CIA report on prisoners of war, which offers an outline of intelligence services, Central Intelligence Agency, "The Responsibilities of the Democratic Republic of Vietnam Intelligence and Security Services in the Exploitation of American Prisoners of War," November 17, 1975, available at http://www.vietnam.ttu.edu/virtualarchive/items.php?item=11270323004. See also Christopher Goscha, "The Early Development of Vietnamese Intelligence Services," in R. G. Hughes, P. Jackson and L. Scott, eds., *Exploring Intelligence Archives* (Londen: Routledge, 2008), pp. 103–15. For a compelling oral history of a Soviet spy in Vietnam, see Xiaobing Li, *Voices from the Vietnam War: Stories from American, Asian, and Russian Veterans* (Louisville: University of Kentucky Press, 2010). See ch. 10, "Russian Spies in Hanoi."

48. Le Duan cited an American as the originator of this terminology, i.e. "special," "limited," and "general war." *Van Kien Dang*, 1965, p. 581.

49. *Van Kien Dang*, 1963, p. 821.

50. *Victory in Vietnam*, pp. 126–27.

51. Pham Hong Thuy, Pham Hong Doi, and Phan Trong Dam, *History of the People's Navy of Vietnam* (Hanoi, Vietnam: People's Army Publishing House, 1985), p. 89.

52. *Victory in Vietnam*, Part II, chapters 4–6 detail the many attacks against American forces leading up to the U.S. deployment of ground troops.

53. Fredrik Logevall, *Choosing War: The Lost Chance for Peace and the Escalation of War in Vietnam* (Berkeley: University of California Press, 1999), p. 189.

Chapter 7

1. One of the best works on the Tonkin incident is Edwin Moise, *Tonkin Gulf and the Escalation of the Vietnam War* (Chapel Hill: University of North Carolina Press, 1996).

2. Lieutenant General Hoang Nghia Khanh, *The Road to the General Head-quarters Staff* (Hanoi, Vietnam: People's Army Publishing House, 2008), pp. 112–13.

3. Combat Operations Department, General Staff of the People's Army of Vietnam, *History of the Combat Operations Department 1945–2000* (Hanoi, Vietnam: People's Army Publishing House, 2005), p. 210.

4. Victory in Vietnam, p. 133.

5. Moise, *Tonkin Gulf*, ch. 3, "The Desoto Patrols," p. 60.

6. Logevall, *Choosing War*, p. 200.

7. *Van Kien Dang*, Toan Tap, 25, Politburo Directive No. 81-CT/TW, August 7, 1964, ed. Vu Huu Ngoan (Hanoi, Vietnam: National Political Publishing House [Nha Xuat Ban Chinh Tri Quoc Gia], 2003), p. 185.

8. *Van Kien Dang*, 1964, p. 186.

9. Ed Moise, *Tonkin Gulf*, ch. 2, "Thoughts of Escalation."

10. Logevall, *Choosing War*, p. 147.

11. Dubbing McNamara the "high priest of rational management," the historian Barbara Tuchman critiqued the Defense Secretary's strategy of incremental escalation for its cool calculation. "One thing was left out of account: the other side. What if the other side failed to respond rationally to the coercive message?" she asked. "Appreciation of the human factor was not McNamara's strong point, and the possibility that human kind is not rational was too eccentric and disruptive to be programmed into his analysis." Barbara Tuchman, *The March of Folly: From Troy to Vietnam* (New York: Knopf, 1984), p. 288. In contrast, Fredrik Logevall notes that McNamara was already exhibiting signs of concern in 1964 that the war was unwise, yet Logevall sees McNamara's "slavish" loyalty to the President as the reason for his continued support of the policy. Logevall, *Choosing War*, p. 127.

12. *History of the Sapper Forces*, Vol. I [Lich Su Bo Doi Dac Cong, Tap Mot], ed. Headquarters and Party Current Affairs Committee of Sapper Command, by Nguyen Quoc Minh, Vu Doan Thanh, Pham Gia Khanh, and Nguyen Thanh Xuan (Hanoi, Vietnam: People's Army Publishing House, 1987), p. 83–85.

13. Lieutenant Colonel Nguyen Quoc Minh, *History of the Sapper Branch Technical Service*, ed. People's Army of Vietnam (Internal Distribution) [Lich Su Nganh Ky Thuat Dac Cong: Quan Doi Nhan Dan Viet Nam (Luu Hanh Noi Bo)] (Hanoi, Vietnam: People's Army Publishing House, 1997), p. 91. See also *History of the Resistance War in Saigon-Cho Lon-Gia Dinh (1945–1975)* [Lich Su Saigon-Cho Lon-Gia Dinh Khang Chien (1945–1975)], ed. War Recapitulation Committee, Ho Chi Minh City Party Committee; Tran Hai Phung, and Luu Phuong Thanh, by Ho Son Dai and Tran Phan Chan (Ho Chi Minh City: Ho Chi Minh City Publishing House, 1994), p. 4. Also *The New York Times*, March 19, 1963, p. 4.

14. Robert S. McNamara, *Argument Without End: In Search of Answers to the Vietnam Tragedy* (New York: Public Affairs, 1999), p. xix. Earlier scholarship

had speculated that the Viet Cong commanders acted on their own initiative in order to garner Soviet support for their cause. Premier Kosygin happened to be visiting Hanoi at the time of the attacks. This view was later discredited once it was revealed that the Soviets had already pledged their support.

15. Colonel General Dang Vu Hiep, with Senior Colonel Le Hai Trieu and Colonel Ngo Vinh Binh, *Highland Memories*, Part IV (Hanoi, Vietnam: People's Army Publishing House, 2000), p. 13.

16. *Highland Memories*, pp. 9–14.

17. Logevall, *Choosing War*, p. 325.

18. *Letters to the South* [Tho Vao Nam], February 1965 (Hanoi, Vietnam: Le Duan, Su That Publishing House, 1985), p. 73.

19. *Letters to the South*, p. 74.

20. *Letters to the South*, Letter to Muoi Cuc (Nguyen Van Linh) and the Cochin China Party Committee [Xu Uy Nam Bo], February 1965, p. 75.

   Le Duan's strategy represented, of course, a form of deterrence. By crippling the ARVN forces, he believed that American decision-makers would be dissuaded from escalating their commitment to the South. In fact, the increased attacks on both ARVN and American forces produced the opposite result. They served only to strengthen those American decision-makers' desire to escalate. The problem with Le Duan's analysis was that it assumed a rational, as opposed to an emotional, decision-making process on the part of top American officials. It also required the American decision-makers to share Le Duan's perception of American vulnerability.

21. James Fearon, "Rationalist Explanations for War," *International Organization*, vol. 49, no. 3 (1995), pp. 379–414.

22. Truong Nhu Tang, *A Vietcong Memoir* (New York: Harcourt, Brace, Jovanovich, 1985), p. 58.

23. See William L. Langer and S. Everett Gleason, *The Undeclared War, 1940–1941* (Gloucester, MA: P. Smith, 1968). For a penetrating analysis of President Franklin Roosevelt's policy toward Japan during the prelude to Pearl Harbor, see Marc Trachtenberg, *The Craft of International History: A Guide to Method* (Princeton, NJ: Princeton University Press, 2006), ch. 4, "Developing Interpretation Through Textual Analysis: The 1941 Case."

24. Lien-Hang T. Nguyen cites the postwar writings of General Tran Van Tra as evidence of southern communists' resistance to Le Duan's push for conventional warfare. See Nguyen, *Hanoi's War*, ch. 2.

25. *Van Kien Dang*, Le Duan speech, December 1965, p. 599.

26. *Letters to the South* [Tho Vao Nam], Le Duan, Su That Publishing House, Hanoi, 1985. Letter to Muoi Cuc (Nguyen Van Linh) and the Cochin China Party Committee [Xu Uy Nam Bo], November 1965, p. 124.

27. *Letters to the South*, Letter to Muoi Cuc (Nguyen Van Linh) and the Cochin China Party Committee [Xu Uy Nam Bo], November 1965, p. 145.

28. *Letters to the South*, Letter to Muoi Cuc (Nguyen Van Linh) and the Cochin China Party Committee [Xu Uy Nam Bo], November 1965, p. 161.

29. Nick Turse, *Kill Anything That Moves: The Real American War in Vietnam* (New York: Metropolitan Books, 2013). See also Deborah Nelson, *The War Behind Me: Vietnam Veterans Confront the Truth About U.S. War Crimes* (New York: Basic Books, 2008).

30. Nguyen, *Hanoi's War*, ch. 2.

31. *Van Kien Dang*, 1965, Speech Given by Party First Secretary Le Duan to the Twelfth Plenum of the Party Central Committee, December 1965, p. 568.

32. *Van Kien Dang*, Le Duan speech, December 1965, p. 568.

33. *Van Kien Dang*, Le Duan speech, December 1965, p. 569.

34. *Van Kien Dang*, Le Duan speech, December 1965, p. 575.

35. *Van Kien Dang*, Le Duan speech, December 1965, p. 579.

36. *Van Kien Dang*, Le Duan speech, December 1965, p. 586.

37. *Van Kien Dang*, Le Duan speech, December 1965, p. 590.

38. *Van Kien Dang*, Le Duan speech, December 1965, p. 592.

39. *Van Kien Dang*, 1966, Speech Given by Chairman Ho Chi Minh to a Conference of High-level Cadres Held to Study the Resolution of the Twelfth Plenum of the Party Central Committee (January 16, 1966), pp. 4–17.

40. *Van Kien Dang*, Resolution of the Politburo, August 1968, p. 409.

41. *Van Kien Dang*, Resolution of the Politburo, August 1968, p. 376.

42. *Major Events: The Diplomatic Struggle and International Activities During the Resistance War Against the Americans to Save the Nation, 1954–1975* (Hanoi, Vietnam: Ministry of Foreign Affairs, 1987). See cables for January and February 1969, in particular January 1, 1969, p. 202, and February 1, 1969, p. 211.

Chapter 8

1. I have relied on two separate English editions: one from 1925 and another from 2005. Luo Guanzhong, *The Romance of Three Kingdoms*, trans. C. H. Brewitt-Taylor (Rockville, MD: Silk Pagoda, 2005). See also Luo Guanzhong, *San Kuo, or Romance of Three Kingdoms*, trans. C. H. Brewitt-Taylor (Shanghai: Kelly & Walsh, 1925). The story of Cun Ming's lute is found in ch. 95.

2. Daniel Kahneman, *Thinking, Fast and Slow* (New York: Farrar, Straus and Giroux, 2011), pp. 193–94.

3. I am adapting this scenario as Kahneman constructed it. I note with regret that this discussion presupposes that productivity is the most valuable trait for academics to possess. It ignores the possibility that creativity and depth of ideas could be more meaningful than the quantity of scholarly output. For the sake of clarifying the continuity heuristic, this simplification is useful.

4. The more specific version of the fundamental attribution error is the actor–observer asymmetry. In a meta-analysis of psychological studies of this effect, one scholar has found little support for the effect's existence, save

for its prevalence in cases where observers attributed negative, as opposed to complimentary, characteristics to the actors in question. For my purposes, it is enough to use the fundamental attribution error as a short-hand label for a specific type of faulty thinking. I take no position on whether or not most people commit this error. Instead, I find that the particular historical actors discussed in this chapter attributed stable, negative dispositions (namely aggression) to the foreign leaders they observed. See Bertram F. Malle, "The Actor–Observer Asymmetry in Attribution: A (Surprising) Meta-Analysis," *Psychological Bulletin*, vol. 132, no. 6 (2006), pp. 895–919.

5. F.O. 371/257. Memorandum by Mr. Eyre Crowe. Memorandum on the Present State of British Relations with France and Germany. (8882. *) Secret. Foreign Office, January 1, 1907.

6. See for example Henry Kissinger, *Diplomacy* (New York: Simon & Schuster, 1994).

7. F.O. 371/257. Memorandum by Mr. Eyre Crowe. Memorandum on the Present State of British Relations with France and Germany. (8882. *) Secret. Foreign Office, January 1, 1907.

8. The fact that the Kaiser remained in power for more than another decade does not diminish Fitzmaurice's point. His objection was to Crowe's assumption that national interests alone determined policy. Even the same individuals can come to perceive their own interests, as well as their nation's interests, differently over time.

9. G. P. Gooch and Harold Temperley, eds., *British Documents on the Origins of the War, 1898–1914* (London: H.M.S.O., 1926–1938), appendix.

10. The international relations theory of constructivism in part challenges the realist school along these lines. My purpose here is merely to elucidate how a static view of the enemy has influenced the history of twentieth-century international conflict, not to debate the merits of one international relations theory over another. See Alexander Wendt's classic article, "Anarchy Is What States Make of It: The Social Construction of Power Politics," *International Organization*, vol. 46, no. 2 (1992), pp. 391–425.

11. For the best recent study of Kennan's career and thinking, see John Lewis Gaddis, *George F. Kennan: An American Life* (New York: Penguin Press, 2011).

12. George F. Kennan, "The Sources of Soviet Conduct," *Foreign Affairs*, vol. 25, no. July 4 (1947). For the classic work on essentializing non-Western behavior and beliefs, see Edward Said, *Orientalism* (New York: Vintage Books, 2003).

13. Marc Trachtenberg has argued that Kennan's impact on the Cold War has been overstated by historians. Regardless of the extent of his influence, my aim here is to assess the shortcuts and assumptions underlying Kennan's analysis in the oft-cited Long Telegram and *Foreign Affairs* article. See Marc Trachtenberg's response to Robert Jervis on John Lewis Gaddis's biography of George Kennan. H-Diplo, May 8, 2012, http://h-net.msu.edu/cgi-bin/logbrowse.pl?trx=vx&list=h-diplo&month=1205&week=b&msg=SQRzDoMRH6ws2OYW4mNKvA&user=&pw=.

14. Dean Acheson, *Present at the Creation: My Years at the State Department* (New York: W. W. Norton, 1969), pp. 149–56.

15. Nathan Leites, *The Operational Code of the Politburo* (New York: McGraw-Hill, 1951).

16. Nathan Leites, *A Study of Bolshevism* (Glencoe, IL: Free Press, 1953).

17. Alexander George, "The Operational Code: A Neglected Approach to the Study of Political Leaders and Decision-Making," *International Studies Quarterly*, vol. 13, no. 2 (1969), pp. 190–222.

18. Margaret Hermann, "Circumstances Under Which Leader Personality Will Affect Foreign Policy." *In Search of Global Patterns*, ed. James Rosenau. (New York: Free Press, 1976). See also Margaret Hermann, "Explaining Foreign Policy Behavior Using the Personal Characteristics of Political Leaders," *International Studies Quarterly* vol. 27 (1980), pp. 7–46. See also Margaret Hermann and Charles Kegley, "Rethinking Democracy and International Peace: Perspectives from Political Psychology," *International Studies Quarterly*, vol. 39 (1995), pp. 511–34.

19. Ole Holsti, "Foreign Policy Viewed Cognitively." In *The Structure of Decision*, ed. Robert Axelrod (Princeton, NJ: Princeton University Press, 1976).

    Ole Holsti, "The 'Operational Code' as an Approach to the Analysis of Belief Systems." Final Report to the National Science Foundation, Grant NO. SOC 75–15368 (Durham, NC: Duke University Press, 1977).

20. See for example Mark Schafer and Stephen G. Walker, "Democratic Leaders and the Democratic Peace: The Operational Codes of Tony Blair and Bill Clinton," *International Studies Quarterly*, vol. 50, no. 3 (2006), pp. 561–83. See also Stephen G. Walker, *Forecasting the Political Behavior of Leaders with the Verbs in Context System of Operational Code Analysis* (Hilliard, OH: Social Science Automation, 2000).

21. In more recent times, numerous foreign policy analysts have made similar claims about Arab thinking. Seymour Hersh even alleged that the neoconservatives influencing the George W. Bush administration relied on Raphael Patai's 1973 book *The Arab Mind* as their bible for understanding Arab behavior. Seymour M. Hersh, "The Gray Zone: How a Secret Pentagon Program Came to Abu Ghraib," *The New Yorker*, May 24, 2004.

22. The exact text reads: "For there is one road which, if past experience is any guide to the future, will most certainly not lead to any permanent improvement of relations with any Power, least of all Germany, and which must therefore be abandoned: that is the road paved with graceful British concessions—concessions made without any conviction either of their justice or of their being set off by equivalent counter-services." Op. Cit. F.O. 371/257, "Crowe Memorandum."

23. Jerrold M. Post, ed., *The Psychological Assessment of Political Leaders: With Profiles of Saddam Hussein and Bill Clinton* (Ann Arbor: University of Michigan Press, 2005), p. 52.

Chapter 9

Parts of this chapter appeared in articles in *Armed Forces Journal* and *Joint Force Quarterly*. I am grateful to the editors for their permission to reprint that material here.

1. For more on the early history and uses of the telescope see Mario Biagioli, *Galileo's Instruments of Credit: Telescopes, Images, Secrecy* (Chicago: University of Chicago Press, 2006).
2. For more on the telescope, see Geoff Andersen, *The Telescope: Its History, Technology, and Future* (Princeton, NJ: Princeton University Press, 2007) and Mario Biagioli, *Galileo's Instruments of Credit: Telescopes, Images, Secrecy* (Chicago: University of Chicago Press, 2006).
3. Nate Silver, *The Signal and the Noise: Why So Many Predictions Fail–But Some Don't* (New York: Penguin Press, 2012), p. 98.
4. Bruce Bueno de Mesquita, *The Predictioneer's Game: Using the Logic of Brazen Self-Interest to See and Shape the Future* (New York: Random House, 2010), p. 167.
5. Abraham Rabinovich, *The Yom Kippur War* (New York: Schockin Books, 2004).
6. Some of the information and quotations in this section stem from discussions between the author and Andrew Marshall, in person, by telephone, and through e-mail exchanges. Not all of Marshall's assertions can be readily verified, as the details of some of these subjects remain classified. Marshall's comments therefore must be viewed with this in mind.
7. See Andrew W. Marshall and Herbert Goldhamer, *Psychosis and Civilization: Two Studies in the Frequency of Mental Disease* (New York: Free Press, 1953).
8. Two useful studies of RAND in the 1950s are Alex Abella, *Soldiers of Reason: The RAND Corporation and the Rise of the American Empire* (Orlando, FL: Harcourt, 2008), and Fred Kaplan, *The Wizards of Armageddon* (Stanford, CA: Stanford University Press, 1991).
9. "Sources of Change in the Future Security Environment," Paper by the Future Security Environment Working Group (Andrew Marshall and Charles Wolf, Chairmen). Submitted to the Commission on Integrating Long-term Strategy (Washington, DC: Pentagon, April 1988).
10. Douglas McGray, "The Marshall Plan," *Wired Magazine*, February 2003.
11. See Mark Mazetti, "Obama Faults Spy Agencies' Performance in Gauging Mideast Unrest, Officials Say," *The New York Times*, February 4, 2011. Available at http://www.nytimes.com/2011/02/05/world/middleeast/05cia.html. See also Paul R. Pillar, "Don't Blame the Spies," *Foreign Policy*, March 16, 2011.

Afterword

1. Philip Tetlock, *Expert Political Judgment: How Good Is It? How Can We Know?* (Princeton, NJ: Princeton University Press, 2005).
2. Daniel Gilbert, *Stumbling on Happiness* (New York: Knopf, 2006).

3. Nassim Taleb, *The Black Swan: The Impact of the Highly Improbable* (New York: Random House, 2007).

4. Dan Ariely, *Predictably Irrational: The Hidden Forces That Shape Our Decisions* (New York: Harper, 2009).

5. Silver, *The Signal and the Noise.*

6. Michael Spence, "Job Market Signaling," *The Quarterly Journal of Economics,* vol. 87, no. 3. (1973), pp. 355–74.

7. Diego Gambetta, *Codes of the Underworld: How Criminals Communicate* (Princeton, NJ: Princeton University Press, 2009).

8. For a classic work on signals and noise in international relations see Roberta Wohlstetter, *Pearl Harbor: Warning and Decision* (Stanford, CA: Stanford University Press, 1967). Another valuable work on how states signal their intentions and how they might try to transmit deceptive signals is Robert Jervis, *The Logic of Images in International Relations* (New York: Columbia University Press, 1989).

9. For more on Shannon, see James Gleich, *The Information: A History, A Theory, A Flood* (New York: Pantheon Books, 2011).

10. Andrea D. Rosati, Eric D. Knowles, Charles W. Kalish, Alison Gopnik, Daniel R. Ames, and Michael W. Morris, "What Theory of Mind Can Teach Social Psychology? Traits as Intentional Terms," Available at http://corundum.education.wisc.edu/papers/TomTraits.pdf.

11. Ray Kurzweil, *How To Create a Mind: The Secret of Human Thought Revealed* (New York: Viking, 2012).

12. Ariely, *Predictably Irrational,* p. 129.

13. Kahneman, *Thinking, Fast and Slow,* p. 56.

14. "World Giving Index 2011: A Global View of Giving Trends," Charities Aid Foundation, 2011. Accessed on February 4, 2013, at https://www.cafonline.org/pdf/World_Giving_Index_2011_191211.pdf.

15. Robert Frank, "The Biggest Gift in the World," *Wall Street Journal,* October 28, 2011.

16. See for example Gerd Gigerenzer, "Surrogates for Theories," *Theory and Psychology,* vol. 8, no. 2 (1998), 195–204; Gerd Gigerenzer, "On Narrow Norms and Vague Heuristics: A Reply to Kahnemann and Tversky," *Psychological Review,* vol. 103, no. 3 (1996), pp. 592–96; Gerd Gigerenzer, "Why the Distinction Between Single-Event Probabilities and Frequencies is Important for Psychology and Vice Versa," in George Wright and Ayton, Peter, eds., *Subjective Probability* (New York: Wiley, 1994), pp. 129–61.

17. Gerd Gigerenzer, "Out of the Frying Pan into the Fire: Behavioral Reactions to Terrorist Attacks," *Risk Analysis,* vol. 26, no. 2 (2006).

18. For a related challenge from within the field of psychology, see Joseph Simmons, Leif Nelson, and Uri Simonsohn, "False-Positive Psychology: Undisclosed Flexibility in Data Collection and Analysis Allows Presenting Anything as Significant," *Psychological Science,* vol. 22, no. 11 (Nov. 2011), pp. 1359–66.

19. Richard K. Betts, *Enemies of Intelligence: Knowledge and Power in American National Security* (New York: Columbia University Press, 2007).

20. Robert Jervis, *Why Intelligence Fails: Lessons From the Iranian Revolution and the Iraq War* (Ithaca, NY: Cornell University Press, 2010).

21. Joshua Rovner, *Fixing the Facts: National Security and the Politics of Intelligence* (Ithaca, NY: Cornell University Press, 2011). For a useful discussion of Rovner's book, see the H-Diplo Roundtable reviews by prominent scholars of intelligence. ISSF Roundtable, vol. III, no. 17 (2012).

22. Daryl Press, *Calculating Credibility: How Leaders Assess Military Threats* (Ithaca, NY: Cornell University Press, 2005).

23. Keren Yarhi-Milo, *Knowing Thy Adversary: Assessments of Intentions in International Relations*, Doctoral Dissertation, University of Pennsylvania, Department of Political Science, 2009. See the more recent book version, *Knowing the Adversary: Leaders, Intelligence Organizations, and Assessments of Intentions in International Relations* (Princeton, NJ: Princeton University Press, 2013).

24. Yarhi-Milo, *Knowing the Adversary*, p. 504.

25. See for example Alexander George, *Presidential Decision Making: The Effective Use of Information and Advice* (Boulder, CO: Westview Press, 1980).

26. Ernest R. May, ed., *Knowing One's Enemies: Intelligence Assessments Before the Two World Wars* (Princeton, NJ: Princeton University Press, 1984).

27. Ernest R. May and Richard E. Neustadt, *Thinking in Time: The Uses of History for Decision-Makers* (New York: Free Press, 1986), p. 166.

28. Christopher R. Browning, *Ordinary Men: Reserve Police Battalion 101 and the Final Solution in Poland* (New York: HarperCollins, 1992), pp. 173–74.

29. Marc Trachtenberg, *The Cold War and After: History, Theory, and the Logic of International Politics* (Princeton, NJ: Princeton University Press, 2012), preface.

SELECT BIBLIOGRAPHY

BECAUSE THIS STUDY COVERS such a wide range of conflicts, I have listed below only the secondary literature of greatest use to this book. The endnotes provide a more thorough account of primary sources used in each chapter, along with journal articles, newspaper accounts, and other relevant materials. For example, the chapters on German foreign policy include endnotes containing references to specific sections of Gustav Stresemann's *Nachlass*, along with citation of the various American, British, and German archival records from collections such as *Akten zur Deutschen Auswaertigen Politik, 1918–1945 (ADAP) Series A and B*. More specific microfilm records are also noted there, such as the Military Intelligence Division reports on German–Soviet relations. I have, however, selected for this bibliography some of the memoirs, intelligence reports, and other firsthand accounts of events that informed this book, as these may assist the reader seeking further exploration of a particular subject.

Abella, Alex. *Soldiers of Reason: The RAND Corporation and the Rise of the American Empire*. Orlando, FL: Harcourt, 2008.

Acheson, Dean. *Present at the Creation: My Years at the State Department*. New York: W. W. Norton, 1969.

Ahamed, Liaquat. *Lords of Finance: The Bankers Who Broke the World*. New York: Penguin, 2009.

Angress, Werner. *Stillborn Revolution: The Communist Bid for Power in Germany, 1921–1923*. Port Washington, NY: Kennikat Press, 1972.

Ariely, Dan. *Predictably Irrational: The Hidden Forces That Shape Our Decisions*. New York: Harper, 2009.

Berman, Larry. *Perfect Spy: The Incredible Double Life of Pham Xuan An, Time Magazine Reporter and Vietnamese Communist Agent*. New York: Smithsonian Books, 2007.

Betts, Richard K. *Enemies of Intelligence: Knowledge and Power in American National Security*. New York: Columbia University Press, 2007.

Boyle, Thomas E. "France, Great Britain, and German Disarmament." Unpub-lished dissertation, State University of New York at Stony Brook, 1972. Available through University Microfilms of America Inc.

Bretton, Henry L. *Stresemann and the Revision of Versailles*. Stanford, CA: Stanford University Press, 1953.

Brown, Archie. *The Rise and Fall of Communism*. New York: Ecco, 2009.

Brown, Judith M. *Gandhi's Rise to Power: Indian Politics, 1915–1922*. London: Cambridge University Press, 1972.

Brown, Judith M. *The Cambridge Companion to Gandhi*. Cambridge, UK: Cambridge University Press, 2011.

Brown, Judith M., ed. *Mahatma Gandhi: The Essential Writings*. New York: Oxford University Press, 2008.

Browning, Christopher R. *Ordinary Men: Reserve Police Battalion 101 and the Final Solution in Poland*. New York: HarperCollins, 1992.

Bueno de Mesquita, Bruce. *The Predictioneer's Game: Using the Logic of Brazen Self-Interest to See and Shape the Future*. New York: Random House, 2010.

Carsten, F. L. *The Reichswehr and Politics, 1918–1933*. New York: Clarendon Press, 1966.

Catton, Philip E. *Diem's Final Failure: Prelude to America's War in Vietnam*. Lawrence: University of Kansas Press, 2002.

Central Intelligence Agency. "The Responsibilities of the Democratic Republic of Vietnam Intelligence and Security Services in the Exploitation of American Prisoners of War." November 17, 1975. Available at http://www.vietnam.ttu.edu/virtualarchive/items.php?item=11270323004.

Chabris, Christopher, and Daniel Simons. *The Invisible Gorilla: and Other Ways Our Intuitions Deceive Us*. New York: Crown, 2010.

Chāruchandra, Guha (Khrishnadas). *Seven Months With Mahatma Gandhi: Being an Inside View of the Non-Co-operation Movement*. Madras, India: Ganesan, 1928.

Cohrs, Patrick. *The Unfinished Peace After World War I: America, Britain, and the Stabilisation of Europe, 1919–1932*. Cambridge, UK: Cambridge University Press, 2006.

Collett, Nigel. *The Butcher of Amritsar: General Reginald Dyer*. London: Palgrave, 2005.

Combat Operations Department, General Staff of the People's Army of Vietnam. *History of the Combat Operations Department 1945–2000*. Hanoi, Vietnam: People's Army Publishing House, 2005.

Cowling, Maurice. *The Impact of Labour, 1920–1924: The Beginning of Modern British Politics*. Cambridge, UK: Cambridge University Press, 1971.

Dutton, David. *Austen Chamberlain: Gentleman in Politics*. Bolton, UK: Ross Anderson Publications, 1985.

Fearon, James. "Rationalist Explanations for War." *International Organization*, vol. 49, no. 3, 1995, pp. 379–414.

Finkelstein, Norman G. *What Gandhi Says About Violence, Resistance, and Courage*. New York: OR Books, 2012.

Fischer, Louis, ed. *The Essential Gandhi: An Anthology of His Writings on His Life, Work, and Ideas.* New York: Vintage Books, 2002.

Freund, Gerald. *Unholy Alliance: Russian–German Relations from the Treaty of Brest-Litovsk to the Treaty of Berlin.* London: Harcourt, Brace, 1957.

Gaddis, John Lewis. *The Landscape of History: How Historians Map the Past.* New York: Oxford University Press, 2002.

Gaddis, John Lewis. *George F. Kennan: An American Life.* New York: Penguin, 2011.

Gambetta, Diego. *Codes of the Underworld: How Criminals Communicate.* Princeton, NJ: Princeton University Press, 2009.

Gandhi, Mahatma. *An Autobiography or the Story of My Experiments with Truth.* Ahmedabad, India: Navajivan Publishing House, 1927.

Gandhi, Mohandas. *Collected Works of Mahatma Gandhi.* New Delhi: Publications Division, Ministry of Information and Broadcasting, 1960–.

Gatzke, Hans. *Stresemann and the Rearmament of Germany.* Baltimore, MD: Johns Hopkins University Press, 1954.

George, Alexander. "The Operational Code: A Neglected Approach to the Study of Political Leaders and Decision-Making." *International Studies Quarterly*, vol. 13, no. 2, 1969, pp. 190–222.

George, Alexander. *Presidential Decision Making: The Effective Use of Information and Advice.* Boulder, CO: Westview Press, 1980.

Gilbert, Daniel. *Stumbling on Happiness.* New York: Knopf, 2006.

Gladwell, Malcolm. *Blink: The Power of Thinking Without Thinking.* New York: Back Bay Books, 2007.

Gleich, James. *The Information: A History, A Theory, A Flood.* New York: Pantheon Books, 2011.

Gorodetsky, Gabriel. *Stafford Cripps' Mission to Moscow, 1940–1942.* New York: Cambridge University Press, 1985.

Gorodetsky, Gabriel. *Grand Delusion: Stalin and the German Invasion of Russia.* New Haven, CT: Yale University Press, 1999.

Goscha, Christopher. "The Early Development of Vietnamese Intelligence Services." In *Exploring Intelligence Archives.* Edited by R. G. Hughes, P. Jackson, and L. Scott. London: Routeledge, 2008.

Goscha, Christopher E. *Historical Dictionary of the Indochina War (1945–1954): An International and Interdisciplinary Approach.* Copenhagen, Denmark: NIAS Press, Nordic Institute of Asian Studies, 2011.

Grossheim, Martin. "Revisionism in the Democratic Republic of Vietnam: New Evidence from the East German Archives." *Cold War History*, vol. 5, no. 4, 2005, pp. 451–77.

Guanzhong, Luo. *The Romance of Three Kingdoms.* Translated by C. H. Brewitt-Taylor. Rockville, MD: Silk Pagoda, 2005.

Guanzhong, Luo. *San Kuo, or Romance of Three Kingdoms.* Translated by C. H. Brewitt-Taylor. Shanghai: Kelly & Walsh, 1925.

Habeck, Mary. *Storm of Steel: The Development of Armor Doctrine in Germany and the Soviet Union, 1919–1939.* Ithaca, NY: Cornell University Press, 2003.

Herman, Arthur. *Gandhi and Churchill: The Rivalry That Destroyed An Empire and Forged Our Age*. New York: Bantam Books, 2008.

Hermann, Margaret. "Circumstances Under Which Leader Personality Will Affect Foreign Policy." In *Search of Global Patterns*. Edited by James Rosenau. New York: Free Press, 1976.

Hermann, Margaret. "Explaining Foreign Policy Behavior Using the Personal Characteristics of Political Leaders." *International Studies Quarterly*, vol. 27, 1980, pp. 7–46.

Hermann, Margaret, and Charles Kegley. "Rethinking Democracy and International Peace: Perspectives from Political Psychology." *International Studies Quarterly*, vol. 39, 1995, 511–34.

Hersh, Seymour M. "The Gray Zone: How a Secret Pentagon Program Came to Abu Ghraib." *The New Yorker*, May 24, 2004. Available at http://www.newyorker.com/archive/2004/05/24/040524fa_fact.

Hiep, Colonel General Dang Vu, with Senior Colonel Le Hai Trieu and Colonel Ngo Vinh Binh. *Highland Memories*. Part IV. Hanoi, Vietnam: People's Army Publishing House, 2000.

Hilger, Gustav, and Alfred Meyer. *The Incompatible Allies: A Memoir-History of German–Soviet Relations, 1918–1941*. New York: MacMillan, 1953.

Historical Chronicle of the Cochin China Party Committee and the Central Office for South Vietnam, 1954–1975. Hanoi, Vietnam: National Political Publishing House, 2002.

History of the COSVN Military Command, 1961–1976. Ministry of Defense and Military Region 7. Edited by Colonel Ho Son Dai. Hanoi, Vietnam: National Political Publishing House, 2004.

History of the Resistance War in Saigon-Cho Lon-Gia Dinh (1945–1975) [Lich Su Saigon-Cho Lon-Gia Dinh Khang Chien (1945–1975)]. Edited by War Recapitulation Committee, Ho Chi Minh City Party Committee; Tran Hai Phung and Luu Phuong Thanh. By Ho Son Dai and Tran Phan Chan. Ho Chi Minh City: Ho Chi Minh City Publishing House, 1994.

History of the Sapper Branch Technical Service: People's Army of Vietnam (Internal Distribution) [Lich Su Nganh Ky Thuat Dac Cong: Quan Doi Nhan Dan Viet Nam (Luu Hanh Noi Bo)]. By Lieutenant Colonel Nguyen Quoc Minh. Hanoi, Vietnam: People's Army Publishing House, 1997.

History of the Sapper Forces. Vol. I [Lich Su Bo Doi Dac Cong, Tap Mot]. Edited by Headquarters and Party Current Affairs Committee, Sapper Command. By Nguyen Quoc Minh, Vu Doan Thanh, Pham Gia Khanh, and Nguyen Thanh Xuan. Hanoi, Vietnam: People's Army Publishing House, 1987.

Hitler, Adolf. *Mein Kampf*. New York: Reynal & Hitchcock, 1939.

Holcombe, Alec. "The Complete Collection of Party Documents: Listening to the Party's Official Internal Voice." *Journal of Vietnamese Studies*, vol. 5, no. 2, 2010, pp. 225–42.

Holsti, Ole. "Foreign Policy Viewed Cognitively." In *The Structure of Decision* Edited by Robert Axelrod. Princeton, NJ: Princeton University Press, 1976.

Holsti, Ole. "The 'Operational Code as an Approach to the Analysis of Belief Systems." Final Report to the National Science Foundation, Grant NO. SOC 75–15368. Durham, NC: Duke University, 1977.

Israel, Fred L. *The War Diary of Breckinridge Long: Selections From the Years 1939–1944.* Lincoln: University of Nebraska Press, 1966.

Jacobson, Jon. *Locarno Diplomacy: Germany and the West.* Princeton, NJ: Princeton University Press, 1971.

Jacobson, Jon. *When the Soviet Union Entered World Politics.* Berkeley: University of California Press, 1994.

Jervis, Robert. *Why Intelligence Fails: Lessons From the Iranian Revolution and the Iraq War.* Ithaca, NY: Cornell University Press, 2010.

Jian, Chen. *China's Road to the Korean War: The Making of the Sino-American Confrontation.* New York: Columbia University Press, 1994.

Kahneman, Daniel. *Thinking, Fast and Slow.* New York: Farrar, Straus and Giroux, 2011.

Kaplan, Fred. *The Wizards of Armageddon.* Stanford, CA: Stanford University Press, 1991.

Kennan, George F. "The Sources of Soviet Conduct." *Foreign Affairs*, vol. 25, no. 4, 1947.

Kent, Susan Kingsley. *Aftershocks: Politics and Trauma in Britain, 1918–1931.* New York: Palgrave MacMillan, 2009.

Kershaw, Ian. *Hitler: 1936–1945, Nemesis.* London: Penguin, 2000.

Khanh, Lieutenant General Hoang Nghia. *The Road to the General Headquarters Staff.* Hanoi, Vietnam: People's Army Publishing House, 2008.

Khong, Yuen Foong. *Analogies At War: Korea, Munich, Dien Bien Phu, and the Vietnam Decisions of 1965.* Princeton, NJ: Princeton University Press, 1992.

Kissinger, Henry. *Diplomacy.* New York: Simon & Schuster, 1994.

Kissinger, Henry. *Ending the Vietnam War: A History of America's Involvement in and Extraction from the Vietnam War.* New York: Simon & Schuster, 2003.

Krüger, Peter. *Die Aussenpolitik der Republik von Weimar.* Darmstadt, Germany: Wissenschaftliche Buchgesellschaft, 1985.

Kumar, R., ed., *Essays on Gandhian Politics: The Rowlett Satyagraha of 1919.* New York: Clarendon Press, 1971.

Kurzban, Robert. *Why Everyone (Else) Is a Hypocrite: Evolution and the Modular Mind.* Princeton, NJ: Princeton University Press, 2010.

Kurzweil, Ray. *How To Create a Mind: The Secret of Human Thought Revealed.* New York: Viking, 2012.

Langer, William L., and S. Everett Gleason. *The Undeclared War, 1940–1941.* Gloucester, MA: P. Smith, 1968.

Lash, Joseph P., ed., *From the Diaries of Felix Frankfurter.* New York: W. W. Norton, 1975.

Le Duan. *Letters to the South [Tho Vao Nam].* Hanoi, Vietnam: Su That Publishing House, 1985.

Leites, Nathan. *The Operational Code of the Politburo*. New York: McGraw-Hill, 1951.

Leites, Nathan. *A Study of Bolshevism*. Glencoe, IL: Free Press, 1953.

Li, Xiaobing. *Voices from the Vietnam War: Stories from American, Asian, and Russian Veterans*. Louisville: University of Kentucky Press, 2010.

Lockhart, Greg. *Nation in Arms: The Origins of the People's Army of Vietnam*. Sydney, Australia: Allen & Unwin, 1989.

Logevall, Fredrik. *Choosing War: The Lost Chance for Peace and the Escalation of War in Vietnam*. Berkeley: University of California Press, 1999.

Logevall, Fredrik. *Embers of War: The Fall of an Empire and the Making of America's Vietnam*. New York: Random House, 2012.

Major Events: The Diplomatic Struggle and International Activities During the Resistance War Against the Americans to Save the Nation, 1954–1975. Hanoi, Vietnam: Ministry of Foreign Affairs, 1987.

Marshall, Andrew W., and Herbert Goldhamer. *Psychosis and Civilization: Two Studies in the Frequency of Mental Disease*. New York: Free Press, 1953.

May, Ernest R., ed. *Knowing One's Enemies: Intelligence Assessments Before the Two World Wars*. Princeton, NJ: Princeton University Press, 1984.

May, Ernest R., and Richard E. Neustadt. *Thinking in Time: The Uses of History for Decision-Makers*. New York: Free Press, 1986.

McNamara, Robert S. *Argument Without End: In Search of Answers to the Vietnam Tragedy*. New York: Public Affairs, 1999.

McNamara, Robert S. *In Retrospect: The Tragedy and Lessons of Vietnam*. New York: Random House, 1996.

Metcalf, Barbara D., and Thomas R. Metcalf. *A Concise History of India*. Cambridge, UK: Cambridge University Press, 2002.

Mikoyan, Anastas. *Tak bylo*. Moscow: AST, 2000.

Moise, Edwin. *Tonkin Gulf and the Escalation of the Vietnam War*. Chapel Hill: University of North Carolina Press, 1996.

Montefiore, Simon Sebag. *Stalin: The Court of the Red Tsar*. New York: Knopf, 2004.

Morgan, J. H. *Assize of Arms: The Disarmament of Germany and the Rearmament, 1919–1939*. New York: Oxford University Press, 1945.

Morgan, Kenneth O. *Consensus and Disunity: The Lloyd George Coalition Government, 1918–1922*. New York: Oxford University Press, 1979.

Murphy, David. *What Stalin Knew: The Enigma of Barbarossa*. New Haven, CT: Yale University Press, 2005.

Naimark, Norman. *Stalin's Genocides*. Princeton, NJ: Princeton University Press, 2010.

Nelson, Deborah. *The War Behind Me: Vietnam Veterans Confront the Truth About U.S. War Crimes*. New York: Basic Books, 2008.

Nguyen, Lien-Hang T. *Hanoi's War: An International History of the War for Peace in Vietnam*. The New Cold War History. Chapel Hill: University of North Carolina Press, 2012.

O'Connor, Timothy E. *Diplomacy and Revolution: G. V. Chicherin and Soviet Foreign Affairs, 1918–1930*. Ames: Iowa State University Press, 1988.

O'Neill, Robert. *The German Army and the Nazi Party, 1933–1939*. London: Cassell, 1966.

O'Sullivan, Christopher. *Sumner Welles, Postwar Planning, and the Quest for a New World Order, 1937–1943*. New York: Columbia University Press, 2008.

Post, Gaines. *The Civil-Military Fabric of Weimar Foreign Policy*. Princeton, NJ: Princeton University Press, 1973.

Post, Jerrold M., ed., *The Psychological Assessment of Political Leaders: With Profiles of Saddam Hussein and Bill Clinton*. Ann Arbor: University of Michigan Press, 2005.

Pribbenow, Merle L. "General Võ Nguyên Giáp and the Mysterious Evolution of the Plan for the 1968 Tết Offensive." *Journal of Vietnamese Studies*, vol. 3, no. 2, 2008, pp. 1–33.

Quinn-Judge, Sophie. "The Ideological Debate in the DRV and the Significance of the Anti-Party Affair, 1967–1968." *Cold War History*, vol. 5, no. 4, 2005, pp. 479–500.

Rabinovich, Abraham. *The Yom Kippur War*. New York: Schockin Books, 2004.

Read, Anthony, and David Fisher. *The Deadly Embrace: Hitler, Stalin and the Nazi-Soviet Pact, 1939–1941*. London: M. Joseph, 1988.

Ricks, Thomas E. *The Generals: American Military Command from World War II to Today*. New York: Penguin, 2012.

Roberts, Geoffrey. *Stalin's Wars: From World War to Cold War, 1939–1953*. New Haven, CT: Yale University Press, 2008.

Rofe, Simon. *Franklin Roosevelt's Foreign Policy and the Welles Mission*. London: Palgrave MacMillan, 2007.

Rovner, Joshua. *Fixing the Facts: National Security and the Politics of Intelligence*. Ithaca, NY: Cornell University Press, 2011.

Rusk, Dean. *As I Saw It, as Told to Richard Rusk*. Edited by Daniel S. Papp. New York: W. W. Norton, 1990.

Said, Edward. *Orientalism*. New York: Vintage Books, 2003.

Salewski, Michael. *Entwaffnung und Militaerkontrolle in Deutschland, 1919–1927*. Muenchen, Germany: R. Oldenbourg Verlag, 1966.

Schafer, Mark, and Stephen G. Walker. "Democratic Leaders and the Democratic Peace: The Operational Codes of Tony Blair and Bill Clinton." *International Studies Quarterly*, vol. 50, no. 3, 2006, pp. 56–83.

Scheidemann, Philipp. *The Making of New Germany: The Memoirs of Philipp Scheidemann*. Vol. 2. Translated by J. E. Mitchell. New York: D. Appleton and Company, 1929.

Schuker, Stephen. *The End of French Predominance in Europe: The Financial Crisis of 1924 and the Adoption of the Dawes Plan*. Chapel Hill: University of North Carolina Press, 1976.

Service, Robert W. *A History of Twentieth-Century Russia*. Cambridge, MA: Harvard University Press, 1997.

Sharma, Suresb K. *The Jallianwala Bagh Tragedy*. Delhi, India: Vista International Publishing House, 2010.

Sharp, Gene. *Gandhi as a Political Strategist: With Essays on Ethics and Politics*. Boston, MA: Porter Sargent Publishers, 1979.

Shirer, William L. *Gandhi: A Memoir*. New York: Simon & Schuster, 1979.

Shore, Zachary. *What Hitler Knew: The Battle for Information in Nazi Foreign Policy*. New York: Oxford University Press, 2003.

Shuster, Richard. *German Disarmament After World War I: The Diplomacy of International Arms Inspection, 1920–1931*. New York: Routledge, 2006.

Silver, Nate. *The Signal and the Noise: Why So Many Predictions Fail—But Some Don't*. New York: Penguin, 2012.

Spence, Michael. "Job Market Signaling." *The Quarterly Journal of Economics*, vol. 87, no. 3, 1973, pp. 355–74.

Steinberg, Jonathan. *Bismarck: A Life*. New York: Oxford University Press, 2011.

Stresemann, Gustav. *Gustav Stresemann: His Diaries, Letters, and Papers*. New York: MacMillan.

Taleb, Nassim. *The Black Swan: The Impact of the Highly Improbable*. New York: Random House, 2007.

Tetlock, Philip. *Expert Political Judgment: How Good Is It? How Can We Know?* Princeton, NJ: Princeton University Press, 2005.

Thayer, Carlyle. *War By Other Means: National Liberation and Revolution in Vietnam, 1954–1960*. Sydney, Australia: Allen & Unwin, 1989.

"The Historic Talks: 35th Anniversary of the Paris Agreement, 1973–2008." Diplomatic History Research Committee of the Foreign Ministry. Edited by Vu Duong Huan [Vũ Dương Huân]. Hanoi, Vietnam: National Political Publishing House, 2009.

Thu, Tong Bi. *Le Duan: Party General Secretary Le Duan*. Hanoi, Vietnam: VNA Hanoi Publishing House, 2007.

Thuy, Pham Hong, Pham Hong Doi, and Phan Trong Dam. *History of the People's Navy of Vietnam*. Hanoi, Vietnam: People's Army Publishing House, 1985.

Trachtenberg, Marc. *History and Strategy*. Princeton, NJ: Princeton University Press, 1991.

Trachtenberg, Marc. *The Craft of International History: A Guide to Method*. Princeton, NJ: Princeton University Press, 2006.

Trachtenberg, Marc. *The Cold War and After: History, Theory, and the Logic of International Politics*. Princeton, NJ: Princeton University Press, 2012.

Turse, Nick. *Kill Anything That Moves: The Real American War in Vietnam*. New York: Metropolitan Books, 2013.

Tuan, Bui Anh, ed. *Ministry of Public Security*. Hanoi, Vietnam: People's Public Security Publishing House, 2004.

Tuchman, Barbara. *The March of Folly: From Troy to Vietnam*. New York: Knopf, 1984.

Victory in Vietnam: The Official History of the People's Army of Vietnam, 1954–1975. The Military History Institute of Vietnam. Translated by Merle L. Pribbenow. Lawrence: University Press of Kansas, 2002.

Volkogonov, Dmitri. *Stalin: Triumph and Tragedy*. New York: Grove Weidenfeld, 1991.

Vu, Tuong. "Dreams of Paradise: The Making of Soviet Outpost in Vietnam," *Ab Imperio: Studies of New Imperial History and Nationalism in the Post-Soviet Space*, no. 2, 2008, pp. 255–85.

Vu, Tuong. "From Cheering to Volunteering: Vietnamese Communists and the Coming of the Cold War, 1940–1951." In *Connecting Histories: The Cold War and Decolonization in Asia (1945–1962)*. Edited by Christopher Goscha and Christian Ostermann. Stanford, CA: Stanford University Press, 2009, pp. 172–204.

Walker, Stephen G. *Forecasting the Political Behavior of Leaders with the Verbs in Context System of Operational Code Analysis*. Hilliard, OH: Social Science Automation, 2000.

Wheeler-Bennett, John. *The Nemesis of Power: The German Army in Politics, 1918–1945*. New York: Palgrave MacMillan, 2005.

White, Stephen. *The Origins of Détente: The Genoa Conference and Soviet Western Relations, 1921–1922*. Cambridge, UK: Cambridge University Press, 1985.

Wolpert, Stanley. *Gandhi's Passion: The Life and Legacy of Mahatma Gandhi*. New York: Oxford University Press, 2001.

Wright, Jonathan Gustav. *Stresemann: Weimar's Greatest Statesman*. New York: Oxford University Press, 2002.

Yarhi-Milo, Keren. "Knowing Thy Adversary: Assessments of Intentions in International Relations." Doctoral dissertation, University of Pennsylvania, Department of Political Science, 2009.

INDEX

abolition movement, 200
Acheson, Dean, 159
Actor Observer Asymmetry, 231
advisors, political, 105
agency and influence, 156
agendas, ideological, 80, 106
aggression
  England and, 96
  passivity and, 69
  Poland and, 78, 134
  Southeast Asian Bloc, 121
  wars of, 120
aggressive nonviolence, 184
agreements
  Locarno, 26, 44–45, 217, 219
  Munich, 94
  Soviet-German, 39–40, 44,
    104–105
Air Force
  Army Air Corp, 94
  Royal, 105
  Soviet, 74
Air Ministry (German), 73
Akerlof, George, 191–192
Alabama Claims Case, 39
algorithms, 172
Allies, 29, 36–43, 60, 100
Amazon, 5
America

Civil War, 29
Cold War strategy, 158, 160–161, 174,
  176–178
foreign policies, 122
Hitler and, 104
loans from, 66
media in, 222
WWII entry, 95
America-centric, 202
American Cold War strategy, 158,
  160–161, 174, 176–178
Amritsar massacre, 14–15, 184
Amritsar pattern break, 18
analysis
  behavioral, 178
  foreign policy, 233
  historical, 119, 140
  of information, 2
  mathematical, 169
  policy, 187
  quantitative, 180
  scientific, 126
Anglo-German relations, 153–154,
  157
anti-Jewish, 92, 94
anti-Polish alliance, 45
Arab-Israeli War, 144
Arab Spring revolution, 179
Ariely, Dan, 191, 196